I0026801

The Evolution of Love

The Evolution of Love

Emil Lucka

MINT EDITIONS

The Evolution of Love was first published in 1922.

This edition published by Mint Editions 2020.

ISBN 9781513266527 | E-ISBN 9781513266961

Published by Mint Editions®

**MINT
EDITIONS**

minteditionbooks.com

Translation by: Ellie Schleussner
Publishing Director: Jennifer Newens
Project Manager: Gabrielle Maudiere
Design & Production: Rachel Lopez Metzger
Typesetting: Westchester Publishing Services

Contents

Translator's Introduction

Since the triumphant days of the Mechanists some twenty-five years ago, the wedge of Pragmatism—a useful tool to be used and discarded—has been driven between materialism and idealism, and it appears that the whole tendency of philosophy is now in the latter direction. Even in England the influence of Bergson has led modern thought away from the pure materialism of the monists, and it seems probable that Benedetto Croce's *Philosophy of the Spirit* will carry the movement a step nearer towards the idealistic concept of reality. And among the latest signs of the new tendency must be counted the brilliant work of Emil Lucka, the young Austrian "poet-philosopher," whose conception of the development of love must rank with the most daring speculations in recent psychology.

In the great reaction of the last century, love, that most cogent motive of human thought and action, fell from its high estate and came to be regarded as an instinct not differing in any essential from hunger and thirst, and existing, like them, from the beginning, eternal and immutable, manifesting itself with equal force in the heart of man and woman, and impelling them towards each other. But Emil Lucka, in his remarkable new book, *The Three Stages of Love* (which was recently published in Berlin, and has already created a sensation in literary circles abroad), leads us on to speculative heights from which we may look back upon the whole theory of evolution not as a bar but as a bridge. "My book is intended as a monograph of the emotional life of the human race," he says in the preface, and "I am prepared to meet with rejection rather than with approval." There has been abundance of criticism and controversy, but Lucka has stated his case and drawn his conclusions with such admirable precision and logic, that his work has aroused admiration and appreciation even in the ranks of his opponents.

Love is a theme which at all times and in all countries has been of primary interest to men and women, and therefore this book, which throws an illuminating ray of light in many a dark place still wrapped in mystery and silence, not only impresses the psychologist, but also fascinates the general reader with its wealth of interesting detail and charm of expression.

The three vitally important points which the author develops are as follows:—

Love is not a primary instinct, but has been gradually evolved in historical time.

Ernst Haeckel's biogenetic law is expanded in a psychogenetic law.

Only man's emotions have undergone evolution, and therefore have a history, while those of woman have experienced no change.

Lucka's book will probably not please the advanced feminists, but the delicate, although perhaps involuntary homage to her sex which is implied in his theories ought to rouse a feeling of gratification in the heart of every right-feeling woman. The very limitations and restrictions which he lays upon her raise and glorify her. For while man has been the "Odysseus wandering through heaven and hell, passing from the bestial to the divine to return again and become human, woman has always been the same, unchangeable and without problems. That which he has set up to-day as his highest erotic ideal, the blending of sexual and spiritual love, has been her natural endowment from the beginning. Never perfect, he falls into error and sin where she cannot err, for her instinct is Nature herself, and she knows not the meaning of sin."

Schopenhauer's "instinct of philoprogenitiveness" has to-day become an article of faith with the learned and the unlearned. This *subconscious instinct for the service of the species* which, in love, is supposed to rise to consciousness, and whose purpose is the will to produce the best possible offspring, is conceded by scientists who reject not only Schopenhauer's metaphysic, but metaphysic in general. Even Nietzsche, that arch-individualist, has proved by many of his pronouncements, and most strikingly by his well-known definition of marriage, that he has not escaped its fascinations. "Schopenhauer ignores all phenomena which are not in support of his myth," says Lucka, who denies this instinct of philoprogenitiveness and would substitute for it a "pairing-instinct." "The experience of others," he argues, "not our own instinct, has taught us that children *may*, not necessarily *must*, be the result of the union of the sexes. Into the mediaeval ideal which reached its climax in metaphysical love, the idea of propagation did not enter. Moreover, the desire for children is frequently unaccompanied by any sexual desire, and therefore to manufacture an instinct of philoprogenitiveness is fantastic metaphysic, and is entirely opposed to intellectual reality. This was well understood in the long period of antiquity which strictly separated the sexual impulse and the desire for children."

Lucka distinguishes three great stages in the evolution of love. In vivid and fascinating pictures he unfolds the erotic life of our primitive ancestors, basing his statements on accepted authorities. The sexual impulse in those remote days, unconscious of its nature and far-reaching consequences, was entirely undifferentiated from any other powerful instinct. Every woman of the tribe belonged to every male who happened to desire her. As is still the case with the aborigines of Central and Northern Australia, the phenomena of pregnancy and childbirth were attributed to witchcraft.[1] The concept of *father* had not yet been formed; the family congregated round the mother and saw in her its natural chief; gynecocracy was the prevailing form of government. In early historical and pre-classical times, promiscuity was systematised by religion in India and the countries round the Mediterranean and survived in the Temple Prostitution and the Mysteries. Man as yet felt himself only as a part of nature, and aspired to no more than a life in harmony with her laws. The worship of fertility and the endless renewal of life was the object of the orgiastic cults of Adonis and Astarte in the East, and Dionysus and Aphrodite in Greece; unbridled licentiousness and blind gratification of the senses their sacrament.

With the growth of civilisation and the development of personality there slowly crept into the minds of men a distaste for this irregular sexuality and a desire for a less chaotic state of things. This longing and the wish for legitimate heirs gradually overcame promiscuity and, in Greece, led to the establishment of the monogamous system. It must not be assumed, however, that the Greek ideal of marriage bore any resemblance to our modern conception. True, the wife occupied an honoured position as the guardian of hearth and children and was treated by her husband with affection and respect, but she was not free. Nor was her husband expected to be faithful to her. Marriage in no way restricted his liberty, but left him free to seek intellectual stimulation in the society of the hetaerae, and gratification of the senses in the company of his slaves. Love in our sense was unknown to the ancients, and although there is a modern note in the legends of the faithful Penelope, and the love which united Orpheus and Eurydice, yet, so Lucka tells us, these instances should be regarded rather as poetic divinations of a future stage of feeling than actual facts then within the scope of probability. Even Plato, in whom all wisdom and ante-Christian culture culminated, was still, in this respect, a citizen of the old world, for he, too, knew as yet nothing of the spiritual love of a man

---

1. *cf.* Hartland's "Primitive Paternity" and Frazer's "Golden Bough."

for a woman. To him the love of an individual was but a beginning, the road to the love of perfect beauty and the eternal ideas.

On the threshold of the second stage of the erotic life stands Christianity, which, in sharp contrast to antiquity and to the classical period, sought the centre and climax of life in the soul. The founder of the "religion of love" *discovered* the individual, and by so doing laid the foundation for that metaphysical love which found its most striking expression in the deification of woman and the cult of the Virgin Mary. How this change of mental attitude was brought about is worked out in a brilliant chapter, entitled "The Birth of Europe." The revivifying influence of Christ's preaching and personality was stifled after the first centuries by the rigid dogma and formalism which had altered his doctrine almost past recognition. The Church was building up its political structure and tolerated no rival. Art, literature, music, all the enthusiasm and profound thought of which the human mind is capable, were pressed into her service. Independent thought was heresy, and the death of every heretic became a new fetter which bound the intellect of man. But about the year 1100, when the mighty edifice was complete, and the pope and his bishops looked down upon kings and emperors and counted them their vassals, when the barbaric peoples which made up the population of Europe had been sufficiently schooled and educated in the new direction, a longing for something new, a yearning for art, for poetry, for beauty, began to stir the hearts of men and women. It found expression in the ideal of chivalry, the Holy Sepulchre and the Holy Grail, and suddenly love, bursting out in a brilliant flame, shed its radiance on the sordid relationship which had hitherto existed between the sexes, and transfigured it. Woman, the despised, to whom at the Council of Macon a soul had been denied, all at once became a queen, a goddess. The drudge, the patiently suffering wife, were things of the past. A new ideal had been set up and men worshipped it with bended knees.

"She shines on us as God shines on his angels,"

sang Guinicelli.

It was in a small country in the South of France, in Provence, that the new spirit was born. The troubadours, wandering from castle to castle, sang the praise of love, genuine love, the earlier ones without admixture either of speculation or metaphysic. The dogma that pure love was its own reward inasmuch as it made men perfect, was framed later on.

"I cannot sin when I am in her mind,"

wrote Guirot Riquier, and Dante, in the "Vita Nuova," calls his beloved mistress "the destroyer of all evil and the queen of all virtues." The monk Matfre Ermengau, who wrote a text-book on love, says:

Love makes good men better,
And the worst man good.

The later troubadours drew a much sharper distinction between spiritual and sensual love. The latter was regarded as degrading and base (at least in principle) and woe to the man who held, or rather, avowed, another opinion. His reward was the contempt of every man and woman of culture. "I ask no more of my mistress than that she should suffer me to serve her," protested Bernart de Ventadour.

It goes without saying that, in spite of this high ideal, sensuality flourished undiminished, and a troubadour who loudly sang the praise of chastity and blatantly professed his entire disinterestedness in the service of his mistress, did not see the least inconsequence in carrying on a dozen intrigues at the same time with other women. Sordello, one of the best known poets of this period, was charged by a contemporary with having changed his mistress over a hundred times, and he himself, impudently bragging, proclaims that

None can resist me; all the frowning husbands
Shall not prevent me to embrace their wives,
If I so wish. . .

Another poet, Count Rambaut III, of Orange, recommended to his fellow-men as the surest way of winning a woman's favour, "to break her nose with a blow of the fist." "I myself," he continued, "treat all women with tenderness and courtesy, but then—I am considered a fool."

As may be expected, sublimated, metaphysical love was not without its caricatures and eccentricities. One of the most grotesque figures of the period of the troubadours was Ulrich von Lichtenstein, a German knight. As a page, we are told, he drank the water in which his mistress had washed her hands. Later on he had his upper lip amputated because it displeased his lady-love, and on another occasion he cut off one of his fingers, had it set in gold and used as a clasp on a volume of his poems which he sent as a present to his inamorata.

At the famous Courts of Love, the most extraordinary questions were seriously discussed and decided. A favourite subject for debate was the relationship between love and marriage, and some of the decisions which have been preserved for us prove without a doubt that those two great factors in the emotional life were considered irreconcilable. At the Court of the Viscountess Ermengarde of Narbonne, the question whether the love between lovers was greater than the love between husband and wife was settled as follows: "Nature and custom have erected an insuperable barrier between conjugal affection and the love which unites two lovers. It would be absurd to draw comparisons between two things which have neither resemblance nor connection."

The contrast between the new, spiritualised love and the older, sexual, instinct created that dualism so characteristic of the whole mediaeval period. Sexuality and love were felt as two inimical forces, the fusion of which was beyond the range of possibility. While on the one hand woman was worshipped as a divine being, before whom all desire must be silenced, she was on the other hand stigmatised as the devil's tool, a power which turned men away from his higher mission and jeopardised the salvation of his soul. Wagner portrayed this dualism perfectly in *Tannhauser*. "A man of the Middle Ages," says Lucka, "would have recognised in this magnificent work the tragedy of his soul."

It was but a small step from the worship of a beloved mistress to the cult of the Virgin Mary. The Church, hostile at first, finally acquiesced, and "through her official acknowledgment of a female deity, open enmity between the religion of the Church and the religion of woman was avoided." A woman, that is to say, the Virgin Mary, had stepped between God and humanity as mediator, intercessor and saviour.

Both Dante, the inspired woman-worshipper of the Middle Ages, and the more modern Goethe, saw in metaphysical love the triumph over all things earthly. And far above either of these intellectual heroes looms the awe-inspiring figure of Michelangelo, the scoffer, to whom love came late in life; in his ecstatic adoration of Vittoria Colonna, the enthusiasm of Plato and the passion of Dante are blended in a more transcendent flame.

Sexual Mystics and the Brides of Christ present the darker aspect of metaphysical love. All the latter, including even Catherine of Siena (a clever politician who kept up a correspondence with the leading statesmen of her time), Marie of Oignies, and St. Teresa, are stigmatised as victims of hysteria and consigned to the domain of pathology.

While the first stage was characterised by the reign of unbridled sexual instinct, the second by the conflict between spiritual and sensual love, the third stage represents our modern conception, the blending of spiritual and sensual love, which is "not the differentiated sexual instinct, but a force embracing the psycho-physical entity of the beloved being without any consciousness of sexual desire." It shares with the purely metaphysical love the lover's longing to raise his mistress above him and glorify her without any ulterior object and desire. "In this stage there is no tyranny of man over woman, as in the sexual stage; no subjection of man to woman, as in the woman-worship of the Middle Ages; but complete equality of the sexes, a mutual give and take. If sexuality is infinite as matter, spiritual love eternal as the metaphysical ideal, then the synthesis is human and personal." The apotheosis of this perfect love Lucka finds in the *Liebestod* (the death of the lovers in the ecstasy of love), in Wagner's *Tristan und Isolde*.

An interesting chapter on erotic aberrations, the demoniacal and the obscene, completes the third part of the book.

There may be much in Lucka's theories which will rouse the scepticism of the monists; some of his deductions may appear to his readers a little strained, but no thinking man or woman can read his brilliant *Conclusion* without denying him the tribute of sincere admiration. In this last chapter he applies Haeckel's biogenetic law to the domain of the spirit. As the human embryo passes through the principal stages of the development of the individual from lower forms of life, so the growing male must pass through the stages of psychical development through which the race has passed. The gynecocratic government of prehistoric time is revived in the nursery, where the mother rules supreme and the sisters dominate. The normal, healthy school-boy, preferring the company of his school-fellows to all others, shunning his mother and sisters, ashamed of his female relatives, is the modern individual representative of those early leagues and unions of young men who opposed matriarchy and finally brought about its overthrow and the establishment of male government. The promiscuous sexuality characteristic of adolescence reproduces the first, merely sexual, stage of the erotic life of the race in the life of the individual. As a rule this phase is followed by a period of woman-worship; love has conquered the sexual instinct and the latter is felt as base and degrading. Atavism is not so much the persistence of the earlier, as the absence of the later stages of psychical development.

I need not emphasise the fact that the three stages are often intermingled and not traceable with equal clearness in the life of every individual. Many men never advance beyond the first stage and others are fragmentary and undeveloped; but certain phases are more or less distinguishable in every well-endowed male individual. Lucka finds a perfect illustration of his theory in the life and works of Richard Wagner, whose operas *The Fairies* (based on Shakespeare's *Measure for Measure*), *Tannhauser*, and *Tristan und Isolde*, successively illustrate the three stages through which the great poet-composer and impassioned lover passed, and reflect the principal halting-places in the erotic evolution of the race. In *Parsifal*, Wagner's last and maturest work, he conjectures a potential fourth stage, divined by the genius of the great musician and thinker, a sublimation of our modern ideal, a stage when love will be freed from all sexual feeling (a conception not unlike Otto Weininger's), but to which we have not yet attained and which we are even unable fully to grasp.

I have not been able to do more than touch upon the principal features of this book, the fame of whose brilliant author has long spread beyond the boundaries of his own native country. Emil Lucka was born in Vienna in 1877, and has already achieved a number of remarkably fine books, most of which have been translated into Russian, French, and other foreign languages. He is as yet unknown in England, this being the first of his works to appear in English.

ELLIE SCHLEUSSNER

THE FIRST STAGE
THE SEXUAL INSTINCT

To the generations slowly rising from the dark abyss of time to the twilight of the Middle Ages, the satisfaction of the sexual instinct offered fewer difficulties than the gratification of any other need or desire. With every unpremeditated and cursory indulgence the craving disappeared from consciousness and left the individual free to give his mind to the acquisition of the necessities of life which were far more difficult to obtain. Primitive, prehistoric man lived in the moment. When there was plenty of food he gorged to repletion, heedless of the starvation which might be his fate to-morrow or the day after. His thought had neither breadth nor continuity. It never occurred to him that there might be a connection between an abrupt and quickly forgotten embrace and the birth of a child by a woman of the tribe after what appeared to be an immeasurable lapse of time. He suspected witchcraft in the phenomena of pregnancy and childbirth (to this day the aborigines of Central and Northern Australia do not realise the connection between generation and birth). As a rule it was remembered that a certain woman had given birth to a certain child by the fact of her having carried it about and fed it at her breast. Occasionally it was forgotten to which mother a child belonged; perhaps the mother had died; perhaps the child had strayed beyond the boundaries of the community and the mother had failed to recognise it on its return. But it was clear beyond all doubt that every child had a "mother." The conception of "father" had not yet been formed. Experience had taught our primitive ancestors two undeniable facts, namely "that women gave birth to children" and "that every child had a mother."

We must assume that sexual intercourse was irregular and haphazard up to the dawn of history. Every woman—within the limits of her own tribe, probably—belonged to every man. Whether this assumption is universally applicable or not, must remain doubtful; later ethnologists, more particularly *von Westermarck*, deny it because it does not apply to every savage tribe of the present day. Herodotus tells us that promiscuity existed in historical times in countries as far removed from each other as Ethiopia and the borders of the Caspian Sea. There can be no reasonable doubt that sexual intercourse took the form of group-marriage, the exchange or lending of wives, and other similar arrangements.

The relationship between mother and child having been established by Nature herself, the first human family congregated round the mother, acknowledging her as its natural chief. This continued even after the causal connection between generation and birth had ceased to be a mystery. In all countries on the Mediterranean, more especially in Lycia, Crete and Egypt, the predominance of the female element in State and family is well attested; it is reflected in the natural religions of the Eastern races—both Semitic and Aryan—and we find innumerable traces of it in Greek mythology. The merit of discovering this important stage in the relationship of the sexes is due to *Bachofen*. "Based on life-giving motherhood," he says, "gynecocracy was completely dominated by the natural principles and phenomena which rule its inner and outer life; it vividly realised the unity of nature, the harmony of the universe which it had not yet outgrown. . . In every respect obedient to the laws of physical existence, its gaze was fixed upon the earth, it worshipped the chthonian powers rather than the gods of light." The children of men who had sprung from their mother as the flowers spring from the soil, raised altars to Gaea, Demeter and Isis, the deities of inexhaustible fertility and abundance. These early races of men realised themselves only as a part of nature; they had not yet conceived the idea of rising above their condition and setting their intelligence to battle with its blind laws. Incapable of realising their individuality, they bowed in passive submission to nature's undisputed sway. They were members of a tribe, and the fragmentary existence of the single individual was of no importance when it clashed with the welfare of the clan. The family—centred round the mother—and the tribe were the real individuals, in the same way as the swarm of bees, and not the individual bee, makes the whole. They lived in complete harmony with nature; they had no spiritual life, no history, for civilisation and the creation of intellectual values which are the foundation of history depend on the rise of a community above primitive conditions. Differentiation had hardly begun to exert its modifying influence; all men (not unlike the Eastern Asiatics of our day) resembled each other in looks, character and habits.

In the countries on the Mediterranean (as well as in India and Babylonia) the first stage of sexual intercourse, irresponsible and promiscuous, was systematised by religion. The annual spring-festivals in honour of Adonis, Dionysus, Mylitta, Astarte and Aphrodite, celebrated unbridled licentiousness. The whole community greeted the re-awakening vitality of the earth by an unrestrained abandonment to passion. Man aspired to be no more than the flower which scatters its seed to the winds. The incomprehensible lords of cupidity and rank vegetation did not suffer the individualisation of desire. The complete union of the male and female qualities, as manifested both in nature and man, was solemnised in the Orgies, and not by any means the relationship of an individual man to an individual woman, or sexuality connected with individuals and dominated by them. Nor was this unfettering of instinct a symbolical act; for it to be so, man must have stood over against nature as an intellectual being, mirroring and transforming her acts by his own deeds. He was as yet far from this. His ambition did not reach beyond the desire to fulfil nature in himself. Before the majesty of sex—worshipped in the vague, shadowy mothers of mankind, Rhea, Demeter, Cybele, and their human offspring, the phallic Dionysus and the hundred-breasted goddess of Ephesus—the individual with his piteous limitations shrank into insignificance. Sex was immortal, sex and primary matter, the contrasted by Aristotle with the, the form. "The female principle is the mother of the body, but the mother of the spirit is the male." The substance of those ancient cults was birth and death, meaningless, purposeless, apparently without rhyme or reason; their sacrament the perpetual union of the sexes. Between the succeeding generations there was but one bond, the natural bond of motherhood. It was the first tie realised by mankind, a tie not felt as a concrete relationship between two individuals, but as a general, maternal, natural force. The presiding divinities were the "mothers," the eternal, incorporeal deities, enthroned outside time and space, and therefore immortal givers of life and preservers of mankind. Before their silent greatness the desire of man to know his whence and whither, to win shape and individuality, became blasphemy. They had given immortality to sex, but upon the individual they had laid the curse of death.

Thus we have first a stage of fatherless, natural conception, corresponding with the philosophical theories which maintained that all created things had sprung from the elements. Later ages discovered a spiritual principle, a becoming, or an eternal being, and finally a conflict between spirit and matter.

But the general attitude towards sexual intercourse underwent a change as soon as here and there individuals appeared who were conscious of their individuality. Natural selection could not come into play in a community the members of which resembled one another so closely that all personal characteristics were obliterated in a general monotony. One woman was as good as another, although in all probability a healthy, youthful and strong individual would be preferred to a sickly, puny specimen. But apart from this, the wish to choose a partner instead of being content with the first comer, must have coincided historically with the outward, and later on with the inward differentiation of the race. I cannot prove my theory by quoting chapter and verse from ancient writers, but obviously a feeling of preference could not have arisen until individuals had begun to show very noticeable traces of difference. Therefore with growing differentiation a new factor—modest at first and operating within narrow limits—the factor of choice, had come into the sexual life. The slow development of personality gave birth to the feeling which rebelled against universal sexual intercourse and gynecocracy in general. The men desired to shape their own world; they had no share in the immortality of maternal life. As (relatively speaking) single individuals they stood over against the material bond of the generations living in the chain of the mothers. Demigods, the sons of the gods of light and mortal mothers, were credited with the salvation of men from a confused, chaotic existence, and the introduction of new conditions of life, no longer based on the dictates of nature but on the moulding genius of man. "Hercules, Theseus and Perseus overthrew the ancient powers of darkness. They laid the foundations of man's great achievement, civilisation, and were the first to worship the gods of light. They delivered humanity from the gross materialism in which it had hitherto been steeped; they were the awakeners of spiritual life, which is a higher life than the life of the senses; they were as incorruptible as the sun from whence they came, the heroes of a new civilisation distinguished by gentleness, a higher endeavour and a new dispensation." (Bachofen.)

Heinrich Schurtz has proved (though not in connection with matriarchy) that side by side with the family, unions of unmarried men existed in many countries at a very early time. The object of these unions, which had nothing of the rigidity of blood-relationship, was fellowship. As soon as the boys had outgrown the care of their mother they were compelled to combine for the purpose of playing games and later on for war and hunting; these men's unions therefore were the outcome of the necessary conditions of life. It is obvious that innovations and inventions of all sorts originated in these unions rather than with the temperamentally conservative women, and that we have to look upon them as the hotbed of all spiritual and social evolution. These confederations and leagues not based on a natural or blood-relationship, but on a feeling of brotherhood and friendliness, might well have been an attack upon the natural ties of the family, an expression of a feeling of hostility to and contempt for women, and probably stood in close relationship to a striking characteristic of the past: a widely spread homosexuality.

Whether Schurtz gives us a correct picture of these men's unions or not, there can be no doubt that the struggle against matriarchy originated in them. This struggle led eventually to the victory of the male principle, the acknowledgment of the authority of the father, the institution of male government which deprived women of all legal rights, and the dominion of the spiritual; the victory of the gods of light over the dark lords of fertility. This revolution of principles was perhaps the completest revolution humanity has ever known.

A long road, marked by numerous compromises and limitations, led from casual intercourse to the final establishment of the monogamous system. Free intercourse had been sanctioned by the gods, who suffered no restrictions and modifications, and sacrifices in the shape of a temporary universal unfettering of instinct were required to pacify their anger and reconcile them to the new system. The first and most important of these compromises was the temple-prostitution practised by many nations in Asia Minor, the Greek Archipelago, India and Babylonia. Many a girl gained in this way the marriage portion which enabled her later on to find a husband, to whom she invariably remained strictly loyal. Thus all religious requirements were satisfied. At first this was an annually recurring rite, but gradually it became an isolated ceremony in the life of every female individual. "In the place of the annual surrender," says Priester, "we now have a single act; the hetaerism of the matrons is succeeded by the hetaerism of the maids; instead of being practised during marriage, it is practised in spinsterhood; the blind surrender has given way to a yielding to certain individuals.". . .

With the growth of civilisation a few girls, the hierodules, were set apart for the purpose of pacifying the offended deities and their act ransomed the rest of the female citizens.

It was not on erotic grounds, but for political and social reasons that the Greek introduced monogamy. The reason which weighed in the scales more heavily than all others was the necessity for legitimate offspring. It was natural that a man of property should desire a legitimate heir who would inherit it on his death. The right of succession from father to son, incorporated later on in the Roman Right, originated during this period. But this was not the only advantage connected with the possession of a son: religion taught that after death the body required sacrificial food which could only be provided by the legitimate male descendants of the deceased. (The same belief was held by the Indians and Eastern Asiatics.) In several Greek States marriage was compulsory and bachelors were fined. At the same time the contraction of a marriage did not interfere with the personal freedom of the man; he was at liberty to go to the hetaerae for intellectual stimulation (unless he happened to prefer the friends of his own sex) and to his slaves for the pleasures of the senses. His wife, although she was not free, was respected by him as the guardian of his hearth and children. There was but one legal reason for divorce: sterility, which frustrated the object of matrimony. Conjugal love as we understand it did not exist; it is a feeling which was entirely unknown to the ancients.

With the exception of the gradually weakening hold of religion on the imagination of the people towards the decline of the Roman Empire, no perceptible change occurred in the social life of the old world until the dawn of the Middle Ages. To quote Otto Seeck: "A wife had no other task than to produce legitimate offspring; and yet she gave herself airs and graces, embittered her husband's life with her jealousy and bad temper or, worse even, set all tongues wagging with her evil conduct. Is it to be wondered at that marriage was merely regarded as a duty to the State, and that a great number of men were not sufficiently patriotic to take such a burden upon their shoulders?"

Thus the victory of the male spiritual principle over universal sexual intercourse ushered in the second stage which checked the sexual impulse and directed it upon certain individuals, a distinction however, which bears no relation to love.

Monogamy had conquered, in principle at least and as an ideal.

The profoundly mystical core of the most powerful Greek tragedy which has come down to our time, the *Orestes* of Aeschylus, represents the victory of the new gods of light over the old maternal powers. Orestes has sinned against the old law, for in order to avenge his father's death, he has slain his mother. The sun-god Apollo and the sinister Erinnys, the upholders of the old maternal right, are waging war over the justifiableness of the deed. To the Erinnys, matricide is the foulest of all crimes, for man is more nearly related to the mother than to the father. But Apollo had commanded the deed, so that the father's murder should not remain unavenged.

Not to the mother is the child indebted
For life; she tends and guards the kindling spark
The father lighted; she but holds his pledge.——

he explains. And the answer is the lament of the Erinnys:

Thus thou destroy'st the gods of ancient times!

Athene, the virgin goddess, the motherless daughter of Zeus, appearing as mediator between the opponents, decides in favour of the new dispensation which places the father's claim above the mother's. Orestes is free of guilt; his deed was justifiable according to the canons of the new law. The tragedy is the symbolical commemoration of the victory of the male principle in Greece. But Athene is the embodiment of the new hermaphroditic ideal of the Greek which stood in close connexion to their homosexuality, and with which I propose to deal later on.

There is a psychical law ordaining that nothing which has ever quickened the soul of man shall be entirely lost. Were it not so, the storehouses of the soul would stand empty. New values are created, but the old verities endure; as a rule they are relegated to a lower sphere, to inferior social layers, but they persist and frequently merge into the new. This law applies without exception to the relationship between the sexes; we shall come upon it again and again. During the second stage, characterised by the spiritual love foreign to the ancients, the purely sexual impulse continued as an unimpaired force, but it had lost its prestige and was not only regarded as ignoble and base, but also stigmatised as sinful and demoniacal. The hearts of men were stirred by new ideals.

A similar attitude, perhaps not quite so uncompromising because the contrast was less pronounced, existed in classical Greece. The more highly developed, self-conscious Hellenic genius, shrinking from promiscuous intercourse, had systematised the instinct and set up a new ideal in Platonic love. But below the surface raged the unbridled natural force, and in perfect harmony with the Greek spirit—it was not hysterically hidden, but assigned a place in the new system. Wrapped in the obscurity of the Mysteries, concealed from the gaze of the new gods of light, it attempted to assuage its inextinguishable thirst. The Mysteries were the annual tribute paid as a ransom by Apollo-worshipping Hellas to chaotic Asia, so that she might be free to pursue her higher psycho-spiritual aims. The brilliant civilisation of Athens was based on the dark cult of the Mysteries. On the festivals of the hermaphroditic Dionysus and Demeter, which are identical with the cults of Adonis and

Mylitta, the impersonal, generative elements were worshipped. Thus, below the surface of the Greek State, founded on masculine values and attempting to restrict intercourse for the benefit of a more systematised progeniture, flourished the orgiastic cult of the ancient Eastern deities, who had vouchsafed to mortals a glimpse of the great secret of life in the ardour of procreation and conception. The women upheld the religion of passion as an end in itself; bacchantes, men in female attire, emasculated priests, sacrificed to the blindly bountiful gods. We are told that Dionysus conquered even the Amazons and converted them to his worship. Euripides described in the *Bacchantes*—the subject of which is the war between the uncontrolled sexual impulse and the new order of things—how Dionysus traversed all Asia and finally arrived in Hellas accompanied by a crowd of abandoned women. But his religion was more than a cult of wine and sensual pleasure, it embraced a gentle worship of nature, throwing down the barrier between man and beast—impassable by the spirit of civilisation—and lovingly including every living creature. We read in the *Bacchantes* that the women who had fled from the town to follow the irresistible stranger, Dionysus, dwelled in the mountains, binding their hair with tame adders, carrying in their arms the cubs of wolves and the young deer, and feeding them with the milk of their breasts; that milk and wine welled up when they struck the earth with the thyrsus; and so on. Dionysus implores Pentheus, the representative of the Hellenic masculine system, not to venture undisguised among the maenads: "They'll murder you if they divine your sex," and, knowing the secret of the male and female temper:

> . . . . *First let*
> *His mind be clouded by a slight disorder*
> *For, conscious of his manhood he will never*
> *Wear women's garb; insane, he's sure to wear it.*

Pentheus, recognising in Dionysus the foe of a more spiritual conception of the law, the *effeminate stranger* who had driven the women to madness, is torn to pieces by the frenzied bacchantes who fall upon him, led by Agave, his mother, and sacrificed to the *bull-god* Dionysus. At the conclusion of this strange and profound epos, Agave recovers her senses and curses the acts which she has committed in her madness. . . women submit to the new spiritual dispensation. We realise now why Hera, the tutelary goddess of the newly introduced monogamous system, hated Dionysus and attempted to kill him before he was born.

The subject treated in the beautiful myth of Orpheus is the relationship between the primitive sexual impulse and its individualisation on a single personality. For seven months Orpheus bewails the death of Eurydice and regards all other living creatures with indifference. This loyalty offends and infuriates the women of Thracia, who divine in it a spirit inimical to a life in harmony with nature. One night, during the celebration of the Dionysian rites, they attack the poet—the representative of the higher Hellenic poetical ideals—and rend him limb from limb. But as the head of the murdered singer floats down the river, the pale lips still frame the beloved name: Eurydice! It is certain that in those remote legendary days such love did not exist. But the prophetic Greek spirit contrasted promiscuous intercourse with love for a single woman.

So far we have encountered only a general, not an individualised, sexual instinct and, in a limited measure at least, a struggling tendency towards individualisation. But even so it was merely a question of instinct, and did not bear the least resemblance to love as we understand it to-day. *Love* did not exist in the old world. I admit that in the legend of Orpheus we are face to face with a sentiment which is not unlike modern love, but, as far as I am aware, this is an isolated case in Greek history, and may be regarded as a divination of something new, just as we find unmistakable anticipations of Christianity in Plato's writings. Such phenomena—the occasional occurrence of which I do not altogether deny, although I regard them as on the whole improbable as far as the sphere of my research is concerned—are not infrequently met with in history, but their effect upon civilisation was nil; they were presentiments, incomprehensible in their day, and for this very reason probably preserved as curiosities.

In spite of the fact, however, that in those far-off days spiritual love of a man for a woman was unknown, we find Plato contrasting "a base and degraded Eros with a divine Eros." Pausanias says in the "Symposium":

"The man who loves with his senses only, loves women and boys equally well. He loves the body more than the soul. . . His only striving is to obtain the object of his desire, and he cares not whether it be worthy or unworthy. The Eros he worships is the ally of that younger goddess in whom male and female attributes are blended. But the other Eros is the companion of Aphrodite, Urania, the divine; unbegotten by a father, unconceived by a mother, she is the offspring of the male element, the elder one, unstained by passion. . . The sensualist who loves the body more than the soul is base. His love passes away like the object of his passion. But the companion of the Olympic goddess is the Eros who fills the hearts of the lovers with the longing for virtue. The other Eros is the confederate of the debased Aphrodite." And Aristophanes, another of the participators in the feast, says: "The yearning does not seem to be a desire for the pleasures of the senses, the one taking delight in his intercourse with the other; far from it, it is obvious that each soul is craving for something which it cannot express in words, but can only divine and conjecture." And the mysterious Diotima revealed to Socrates an entirely novel principle in erotic life; the principle which guides man beyond the pleasures of the senses and—through love—leads him to the divine. "The slave of his senses runs after women; but he who loves with his soul and strives to win immortality through virtue and wisdom, seeks a great and beautiful soul that he may surrender himself to it completely." But in the opinion of the classical ages, a beautiful soul was only to be found in the body of a man; woman belonged to the lower, animal spheres; she was destined for the pleasure of the senses and the propagation of the race. Plato's theory of ideas is the philosophical victory of the male-spiritual principle over nature, matter and their warden: woman. (Perhaps it is even the revenge of the Greek genius for man's original enslavement.) "Love between men," continues the seer, "forms a stronger tie, a closer friendship, than love between parents and children; it has a mutual share in children which are immortal and far more beautiful than the children of men." She teaches Socrates that this noble love is at the root of all the magnificent creations of the spirit, as carnal love is the origin of human life. "Until he becomes aware that the beauty of all bodies is closely related, a man must love an individual with all his heart. If a man will follow after beauty, he is foolish not to conceive the beauty of all bodies as one and the same. As soon as he has learned this, he will become a lover of all beautiful forms; his fervent passion for one will diminish, he will scorn the individual and hold it cheap."

With the Hellenic homosexuality an element foreign and even hostile to the original and natural bi-sexual sensuality crept into the erotic life of the human race; it found its classical representation in the Platonic dialogues "Symposium" and "Phaedros." In conscious opposition to all sexuality Platonic love (what is usually called Platonic love is based on an obstinate misunderstanding) turns to the purely spiritual, that is to say, the conceptions of truth, beauty and goodness; it is a yearning for the supernatural, and it knows itself as the path to it. In the mutual love of all noble souls lies the germ of all higher things; it is the way to the gods of light which, in this connection, are conceived philosophically as ideas, though in the true Hellenic spirit as objective ideas, the prototypes and culminations of everything human. To grasp the meaning of Platonic love it is essential to realise that—unlike the spiritual woman-worship peculiar to the Middle Ages—it is not a personal feeling of one individual for another; platonically speaking, the love for an individual is only a first stage; the path which leads to the love of beauty and the eternal ideas. The characteristic of this metaphysical love which Plato was the first to conceive, was therefore love for the universal, and not love for an individual. The latter, as we shall find later on, is the characteristic of the true or, more modestly speaking, specifically European conception of love. Platonic love, finally, was the perception of perfection, the Socratic knowledge; its alpha and omega was not, as the mystic and true erotic would have it, its ardour and passion, the fulness of its own being. It had an alien purpose: the knowledge of things divine, by a later period Christianised and understood as the divine mysteries. To Plato, the essence and climax of antique, ante-Christian culture, every individual, even the beloved mistress, was but a preliminary, a finger-post, pointing the way to the perception of perfect beauty. True virtue is the outcome of profound knowledge; it transforms men into gods. The purely spiritual woman-worship of the Middle Ages was only another aspect of this yearning to attain to virtue and perfection through the love of an individual. We must not lose sight of the fact that it was already strongly emphasised and upheld in the Platonic ideal of love.

In the dark excesses of the Mysteries the beauty of the human form counted for nothing; voluptuousness and intoxication ruled. In the Asiatic cult of the sexes there was no room for beauty, no time for selection. The Greeks were the discoverers of the beauty of the human form. Beauty kindled the flame of love in their souls, beauty was the gauge which determined their erotic values. Their ideal was a *kalokagathos*, a youth beautiful in body and soul.

In "Phaedros" Plato contrasts with far greater force than in the "Symposium" him "who craves for sensual pleasure like the beasts in the fields" with him "who strives after beauty and perfection." To the latter "the face of the beloved is the reflection of the sublimely beautiful." He would like to sacrifice to her, as to the immortal gods. All beautiful bodies represent to him in an increasing measure the idea of the beauty of form, which again is subordinate to the beauty of the soul. It points the way to metaphysical beauty, the eternal and imperishable idea of mankind. Socrates could scorn the beauty of the individual because he saw in it merely an imperfect reflection of perfect beauty. In its truest sense Platonic love is, therefore, impersonal; it is not spiritual love for a human being, but a peculiar characteristic of the Greek cult of beauty. We shall again meet this principle of beauty-worship in metaphysical love, the adoration of woman; thanks to Plato, it has for all time become the inalienable property of the human mind. The striving to rise above all individualism was another ideal which a later period revived. But the pivot round which the emotions revolved was the love for a beloved individual, the modern, European, fundamental motive, as opposed to the antique Platonic cult of ideas. Thus Plato, too, was a citizen of the old world, at whose threshold stood universal sexual intercourse, tolerating nothing personal, knowing of no individuals, acknowledging only unchecked, uncontrollable instinct, and whose decline was again characterised by the extreme impersonality of ideas. It had traversed the path of human existence in a huge cycle. Starting from an unconscious existence in complete harmony with nature, it had passed through individualised man to the loftiest spiritual conceptions in the impersonal world of ideas.

The Hellenic ideal of beauty was almost invariably realised in the male form. The Greeks of the classical period disdained woman; she was for them inseparably connected with base sensuality, but their contempt had its source partly in a feeling of horror. The days when matriarchy was the form of government were not very remote; it survived in a great number of myths and also, subconsciously perhaps, in the soul of man. To the Greek mind woman was the embodiment of the dark side of love, and it was merely the logical conclusion of this conception when, at a later period, she was regarded as the devil's tool. It is certain that the origin of the idea must be sought in Plato's time.

In intercourse with women man dimly felt the vague elementary condition from which he had struggled hard to emerge, and fled to the more familiar companions of his own sex. Would not love between man and man deliver him from the basely sensual, strengthen his spirituality and lead him to the gods? In this connection Zeus is called in "Phaedros", the maker of friendships. Plato, in propounding this doctrine, drew thereby the most radical conclusion of the new, apparently male, but at heart hermaphroditic ideal of civilisation, conceived in the heroic epoch and elaborated and brought to perfection by the Greek of classical times. This ideal was the victory of the spiritual principle over promiscuous sexuality and irresponsible propagation and, quite in the true Hellenic spirit, it was again interpreted materially.

Because individualised love was an unknown quantity to the ancients, they ornamented their sarcophagi with symbols of ecstatic life, with dancing and embracing fauns and maenads. Generations passed away, but new ones arose, embracing and begetting life—for life was eternal. Death was vanquished in the ecstasy of the nameless millions, for the true meaning of life lay in the preservation of the species. The death of the individual did not have a deep and poignant meaning until the soul had become the centre and climax of life. An individual had passed away for ever—nothing could recall him. Death had become the final issue, the terror, because it destroyed the greatest of all things: self-conscious man. But love, too, had changed; it was no longer sexual impulse, depending on the body and perishing with it, but a craving of the soul, conscious of itself and stretching out feelers far beyond the earth. A new pang had come into the world, but also a new reconciliation.

THE SECOND STAGE
LOVE

I

The Birth of Europe

The memory of the figure and preaching of Christ had so powerfully influenced the centuries that it had gradually permeated and transformed not only the Platonic doctrine of ideas—that maturest fruit of Greek wisdom—but also the Semitic mediaeval monotheism. Something new had sprung into being, something which expressed a hitherto unknown feeling for life and for humanity, vague and uncertain in the beginning, but growing in clearness and uniformity. On the throne of the Roman emperors sat a bishop, whose power was increasing with the development of the new civilisation, and whom the final victory of the new transcendental world-principle had made master of the world. The building up of this new civilisation had absorbed the intellectual force of a thousand years; it had monopolised thought and every form of energy. The reward was great. For the first time in the annals of the world the questionings of brooding intelligence were fully answered, the anguish of the tortured soul was stilled. The purpose of the universe, the destiny of man, were comprehended and interpreted, good and evil being finally known. At the close of the first Christian millenary, all moral and intellectual values were grouped round and dominated by one supreme ideal; the loftiest value in this world and the next, side by side with the greatest secular power, were in the hands of the Church; together with the imperium she had succeeded to the spiritual and ethical inheritance of the dead civilisations. Without her uncouth barbarism reigned, and it was her task, while elaborating the system of the universe for which she stood, to teach and convert the new nations, to spread a uniform Christian civilisation.

On the mere face of it it must seem strange that a religion which had grown on foreign soil, out of foreign spiritual assumptions, should have been accepted so readily and quickly by nations to whom it must have been alien and unintelligible. The love of war and valour of the Teutonic tribes and Christian asceticism were diametrically opposed ideals, and very often their relationship was one of direct hostility. I need only remind the reader of the contempt expressed for the chaplain by Hagen (in the "Song of the Niebelungen"). On the other hand, the ancient Celtic and Teutonic races shared one profound characteristic with the Christian world, the consequences of which were sufficiently far-reaching to raise the religion of Christ to the religion of Europe. The characteristic common to the still uncultivated European spirit and Christianity, and meaningless alike to the Asiatic barbarians, the Jews of the Old Testament and the Greeks, was the importance which both attached to the individual soul. Through the Christian religion this new intuition which saw in the soul of man the highest of values, became the centre and pivot of life and faith—a position to which even Plato, to whom the objective, metaphysical idea was the essential, never attained. It had been the most personal experience of Christ, and centuries after his death the nations rediscovered it as their highest value. It entitled Christianity to become the natural religion of Europe, and the soul of its new system of civilisation. It formed the most complete contrast to all Asiatic cults, Brahminism and Buddhism, a fact which, since Schopenhauer, one is inclined to overlook. To the Indian, the soul of man is not an entity; his consciousness is a republic, as it were, composed of diverse spiritual principles and metaphysical forces which are not centralised into an "I-centre," but exist impersonally, side by side. This may be a great conception, but it is foreign to the feeling of the citizen of Europe. To the latter the I, the soul, the personality, is the pivot round which life turns. The evolution of the European world-feeling is in the direction of the independent development of all psychical forces and their fusion into a unity of ever-increasing intimacy. New values will be created, but the fusing power of the soul will strive with growing intensity to co-ordinate and unify the internal and external life; personality will recreate the world in conformity with its own purposes, that is to say, it will found the system of objective civilisation. The incapacity of the Indian to produce a civilisation perfect in every direction is explained by his one-sided, morally-speculative thought. The world is to him nothing but a moral phenomenon, he admits no other explanation; he seeks its true meaning and the possibility of its salvation in the realisation of the vanity of life, not in the liberating deed, and not in the inward change.

The kernel of matured and spiritualised Christianity, which reached its apex in the German mystics, lies in the soul of man, eager to shed everything which is subjective and accidental, and become spirit, profound, divine reality. Eckhart, the great perfecter of this European religion, deliberately and in direct contradiction to the dogma of his time, placed man above the "highest angels," whom he considered subject to limitations; "man," he argues, "thanks to his freedom, is able to reach a goal to which no angel could aspire. For he is always new, infinitely exalted above the limitations of the angels and all finite reason." Of the relationship between the soul and God he says; "The soul of the righteous man shall be with God, his equal and compeer, no more and no less." The Upanishads, on the other hand, maintain that the core of the world is not to be found in the soul of the individual but in Brahma, the universal soul, outside whom there is no reality. "The individual soul is but a phantasm of the universal soul, as the reflection of the sun in the water is but a phantasm of the sun." The sole purpose of the world is the extinction of individual consciousness, its absorption in Brahma, the end of all suffering: "When feeling has ceased, pain must cease, too, and the world be delivered." The Indian lacks the central conception of love, for which he substitutes knowledge. Primitive Christianity conceived the connection between body and soul, the encumbering of the soul by the body, as it were, as a temptation or a punishment; according to the Vedas, it is merely a delusion to which the sage is not subject. Before his keen vision, the deception falls to the ground, and by this very fact he is delivered. To the feeling of Europe and Christianity, however, life and the universe are genuine, deep realities, the touchstone of the soul. Love is the soul's greatest treasure and the only true path to God; knowledge can never take its place. "The divine stream of love flowing through the soul," says Eckhart, "carries the soul along with it to its origin, to the bourne of all knowledge, to God."

The very general identification of the Christian and Indian mystics—a fact which is accounted for by their common metaphysical tendency—is based on an error; Indian mysticism and Christian mysticism originated in different concepts; here the centre of all being is laid in love and in the soul of man, there it is contained in knowledge and in Brahma. But ultimately, at the termination of the world-process, they will meet, although coming from different directions. "While the soul worships a God, realises a God and knows of a God," says Eckhart, "it is separated from God. This is God's purpose, to annihilate Himself in the soul, so that the soul, too, shall lose itself. For God has been called God by the creatures." The words "The soul creates God from within, is connected with the divine and becomes divine itself," are highly significant. To the Vedantist the soul of man is an emanation from the world-soul: "Although God differs from the individual soul, the individual soul does not differ from God." At this point it is no longer an easy matter to distinguish the feeling of the Christian mystic from the feeling of the Brahmin; though their valuations of man, life and the world differ, nay, are even opposed to each other, they finally meet in God. We read in the Vedanta: "The force which created and maintains the universe, the eternal principle of all being, dwells entirely and undividedly in every one of us. Our self is identical with the supreme deity and only apparently differentiated from it. Whosoever has mastered this truth has become at one with all creation; whosoever has not mastered it, is a stranger and a foe to all creatures."

I do not intend to depreciate Indian wisdom; I merely desire to point out its inherent dissimilarity to Western thought; my task of laying hold of the spirit of Europe in its crises and watching its growth is bound to be advanced by this division.

The religious experience of Christ, based on the realisation of the divine nature of the soul, and the road of the soul to God, has established the fundamental Western principle. A world-system was built up which emanated from the innermost depth of the individual soul and, very consistently, related all existing things, heaven and earth, the creation and the destruction of the world, salvation and perdition, to the soul of man. This was achieved with the aid of a naïve metaphysic, created by the Greek genius and externalised by the crude intellect of barbarians; this metaphysic drew its whole content from a unique revelation, and the essential was frequently hidden by dialectic and speculation. One may safely say that the first millenary strove, if not exactly to set aside the original principle of Christianity, yet to bind it by dogma in such a way that it often became completely obscured. A long training was necessary before the immature nations of barbarians were fit to become citizens of the spiritual world, before they could fully assimilate the new traditions and grasp their innermost meaning, which by this very fact became altered and modified. This process of education came to a temporary conclusion about the year 1100. At last the European nations had outgrown the guardianship of the Church with its antiquated methods; a new, a creative epoch was dawning; the civilisation of Europe, opposed to all barbarism and orientalism, rose like a brilliant star on the horizon of the world. Spontaneous feeling for the race, for nature and for the divine verities had again become possible.

I shall have to exceed the limits of my subject in this chapter, for I propose showing the seeds from which, in the time of the Crusades, the new soul of the European, throwing off the lethargy of the first Christian millenary, began to grow with extraordinary vigour and rapidity; that new soul which experienced a wider, if not deeper, unfolding in the period of the Renascence, and to this day pervades and fertilises our spiritual life. I might have been less digressive, but I hope that two reasons will justify my prolixity; the first is the great importance of the subject from the point of view of a history of civilisation, and the second and more particular one is its close inner relationship to my principal theme. For, in complete contrast with the sexuality on which heretofore the relationship between husband and wife had been based, a new feeling, that of spiritual love, had come into existence and quickly reached its climax. Projected not only on the other sex, but also on God and on nature, it permeated the age and explains its great and unprecedented manifestations: the spiritual love between man and woman (which deteriorated later on into the deification of woman), the new religion of the German mystics, the awakening appreciation of the beauty of nature, the sudden outburst of German poetry—no sooner born than it reached perfection—the specifically European Gothic architecture, so completely independent of the old art. All these new creations had their origin in the strange craving of the period for something novel and romantic, something hitherto unknown. This longing begot the ideal of chivalry and a wealth of half human, half preter-human conceptions, such as the Holy Sepulchre and the Holy Grail. And all at once, something unprecedented, something of which the race had as yet no experience, had come to pass: love, which had nothing in common with sensuality, which was even deliberately hostile to it, love which welled up in one soul and flowed into the other—presupposing personality—love was there! If, therefore, I have gone into detail, I hope that it has served to elucidate the principal theme of this part of my book, namely, the spiritual part of man for woman aspiring to the metaphysical, which is so alien to our modern feeling.

It is necessary to begin by sketching a background which shall set off the new phenomenon. The spiritual achievement of the first millenary was the construction of the Christian system of the universe the Church had complete knowledge of all things in heaven and earth—symbols merely of the eternal verities; her wisdom almost equalled divine wisdom, for the secrets of life and death had been revealed and surrendered to her; St. Chrysostom's words uttered in the fourth century, "The Church is God," had become a fact. The profoundest wisdom, the greatest power, were hers; the loftiest ideal had been realised as it has never been realised before or since. As the wisdom of the Church had been a direct gift of God, so her power, too, had divine origin and reached beyond this earthly life. The Church alone held the key to eternal bliss, her curse meant everlasting damnation. To be excommunicated was to be bereaved of temporal and eternal happiness. A man who had been excommunicated was worse off than a wild beast; he was surrendered to the devils in hell, and he knew it. There was but one road to salvation: to do penance and humbly submit to the Church. This has been symbolised for all times by the memorable submission of the Roman-German emperor, who stood for three days, barefooted and fasting, in the snow in the courtyard of Canossa, before he was received back into the kingdom of God. The kingdom of God was synonymous with the Church; Jews and pagans were the natural children of the devil, but the dissenter, the heretic who dared to question a single proposition of the divine system, or was bold enough to think on original lines—in other words in contradiction to tradition—voluntarily turned his back on God, and with seeing eyes went into the kingdom of the devil. He was wholly evil, and no earthly punishment fitted his crime. The emperor Theodosius, as far back as A.D. 380, had called such heretics "insane and demented," and the burning of their bodies at the stake which prevented their souls from falling into the hands of the devil, was looked upon as a great and undeserved mercy. But not only during their lifetime, but after their death, too, the hand of the Church fell heavily on all those who had strayed beyond her pale; their bodies were dragged from their graves and thrown into the carrion-pit. A man whom the Church had excommunicated was buried in the cemetery of a German convent. The Archbishop of Mayence ordered the exhumation of the body, threatening to interdict divine service in the convent if his command were disobeyed. But the abbess, Hildegarde of Bingen (1098–1179), a woman of great mental power and an inspired seer, opposed him. Having received a direct message from God, she wrote to the bishop as follows: "Conforming to my custom, I looked up to the true light, and God commanded me to withhold my consent to the exhumation of the body, because He Himself took the dead man from the pale of the Church, so that He might lead him to the beatitude of the blessed. . . It were better for me to fall into the hands of man than to disobey the command of my Lord." The saint had interpreted the will of God, and the archbishop, sanctioning a sudden rumour that the deceased had received absolution at the eleventh hour, yielded. But the bishop's yielding by no means countenanced the belief that God might, for once, tolerate the body of an excommunicate in sacred ground, far from it—the vision of the abbess Hildegarde had merely served to correct an error.

All those who dared to oppose the clergy by word or deed were doomed to everlasting perdition—this was a fact which it were futile to doubt; at the most, a man shrugged his shoulders at certain damnation for the sake of mundane pleasures—a rich legacy in the hour of death might save him. Not infrequently the fear of the devil was transformed into indifference, and sometimes even into demonolatry. A single ungodly thought might involve eternal death, and as many a man, more particularly many a priest, realised his inability to live continuously in the presence of God, he surrendered his soul to the anti-god, not from a longing for the pleasures of the senses, but from despair. The worship of the devil, far from being an invention of fanatical monks, actually existed, and was often the last consolation of those who held themselves forsaken by God. The hierarchy did not hesitate a moment to make the utmost use or the power conferred upon them by the mental attitude of the people. The government of kings and princes, in addition to the ecclesiastical government, could only be a transient, sinful condition; the time was bound to come when the pope would be king of the earth, and the great lords of the world his vassals, appointed by him to keep the wicked world in check, and deposed by him if he found them incapable, worshippers of the devil, or disobedient to the Church. The whole world was a hierarchy whose apex reached heaven and bore, as the representative of its invisible summit, the pope. He stood, to quote Innocent III, "in the middle, between God and humanity." The same great pope has left us a document entitled *On the Contempt of the World*, which treats of the absolute futility of all things mundane. There is no reason to look upon the union of this unquenchable thirst for power and complete "other-worldiness" as a contradiction. The kingdom of God, Augustine's *Civitas Dei*, must of necessity be established that the destiny of the world may be fulfilled. Every pope must account to God for his share in the advancement of the only work which mattered, and the greater the power the ruler of this world had acquired over the souls of men, the more he trembled before God, weighed down by the burden of his enormous responsibility. "The renunciation of the world in the service of the world-ruling Church, the mastery of the world in the service of renunciation, this was the problem and ideal of the middle ages" (Harnack). But not only the pope, every priest, as a direct member of the kingdom of God, was superior to the secular rulers. This was taught emphatically by the great St. Bernard of Clairvaux, for instance, and Gregory VII, the wildest fanatic of the kingdom of God, said, in writing to a German bishop: "Who then who possesses even small knowledge and reasoning power, could hesitate to place the priests above the kings?" Even the emperor Constantine, though he was still largely under the sway of the imperial idea, distinctly acknowledged the bishops as his masters; according to the legend he handed to the Bishop of Rome the insignia of his power, sceptre, crown and cloak, and humbly held the bridle of the prelate's horse.

The theoretic backbone of this mental attitude was the doctrine of the Fathers of the Church and the older scholasticism, pronouncing the illimitable power of human perception; the world's profoundest depths had been fathomed, its riddle finally solved; there was consequently no room for philosophy, the endless meditation on the meaning of the world and the destiny of man. Science had but one task: to bring logical proof of the revealed religious verities. The greatest champion of this view was Anselm of Canterbury (1033–1109), who in his treatise, *Cur Deus Homo* proved that God was compelled to become man in order to complete the work of salvation. Abélard preached a similar doctrine, but carried away by the fervour of thought, arrived at conclusions which he was forced to recant ignominiously; for at the end of his chain of evidence he did not always find the foregone conclusion which should have been there. This system of a final and infallible knowledge of the world is the very foundation of ecclesiastical government. The priest alone has all knowledge, for he has the doctrine of salvation. Had it occurred to any man to defend his own opinions in contradiction to the system of the Church, that man would speedily have come to the conclusion that the devil had tempted him to false observations, or false deductions, and his submission to the Church would have been the outward sign of his victory over the evil which had blinded his spiritual vision. A man had to choose between the worship of God and the worship of the devil, there was no alternative. Nobody knew the limits of human knowledge; everybody, the learned ecclesiastic as well as the unlearned, plain man, believed others to be in possession of the key to profound secrets and unlimited power. One thing only was needful: to possess one's self of the philosopher's stone; therefore the belief in witchcraft and the fear of certain men supposed to be endowed with supernatural power—the priests—were but the obvious results of a world-system, founded on a revealed and exact religion.

The Latin poets, whose study would probably have counteracted the universal barbarism, were regarded as dangerous, the gods of antiquity being identified with the demons of the Scriptures. This view was responsible for the loss of many a valuable manuscript. The favourite haunts of the demons were the convents, originally designed as battlefields on which the struggles with the demons were to be fought out, but frequently perishing in superstition and ignorance. Every monk had visions of devils; miracles occurred continually; the torturing problem was as to whether they were worked by God or the devil. Nature was merely a collection of mystic symbols, divine—or perhaps diabolical—allegories, whose meaning could be discovered by a correct interpretation of the Bible. Everything which could possibly happen was recorded in the Scriptures; they contained the true explanation of all things. It was only a matter of selecting the right word and interpreting it correctly, for every word was ambiguous and allegorical. Every natural occurrence—an eclipse of the sun, a comet, or even a fire—stood for something else; it was the symbol of a spiritual event concealed behind a phenomenon. The allegorical interpretation of the Bible was carried to the point of abstruseness because every word was considered of necessity to have an unfathomably profound meaning. The following amazing interpretation is by the highly-gifted German poet and mystic, Suso: "Among the great number of Solomon's wives was a black woman whom the king loved above all others. Now what does the Holy Ghost mean by this? The charming black woman in whom God delights more than in any other, is a man patiently bearing the trials which God sends him." Abélard's interpretation of the black woman is even worse; he maintained that though she was black outside, her bones, that is her character, were white. A really remarkable deed of bad taste was committed by the monk, Matfre Ermengau, the author of the *Breviari d'Amor*, at a time when civilisation had already made considerable strides. He sent his sister a Christmas present, consisting of a honey-cake, mead, and a roast capon, accompanied by the following letter: "The mead is the blood of Christ, the honey-cake and the capon are His body, which for our salvation was baked and pierced at the Cross. The Holy Ghost baked the cake in the Virgin's womb, in which the sugar of His divinity amalgamated with the dough of our humanity. In the Virgin's womb the Holy Ghost also spiced the mead and prepared it from wine; the spice is divine virtue, the wine is human blood. In addition He caused the holy capon to issue from the egg; the yolk of the egg is the deity, the white is humanity, the shell is the womb of the Virgin Mary. . . ," etc.

The religion of Christ was lost, man had become a stranger to his own soul—celestial warnings, signs of the Judgment Day, daemonic temptations, surrounded him, as far as he paid heed to anything supersensuous on all sides. The French chronicler, Radulf Glaber (about A.D. 1000), might have been writing a satire on antiquity when he warned his contemporaries of the demons lurking everywhere, but more especially dwelling in trees and fountains. Of a learned man who was studying the classic poets, he said: "This man, confused by the magic of evil spirits, had the impudence to propound doctrines contradictory to our holy faith. In his opinion everything the ancient poets had maintained was true. Peter, the bishop of the town, condemned him as a heretic. At that time there were many men in Italy believing this false doctrine; they perished by the sword or at the stake." We have a letter, written at the same time by Gerbert, who later on became Pope Sylvester II, to a friend, beseeching him to obtain for him manuscripts of the Latin philosophers and poets. He wrote textbooks of astronomy, geometry and medicine, and introduced the Arabic numbers and the decimal system into Europe. In consequence he, too, was accused of magic and intercourse with Arabian pagans. A chronicler relates that he sold his soul to the devil and became pope through the devil's agency; and that, when he was on the point of death, he ordered his body to be cut to pieces so that the devil should not carry it away.

To-day we find it difficult to realise such a state of mind. Every man of our period who takes the smallest interest in things spiritual—be he the most orthodox ecclesiastic—at least knows that there are capable people in the world whose opinions differ from his, who seek fresh knowledge; he knows it, even though he may pretend that they are people who have gone astray and have been abandoned by God. No one can be entirely blind to the new values created by human intellect. But the men of the Middle Ages were swayed by a monstrous dualism, and despite their belief in the illimitable power of human cognition, they unquestioningly accepted the sacred tradition and rejected the naïve evidence of the senses and intellect whenever it seemed to contradict the dogma. Thus mediaeval science did not represent what it represented in antiquity, and what it represents now, the study of the true relationship of things, but rather the application of truths revealed once and for all. There was nothing more to be discovered, and therefore scientists took a delight in logical and dialectical speculations which to a man of our day seem senseless and childish. Far into the Renascence, natural history was a medley of ancient traditions, oriental fables and superficial observations. The strangest qualities were attributed to animals with which we come almost daily into contact. The following quotations are culled from a Provençal book on zoology: "The cricket is so pleased with its song that it forgets to feed and dies singing." "When a snake catches sight of a nude man, it is so filled with fear that it does not dare to look at him; but if the man is dressed, the snake looks upon him as a weakling and springs upon him." "The adder guards the balsam; if a man desires to steal the balsam, he must first send the adder to sleep by playing on a musical instrument. But if the adder discovers that it is being duped, it closes one of its ears with its tail and rubs the other one against the ground until it is filled with earth; then it cannot hear the music and remains awake." "Of all animals there is none so dangerous as the unicorn; it attacks everybody with the horn which grows on the top of its head. But it takes such delight in virgins that the hunters place a maiden on its trail. As soon as the unicorn sees the maiden, it lays its head into her lap and falls asleep, when it may easily be caught." Of the magnet we learn among other things that it restores peace between husband and wife, softens the heart of all men and cures dropsy. "If a magnet is made into a powder and burnt on charcoal in the four corners of the house, the inhabitants imagine that they cannot keep on their legs and run away, sorely affrighted; thieves frequently profit by this fact. If a magnet is placed under the pillow of a sleeping woman, she is compelled, if she is virtuous, to embrace her husband in her sleep; if she has betrayed him, she will fall out of her bed with fear."

All this information was the common property of the period; Richard of Berbezilh, for instance, an "aesthetic" troubadour, tells us that—like a still-born lion's cub which was only brought to life by the roaring of its dam—he was awakened to life by his mistress. (He does not say whether it was by her roaring.) Conrad of Würzburg compares the Holy Virgin to a lioness who brings her dead cubs, *i.e.*, mankind, to life with loud roaring. Bartolomé Zorgi, another troubadour of the same period, likens his lady to a snake, for—he explains—"she flees from the nude poet and her courage only returns with his clothes." During the whole mediaeval period the unicorn was a well-known symbol of virginity, more especially of the virginity of Mary. The *Golden Smithy* of the German minnesinger, afterwards monk Conrad of Würzburg, contains a rather abstruse poem which begins:

> *The hunt began;*
> *The heavenly unicorn*
> *Was chased into the thicket*
> *Of this alien world,*
> *And sought, imperial maid,*
> *Within thine arms a sanctuary. . . etc.*

Natural history was in a parlous state, and geographical knowledge was equally spurious. The Church was averse to natural research, for the only problem in the world was the salvation of man from everlasting damnation. Not only Tertullian, but several Fathers of the Church, regarded physical research as superfluous and absurd, and even as godless. "What happiness shall be mine if I know where the Nile has its source, or what the physicists fable of heaven?" asked Lactantius. And, "Should we not be regarded as insane if we pretended to have knowledge of matters of which we can know nothing? How much more, then, are they to be regarded as raving madmen who imagine that they know the secrets of nature, which will never be revealed to human inquisitiveness?" Here one is reminded of a remark made in "Phædros" by *the wisest of all Greeks*, who refused to leave town because "what could Socrates learn from trees and grass?" And Julius Cæsar wrote an account of his wars to while away the time when he was crossing the Alps.

Very likely the system of the Church would have been less rigid had it not largely been occupied in dealing with ignorant barbarians. In the case of Celts and Teutons, a complete and unassailable form of dogmatics with its corollary of hieratical intolerance was the only possible system. The traditions of these peoples were far too foreign to Christianity to allow Christian germs to flourish in their soil. And the new nations, accepting what Rome offered to them, were completely unproductive in their adolescence. The achievement of this fatal first millenary might be formulated as follows: "The civilised world of Western Europe was united under the government of the Church of Rome; on all nations it had been impressed in the same combination of words and similes that they were living in a sinful world; they knew when this world had been created and when its Saviour had appeared; they knew that its end would come together with the bodily resurrection of the dead and the terrible day of the Last Judgment; they knew that demons were lurking everywhere, seeking to destroy man's soul, and that the Church alone could save him. All these facts were as unalterable as the return of the seasons."

The fundamental sources of antiquity had been sensuality and asceticism, the elements of the Middle Ages abstract thought and historical faith; now emotion was to become the principal factor. It welled up in the soul and soon dominated all life. The fountain which had been dried up since the dawn of the Christian era, began to flow again in a small country in the south of France. The civilising centre had again shifted westwards, as in the past it had shifted from Asia to Greece, and from Greece to Rome. In the course of the first thousand years Greece and Asia Minor had separated themselves from Europe, and founded a distinct culture, the Byzantine, which exerted no influence on the development of Europe. But not even Italy, the scene of the older civilisation, was destined to give birth to the new; maybe the memory of the antique, ante-Christian, period was too powerful here. Its cradle stood on virgin ground, in Provence, a country wrested from Celts and Teutons by the Roman eagles, ploughed by the Roman spirit, preserving in some of its coast towns, notably in Marsilia, the rich remains of Greek settlements, something of Moorish influence in race and language, and fusing all these heterogeneous elements into a splendid whole. But why this important spiritual centre should have been formed just here it is difficult to say.

For the first time the system of ecclesiastical values was confronted by something novel, which was not—like the old Teutonic ideal of the perfect warrior—tainted by barbarism, but may be described as the system of mundane court values. This new ideal was not founded on an authority which had to be accepted in good faith; it had its direct origin in the passionate yearning of the human soul. Man had re-discovered himself and become conscious of his personal creative force. A very great thing had been accomplished; the seed which, slowly gathering strength, had lain in the soil for a thousand years, had at last burst its husk, and was rapidly growing into the magnificent tree of the European civilisation. In silent opposition to the system of the accepted ecclesiastical values, the new ideal of *pretz e valor e beutatz* (worth and value and beauty), of *cavalaria* and *cortezia* (chivalry and courtesy), was upheld in Provence. Four worldly virtues, wisdom, courtly manners, honesty and self-restraint, were contrasted with the ecclesiastical cardinal virtues. The courts of the princes became centres of new life and art. The new spiritual-aesthetic concept of feasting and enjoyment transformed the former orgies of eating and drinking. Woman, who had heretofore been excluded from male society, was all at once transferred to the very centre of being; for her sake men controlled their brutal tempers and exerted themselves to please by good manners, taste and art. She, whom the Church had done everything to depreciate, who had been denied a soul at the Council of Macon (in the sixth century), had become the very vessel of the soul; man looked up to her and bent his knee before the newly-created goddess.

The cultivation of the new courtly manner coincided with the nascent art of the troubadours. There was no gradual growth and development in the latter; at the very outset it had reached perfection. The first troubadour whose name has come down to us was Guillem of Poitiers, Duke of Aquitania (about 1100); great lords and barons gloried in the exercise of this new art. Every court boasted its poets, hospitably received and loaded with presents; the great ones of the earth were beginning to exercise that patronage of art and letters which in the Renascence reached such extravagant proportions. Every distinguished poet employed salaried musicians, the joglars (jongleurs), who wandered from court to court, singing their masters' new songs. Others again, the comtaires, related romances of love and adventure, gathering round them a rapt throng of lords and ladies. Courtly manners and lofty principles quickly became the recognised ideal; the man who was satisfied with the pleasures of the senses was held in contempt; the greatest reproach was "vilania"; in the "Yvain" of the French epic poet Chrestien de Troyes, this universal feeling is thus expressed:

> *A courtier counts though he be dead,*
> *More than a rustic stout and red.*

Dante and his circle, as well as the best of the troubadours, substituted for the "cortois" of the superficial Chrestien the "cor gentil," the noble heart, which they accounted more precious than rank and wealth and power. "Wherever there is virtue there is nobility," says Dante, "but where there is nobility there need not necessarily be virtue." A time had come when personal distinction was in every man's grasp, no matter whether he was learned or unlearned, a nobleman or a commoner. Certainly the commoner was never on an equality with the aristocrat, partly because he was dependent on the largess of the great. Even Dante was compelled to seek princely patronage, and not until the Renascence do we hear of writers whose sarcastic tongues were so dreaded that they became independent of charity.

In opposition to the monkish ideal of a contemplative life which had hitherto obtained, a new ideal, the ideal of the courtier's life, was upheld; ecclesiastical saintliness was contrasted with knightly honour. Beauty, which at the dawn of the Christian era had fallen into ill repute and had become associated with unholy, and even diabolical, practices, had again come into its kingdom. Above everything it was the beauty of woman which was re-discovered—or rather, in its new, spiritual sense, newly discovered—and claimed the enthusiasm and love of the best men of the period. After a thousand years of gloom and brutality, joy and culture shed their radiance on a renewed world. The ideal of chivalry bore very little resemblance to the old Teutonic ideal of the hero; the older ideal had been based entirely on the appreciation of physical strength; but chivalry was the disseminator of culture, leaving ecclesiastical culture, which hitherto had been synonymous with civilisation, a very long way behind. "Mezura," "masze" (the of the Platonic Greeks) was the new criterion, as compared with the barbarian's want of restraint.

I do not propose to give a description of the life at the courts of Provence. The news of it travelled north, and everywhere roused a desire to imitate it. The need of a renewed life was powerfully stirring all hearts. Men yearned for beauty and spontaneity, for passionate life, unprecedented and romantic. This was especially the case in the north, in France and in Germany, and above all in Wales, the country of the imaginative and highly-gifted Celts. Here life was harder, poorer, more barbaric; the cultured mind suffered more from its brutal surroundings than it did in the favoured south. It was here that the great legends of the Middle Ages, so clearly expressive of the yearning of the period, were first collected. The early Middle Ages had produced epic poems, treating scriptural subjects (such as the Harmony of the Gospels of the monk Otfrit, written in the ninth century), and celebrating the exploits of popular heroes, as, for instance, the German Song of Hildebrand, and the French "Chansons de Geste," which contain episodes from the lives of Charlemagne and his nephew Roland. The true epic, arising from the rich and poetical Celtic tradition, came into existence in the eleventh century in the North of France and immediately burst into extraordinary luxuriance. The legends of the heroes of the dreamy Celtic race—King Arthur and his knights, Merlin the magician, the knights of the Holy Grail—travelling across France, became the common property of the civilised European nations, and filled all hearts with longing and fantastic dreams. Chrestien de Troyes, in his romances, extolled knightly exploits and the service of woman, thus producing by the combination of the older and the newer ideals the novel of adventure which has fascinated the world for centuries. It is a mistake to believe that Don Quixote has struck at the root of it; to this day the masses wax enthusiastic in reading of the doughty deeds of knights, the beauty of ladies and their unswerving, undying love.

In addition to the great and heroic subjects, there were lesser, more intimate, and frequently sentimental, romances, especially enjoyed and widely circulated by the ladies. The baron, riding forth, left his young wife at home, shut up in her bower and surrounded by spies; sometimes even physically branded as his property. A prisoner behind bars, her imagination went out—not to the unloved husband who had married her for the sake of her broad acres, and could send her back to her parents as soon as he found a wealthier bride (he had but to maintain that she was related to him in the fifth degree and the Church was ready to annul the marriage), not to him, her lord and master, but to the unknown knight, the passionate lover, who would gladly give his life to win her. A jongleur arrived with stories of the courts where love was the only ruler; where the knights willingly suffered grief and want, if by so doing they could serve their lady; where the lover, in the shape of a beautiful blue bird, nightly slipped through the barred windows into the arms of his mistress. But the jealous husband had drawn barbed wire across the window, and the lover, flying away at dawn, bled to death before the eyes of his grief-stricken lady. The jongleur would tell of the knight who had fallen passionately in love with a beautiful damsel of whom he had but caught a passing glimpse; month after month he worked at digging an underground passage; every night brought him a little nearer to her bower—she could distinctly hear the dull sounds of his burrowing—until at last he rose through the ground and took her into his arms. These and similar tales, doubtless all of them of Celtic origin—preserved for us in the charming "Lais" of Marie de France—brought tears to the eyes of many a lonely wife and gave shape to her vague longing. There was no reason why a man, and a lover to boot, should not transform himself nightly into a blue bird. Those simple stories in verse fulfilled every desire of the heart; imagination supplied in the north what the south offered in abundant reality. But Marie de France, the first woman novelist of Europe (about the end of the twelfth century), deserves to be remembered for another reason; she was the first poet voicing woman's longing for love and romance—woman's adventure. The charming *Lai du Chevrefoile* ("The Story of the Honeysuckle") relates an episode from the loves of Tristan and Isolde, the famous lovers, legendary even at that time. Tristan and Isolde, Lancelot and Guinevere, Fleur and Blanchefleur—these were the admired and mythical lovers of whom the poets sang and dreamed. All the world knew their adventures; all the world repeated them again and again, reverently preserving the identical words and yet unconsciously remoulding them. At the recital of their loves, hand clasped hand; "on that day we read no more," confessed Dante's ill-fated lovers.

The longing, so characteristic of the North of Europe, to see the world and meet with adventures, was in Provence and Italy less pronounced. These favoured climes possessed so many of the things dreamed of and desired by other countries. Events, strange as fiction, actually occurred. Count Raimond of Roussillon, for instance, imprisoned his wife in a tower because the troubadour, Guillem of Cabestann, was in love with and beloved by her. He waylaid the lover, killed him, cut his heart out of his breast and sent it, roasted, to his countess. When she had partaken of it, he showed her Guillem's head and asked her how she had enjoyed the dish. "So much that no other food shall ever pass my lips," she replied, casting herself out of the window. When the story spread abroad, the great nobles rose up in arms against Raimond, and even the King of Aragon made war on him. He was caught and imprisoned for life, and his estates were confiscated. Guillem and the countess were buried in the church, and for a long time after men and women travelled long distances to kneel at their grave. The charming poems of Melusine and the beautiful Magelone, which to this day delight the reader, were composed during the same period.

Before the eleventh century poetry in the true sense of the word did not exist. There were only Latin Church hymns and legends, perverted reminiscences of antiquity, and, in the vulgar tongue, legends of the saints and simple dancing-songs for the amusement of the lower classes. Thanks to the relentless war which the clergy waged against them, a few only have been preserved. There can be no doubt that Provence was the birthplace of European poetry. The "sweet language" of Provence was the first to reach perfection and perfect maturity. It drove the language of the German conquerors eastwards and prepared the ground for the French tongue.

The beginning of the twelfth century saw the birth of the poetry of the troubadours, which possessed from the first in great perfection everything that distinguishes modern lyric poetry from the antique. Instead of the syllable-measuring quantity, we now have the emphasising accent; the rhyme, one of the most important lyrical contrivances—and in its near approach to music the most striking characteristic of modern lyrical poetry as compared with the antique—reaches perfection together with the complete, evenly-recurring verse which is still to-day peculiar to lyrical art. The poems of many of the troubadours pulsate with passionate life, and bear no trace of the traditional or the conventional. The martial songs of Bertrand de Born stride along with a rhythm reminiscent of the clanking of iron. I quote the first verse of one of these:

Le coms m'a mandat e mogut
Per N'Arramon Luc d'Esparro,
Qu'eu fassa per lui tal chanso,
On sian trenchat mil escut,
Elm e ausberc e alcoto
E perponh faussat e romput.

The count he sent to me one day
Sir Arramon Luc d'Esparro;
A song I was to make him—so
That thousand shields with ring and stay
And mail and armour of the foe
To fragments shivered in dismay.

The poetry of the Provençal troubadours had already passed its prime when, in the other European countries, lyric art was still in its infancy.

The crusade against the Albigenses (1209), undertaken by Gregory VII with the object of killing the new spirit and the new secular civilisation, drove many troubadours to Italy, among others the famous Sordello, who is mentioned in Dante's *Divine Comedy*. Others went to Sicily, to the court of the art-loving Emperor, Frederick II, where a distinct, but not very original, poetic art arose. In Italy the perfection of mediaeval poetry was reached in the "sweet, new style" immortalised by Dante. But not only the great Italians, the trouveres from the North of France also, and—to some extent—the German minnesingers, were influenced by the art, and above all, the ideals which had originated in Provence. The poetry of the earliest Rhenish and Austrian minnesingers closely follows German folklore, and the songs of Dietmar of Aist and others are still quite innocent of any trace of neo-Latin characteristics. But very soon the technical perfection of the Provençal poetry and the Provençal ideal of courtesy and love, famous all over Europe, strongly influenced the German mind.

The new poetry and the ideal of chivalry and the service of woman were the first independent developments able to hold their own by the side of ecclesiastical culture. The rigid Latin was superseded; the soul of man sang in its own language of the return of spring, the beauty of woman, knighthood and adventure. Poetry became the most important source of secular education, and as each nation sang in its own tongue, national characteristics shone out through the individuality of the singer. Provençals, Frenchmen, Germans and Italians realised that they belonged to different races. This was particularly the case during the Crusades when, under the auspices of the Church, the nations of Europe had apparently undertaken a common task.

In Provence, in France and Germany, every poem was set to music, and thus, simultaneously with the lyrical art, secular music was evolved. J.B. Beck, the greatest authority on the music of the troubadours,—the music of the minnesingers has been studied very little,—says, "The poetry of the troubadours and trouveres represents in its totality a collection of songs which in their frequently amazing naïveté and melodiousness, their spontaneity and sound music, intimate congruity of melody and text and extraordinary originality, have been unparalleled to this day." All these songs are distinguished by graceful simplicity; but the ear of the non-musician can hardly perceive the originality on which Beck lays such stress. In any case, the music is inferior to the frequently perfect text. This same period saw the inception of our present system of musical notation.

The new poetry created a desire for "literature," thus giving impetus to the already existent art of illuminated manuscripts. Every prince kept a salaried army of copyists and illuminators, producing the manuscripts to-day preserved and studied in our museums. Studios where this work was carried on existed at various art centres, especially—as far as we are able to tell to-day—at the papal courts at Avignon—that meeting-ground of French and Italian artists—in Paris and at Rheims. These workshops were the birthplace of miniature painting, which reached perfection in the famous Burgundian "Livres d'Heures."

To-day the science of aesthetics is attempting to trace the influence which emanated from the French and even from the earlier English workshops, and spread over the whole continent. It is very probable that the French art of miniature painting of the first half of the thirteenth century was mother of the later North-European art of painting. It was in Northern Europe that, independently of Hellenic and Byzantine influence, a new art originated, of which Max Dvorak says: "It would hardly be possible to find an external cause for the quick and complete disappearance of the elements of the Neo-Latin art. The past was simply done with, and an absolutely new period was beginning. Thus the new art was almost without any tradition." Dvorak calls this complete change the most important in the history of painting since antiquity. George, Count Vitzthum, has proved that the famous Cologne school of painting modelled itself on Northern-French, Belgian, and a quite independent English school of illuminators. It is even suggested that the English style of miniature painting influenced Europe as far as the Upper Rhine. It is also very significant that the Dutch art of the brothers van Eyck, whose sudden appearance seemed so inexplicable, is now proved to have had its source in the North of France. On the other hand, we have drawings of three ecstatic nuns showing decided originality; Hildegarde of Bingen, already mentioned on a previous occasion, has herself ornamented her book, *Scivias*, with miniatures which, according to Haseloff, in spite of their primitive style, reveal a bizarre plastic talent, and are therefore closely related to her intuitions. Alfred Peltzer speaks of "fantastic figures surrounded by flames." The two other nuns were Elizabeth of Schönau, and Herrad of Landsberg; these two were entirely under the influence of the dawning mysticism.

I will here quote a few more passages from Dvorak, who, in dealing with the individual arts, does not lose sight of the whole. "Simultaneously with a new literature," he says, "we have a new art of illustration, new miniatures, no longer drawing inspiration from antiquity. . . We meet the new style in its full perfection wherever it is a matter of a new technique (in the art of staining glass, for instance, or of illustrating profane literature). . ." He speaks of a new decoration of manuscripts invented in Paris in the first half of the thirteenth century. Thus the close and causal connection between the new poetry and the illumination of books is clearly apparent, and it may be said without exaggeration that the Provençal lyric poetry and the North-French and Celtic cycles of romance led up to the new European style of painting which did not come to perfection until two centuries later. (Nothing positive can be said about the influence of France on Italian art; the monumental character and the art of Cimabue, Giotto and the Sienese does not, however, suggest that they were much influenced by the art of miniature painting, but rather hints that they drew inspiration from antique frescoes.)

I must add a few words on the subject of those miniatures which are not easily accessible to the layman, but reproductions of which are frequently met with in books on the history of art. In addition to religious subjects, the whole courtly company which lives and breathes in the legends of the Round Table, kings and knights, poets, minstrels, and fair damsels, hawking, jousting, banqueting and playing chess, everything which stirred the poet's imagination, is depicted. The spirit of the romances which in modern times enchanted the English Pre-Raphaelites, six centuries ago provided food and stimulus to the industrious illuminators whose names have long been forgotten.

If the art of miniature painting never rose—excepting in its wider consequences—to universal significance, mediaeval architecture stands before our eyes magnificent as on the first day. Until the middle of the twelfth century the monumental structures of Europe were directly influenced by the later Hellenic civilisation. The Byzantine basilica was slowly transformed into the Neo-Latin house, and thus, in this important domain also, Europe drew her inspirations from antiquity. But only the ground-plan of the Gothic cathedral, that is to say, the idea of a nave with side-aisles, was traditional and borrowed from Neo-Latin models. From this invisible ground-plan rose something absolutely original and autochthonic. This new, specifically Central-European style of architecture was developed on soil where there were no antique buildings to stem the new life with their overwhelming domination, and to bar the way of artistic inspiration with their ominous "I am perfection!" In every branch of art antiquity had proved itself a foe, until at last the Renascence was sufficiently mature to assimilate and overcome the antique inheritance so completely that it became an excellent fertiliser for the new art. The essence of the Gothic style is the dissolution of all that is heavy and material—the victory of spirit over matter. Walls were broken up into pillars and soaring arcades; monotonous facework was tolerated less and less, and every available inch was moulded into a living semblance. The result may be studied in the incomparable façades of many of the cathedrals in the North of France; and in tower-pieces almost vibrating with life and passion such as that of St. Stephen's in Vienna. The conflict between matter and pure form is settled—for the first and only time—in Gothic architecture. The Greek temple with its correct proportions possessed no more than perfection of form without spiritual admixture; it was perfect as marble statues, which are an end in themselves, and do not point the way to spiritual truths. Gothic architecture is probably unique in its blending of æsthetic perfection of form and infinite spiritual wealth; in the fusion of these two elements in a higher intuition. It is the balance of the two characteristics of genius, inexhaustible wealth and the striving for harmonious expression. It marked the first powerful working of the Teutonic spirit on the world; its metaphysical yearning together with a genuine love of nature, found in this art its own peculiar traditionless expression, just as it found expression in the newly-evolved mysticism which no longer re-echoed Aristotle and his commentators, but drew inspiration from its own intuition. For this reason Gothic architecture never became acclimatised in Italy. The soaring tower, more especially, never appealed to the Italian architect.

Ornamentation and capitals, previously a combination of geometrical figures, which may have been architecturally great and imposing, but was always more or less formal and rigid, disappeared; the new masters, whose names have been forgotten, looked round them and drew inspiration from nature. The forest trees of Central Europe became pillars; grouped together, apparently haphazard, they reflected a mystical nature pulsing with mysterious life. Spreading and ramifying, growing together in an impenetrable network of foliage, they bore buds, leaves and fruits. Every pinnacle became a sprig, even the pendant icicles reappeared in the gable-boards. But the assimilation of natural objects did not cease there; tiny animals, light as a feather, run over the tendrils, lizards, birds, even the gnomes of German mythology, find their way into the Gothic cathedral. Not the traditional Greek acanthus leaf, but the foliage of the

North-European oak grows under the hands of the sculptor. Even the cross is twisted into a flower; the sacro-sanct symbol of the Christian religion is newly conceived, newly interpreted and moulded so that it may have a place. The Gothic cathedral with its soaring arches free from all heaviness is the perfect expression of that cosmic feeling that inspired Eckhart and reached its artistic perfection in Dante.

But the soul of the mystic in stone contains the same elements as the soul of Eckhart, who was also a schoolman. The confused and complex scholastic world of ideas which corresponded so well with the mediaeval temper and, together with the new art, had emanated from Paris, is closely akin to Gothic architecture. For the Gothic style and scholastic thought share the characteristics of the infinitely constructive and infinitely cleft, the infinitely subtle and ornamental—perhaps the last trace of the spirit of the north as compared with the simplicity of the south.

As if from fertile soil, a world of sculptured men and beasts sprang from the façades of the new cathedrals. The figures on the cathedrals of Naumburg, Strassburg, Rheims, Amiens and Chartres are far superior to the artistic achievements of the dawning renascence in Italy. They are real men, full of life and passion, no longer symbols of the transcendental glory of the world beyond the grave. "All rigidity had melted, everything which had been stiff and hard had become supple; the emotion of the soul flows through every curve and line; the set faces of the statues are illuminated by a smile which seems to come from within, the afterglow of inward bliss" (Worringer).

A longing went through the world, stimulating faith in miracles and a desire for adventure, a longing which no soul could resist. Nothing certain was known of countries fifty miles distant; the traveller must be prepared for the most amazing events. No one knew what fate awaited him behind yonder blue mountains. The existence of natural laws was undreamt of; there was no improbability in dragons or lions possessing power of speech. A period incapable of distinguishing between the natural and supernatural will always indulge in those fancies which are best suited to its temper. Be the native country never so poor, the long darkness and cold of the winter never so hard to bear, far away in the East, or in Camelot, the kingdom of King Arthur, life was full of beauty and sunshine. The legends of King Arthur powerfully affected the imagination; they were read, secretly and surreptitiously, in all convents; on a sultry summer afternoon, during the learned discussion of their preceptor, one after another of the pupils would fall asleep; the preceptor, suddenly interrupting himself, would continue after a short pause: "And now I will tell you of King Arthur," and all eyes would sparkle as the pupils listened with rapt attention. Francis of Assisi called one of his disciples "a knight of his Round Table," and three hundred years later Don Quixote lost his reason over the study of those legends; some of the finest works of art of the present time, Wagner's "Lohengrin," "Tristan and Isolde," and "Parsifal," take their subject from the inexhaustible treasure of the Celtic epic cycle. The longing for experience and adventure had laid hold of the imagination to an extraordinary degree. The recital of wondrous adventures no longer satisfied the listener; he yearned to participate in them. The young knight, trained in athletics and courtesy, and possessing a little knowledge of biblical history, left his father's castle to face the unknown world. There was a sanctuary, mysterious, almost supernal, carefully guarded in the dense forest of an inaccessible mountain. A knight whose heart was pure, and who had dedicated himself to the lifelong service of the divine, could find it; but he would have to wander for many years, through forests and glens and strange countries, alone and solitary, before his eyes would behold the most sacred relic in the world, the Holy Grail.

The time was ripe for a great event, a universal and overwhelming enterprise which could absorb the passionate longing. Maybe that the wisdom of the great popes—half unconsciously, certainly, and under the pressure of the age, but yet led by an unerring instinct—guided this stream into the bed of the Church; the vague craving found a definite object: the Crusades were organised. The Holy Sepulchre, the most sacred spot on earth, was in the hands of the heathens; it was despised and defiled—what greater thing could a man do than hasten to its rescue and wrest it from the grasp of pagans, giants and sorcerers? In the fantastic imagination of the men of that period the Lord's sepulchre was nothing but the earthly realisation of their yearning for the Holy Grail.

As far back as A.D. 1000 Gerbert had sent messengers to all nations, exhorting them to hoist their banners and march with him to the Holy Land. It had been prophesied that he should be the first to read Mass in Jerusalem; a few ships were actually equipped at Pisa—the first attempt at a Crusade. But at that time Europe was not yet quite prepared for the extraordinary, almost incomprehensible, enterprise—the conquest of a country which hardly anybody had ever seen and in which nobody had any practical interest. Before such an enterprise could be carried out all hearts must be filled by that uncontrollable and yet vague longing, so characteristic of the great period of fantasy. The suggestion that the wealth of the East, exciting the greed of the western nations, led to the Crusades, is an absolutely indefensible idea. Doubtless, rumours of the fabulous treasure of the Orient had stirred the imagination of Europe, appealing far less, however, to the cupidity of the individual than to his desire for something strange, new and incredible. It was impossible to foresee the result of the first Crusade; the crusader went to a strange land in order to fight—the return was in God's hand. There have been at all times men coveting wealth, but to make such men the instigators and organisers of the Crusades is a deliberate attempt to represent a characteristic and unique event in the history of the world in the light of a commonplace and every-day occurrence. In the first enchanted wood a man might chance upon a beautiful princess sitting beside a fountain, nude and weeping; but it was equally possible that a giant would rush upon the Christian knight, break his shield and exact heavy penalties. It was possible to win the kingdom of a sultan or emir—it could be achieved by bravery and in a duel—and become a great king, for a king in those days was no more than a large landed proprietor. Such dreams were actually fulfilled in the most extraordinary way. Gottfried of Bouillon, a poor Alsatian knight, might have become King of Jerusalem, had he not refused to wear a crown of gold in a land where his Saviour had worn a crown of thorns, and contented himself with the title of "Protector of the Holy Land."

The embattled citadel of Jerusalem, like the Holy Grail, was pictured as being situated outside the world. *There* the longing which had become so vast that it had outgrown the earth, would be stilled. A direct way must lead from Jerusalem, the centre of the earth—it still takes this position in Dante's *Divine Comedy*—to Paradise. Was it not the spot where the Cross of the Saviour had been raised? Had not once before heaven opened above the city to receive His risen body? Was it not the scene of countless miracles in the past? Why should it be different now? Men knew practically nothing of Palestine; they had in their minds a fantastic picture tallying, in every respect, with Biblical accounts; doubtless, the footprints of the Redeemer could easily be traced everywhere; the possession of the country promised the fulfilment of transcendental dreams.

The impulse and the strength necessary for the organisation of the Crusades were spiritual phenomena inherently foreign and even hostile to the Church; but thanks to the mental superiority of the popes of that period, and the overpowering conception of a divine kingdom, they became the instruments of the greatest triumphs vouchsafed to the Church of Rome. The hosts, driven across the sea by inner restlessness and ill-defined longing, in reality fought for the aggrandisement of the Church. The great Hildebrand resolved to lead all Christendom to Jerusalem, to found on the site of the Holy Sepulchre the divine kingdom preached by St. Augustine, and invest—a risen Christ—the emperor and all the kings of the earth with their kingdoms.

The crusader and the knight in quest of the Holy Grail present together a paradoxical combination of the Christian-ecclesiastical and the mundane-chivalric spirit, which is quite in harmony with the spirit of the age. These two worlds, inward strangers, formed—in the Order of the Knight-Templars, for instance—a union which, while possessing all the external symbols of chivalry, attributed to it heterogeneous, ecclesiastical motives; the glory of battle and victory, the caprice of a beautiful damsel, were no longer to become the mainsprings of doughty exploits; henceforth the knight fought solely for the glory of God and the victory of Christianity. In addition to King Arthur's knights, the classical Middle Ages worshipped the ideal of these priestly warriors who waded through streams of blood to kneel humbly at the grave of the Saviour, of those seekers of the Holy Grail who dedicated themselves to a metaphysical task. King Arthur's Round Table served the actual orders of knighthood as a model. Not only the Franciscans of Italy, but also slow, German mystics, such as Suso and the profound Johannes Tauler, delighted in borrowing their similes and metaphors from knighthood. Tauler speaks of the "scarlet knightly robes" which Christ received for His "knightly devotion": "And by His chivalric exploits he won those knightly weapons which he wears before the Father and the angelic knighthood. Therefore Christ exults when His knights elect also to put on such knightly garments. . . ," etc.

Not infrequently the Saracens behaved far more generously than the Christian armies. A German chronicler, Albert von Stade, tells us that A.D. 1221 "the Sultan of Egypt of his own free will restored the Lord's Cross, permitted the Christians to leave Egypt with all their belongings, and commanded all prisoners to be set free, so that at that time 30,000 captives were released. He also commanded his subjects to sell food to the rich and give alms to the poor and the sick." Occasionally the pope entered into an alliance with the enemies of Christendom against the emperor, if the latter proved troublesome. A.D. 1246 the Sultan of Egypt (Malek as Saleh Ejul) taught Innocent IV, the speaker of all Christendom, the judge of the Christian peoples, the following lesson: "It is not befitting to us," he wrote to him, "that we should make a treaty with the Christians without the counsel and consent of the emperor. And we have written to our ambassador at the court of the emperor, informing him of what has been proposed to us by the Pope's nuncio, including your message and suggestions."

The most pathetic symptom of the restlessness of the age was the Children's Crusade in 1212, which, even at its actual occurrence, caused helpless amazement. The reports of two German chroniclers are sufficiently interesting to be quoted verbally: "In the same year happened a very strange thing, a thing which was all the more strange because it was unheard of since the creation of the world. At Easter and Whitsuntide many thousands of boys from Franconia and Teutonia, from six years upwards, took the Cross without any external inducement or preaching, and against the wish of their parents and relations, who sought to restrain them. Some left the plough which they had been guiding, others abandoned their flocks, or any other task which they had been set to do, banded together, and with hoisted banner began to march to Jerusalem, in batches of twenty, fifty and a hundred. Many people enquired of them at whose counsel and admonishment they were undertaking this journey, (for it was not many years ago that many kings, a great number of princes and countless people had travelled to the Holy Land, strongly armed, and had returned home without having accomplished their desire,) telling them that in their tender years they had not yet sufficient strength to achieve anything, and that therefore this thing was foolish and undertaken without due consideration; the children answered briefly that they were obeying God's will, and would willingly and gladly suffer all the trials He would send them. And they went their way, some turning back at Mayence, others at Piacenza, and others at Rome; a small number arrived at Marseilles, but whether they crossed the sea or not, and what happened to them, no one knows; only that much is certain, that of all the thousands who went forth, only very few returned." Another chronicler wrote: "And at this time boys without a leader or guide, left the towns and villages of all countries, eagerly journeying to the lands across the sea, and when asked whither they were wending, they replied: 'To Jerusalem, to the Holy Land.' Many of them were kept by their parents behind locked doors, but they burst open the doors, broke through the walls and escaped. When the Pope heard of these things he sighed heavily and said: 'These children shame us, for they hasten to the recovery of the Holy Land while we sleep.' No one knows how far they went and what became of them. But many returned, and when they were asked the reason of their expedition, they said they knew not. At the same time nude women were seen hurrying through towns and villages, speaking no word."

If it had not been for the Crusades, something else must have happened to relieve the unbearable tension. The world was longing for a great deed, a deed overstepping the border-line of metaphysics, and its enthusiasm was sufficient guarantee of achievement. In the case of the individual, vanity and boastfulness played no mean part. Thus the Austrian minnesinger, Ulrich of Lichtenstein, proposed taking the Cross "not to serve God but to please his mistress." It is quite probable, though not historically proved, that this veritable Don Quixote dreamed of decorating the Holy Sepulchre with his lady's handkerchief, but in the end he remained at home. A journey to foreign lands, to return after years of yearning for the beloved, her loyalty, or her treachery, supplied the romantic imagination of the age with endless material. The story of the Count von Gleichen and his two wives is famous to this day. A charming Provençal song tells of a maid who, day after day, sat by a fountain weeping for her lover. At this spot they had bidden farewell to each other, and here she was awaiting his return. One day a pilgrim arrived, and she at once asked for news of her knight. The pilgrim knew him and had a message for her. After a short conversation he threw back his cowl and drew the delighted maiden into his arms, for it was he himself, her lover, who after many years of absence had returned and was first visiting the spot where, years ago, he had said good-bye to her.

But there was another motive, a religious one, which, joined to the universal lust of adventure, dominated the whole mediaeval period to an extraordinary degree; that motive was the idea of doing penance and—after all the failures of life—returning to God. The Crusades offered an opportunity for combining one's heart's desire with this spiritual need. Of all good works there were none more pleasing to God, and every participator was promised forgiveness of his sins. In the troubadours' songs of the crusaders there is a strong yearning for penance and sanctification, quite independent of the idea of the delivery of the Holy Sepulchre from the rule of the infidels.

All I held dear I now abhor,
My pride, my knightly rank and fame,
And seek the spot which all adore,
The pilgrim's goal—Jerusalem.

sang Guillem of Poitiers, one of the gayest of the troubadours.

Only very few of the more thoughtful minds realised that divine thoughts have their source in the soul of man, and that these Crusades were obviously a senseless undertaking (not to mention the fact that God does not need human assistance). "It is a greater thing to worship God always in humility and poverty," said the abbot, Peter of Cluny, "than to journey to Jerusalem in great pomp and circumstance. If, therefore, it is a good thing to visit Jerusalem and stand on the soil which our Lord's feet have trod, it is a far better thing still to strive after heaven where our Lord can be seen face to face." Both the great scholastic, Anselm of Canterbury, and Bernard of Clairvaux, were of the same opinion. "They shall aspire not to the earthly, but to the heavenly Jerusalem, and travel there not with their feet, but with the desire of their hearts." And "They seek God in external objects, neglecting to look into their hearts, in whose innermost depths dwells the divine." And yet those same men, who even then seemed to have outgrown biblical religiosity, were under the spell of the all-absorbing idea of the age. Bernard solved the contradiction in the following way: "It is not because His power has grown less that the Lord calls us feeble worms to protect His own; His word is deed, and He could send more than twelve legions of angels to do His bidding; but because it is the will of the Lord your God to save you from perdition, He gives you an opportunity to serve Him." In these words a significant change of the fundamental idea can already be traced. Peter of Cluny worked for the Crusades, and Bernard, one of the most influential and venerable personalities of the Middle Ages, a man before whose word the popes bowed down, journeyed through the whole of France, inciting all hearts to fanatical enthusiasm. Whoever heard him preach forsook his worldly possessions and took the cross, clamouring for Peter himself to lead all Christendom. "Countless numbers flocked to his banner, towns and castles stood forsaken and there was hardly one man to seven women. The wives were made widows during the lifetime of their husbands." Thus Bernard wrote to the Pope, travelling through Germany, healing the sick by his mere presence, and preaching to the people in a tongue no one could understand. But the personality of this physically delicate man, whose body was only kept alive by his spirit, touched all hearts. The prudent Emperor, Conrad, resisted for a long time, and would have nothing to do with such an aimless enterprise. But Bernard's first sermon in the cathedral at Speyer, on Christmas Day, moved him to tears. Bernard left the pulpit and pinned the cross on the shoulder of the kneeling emperor. By this symbolical act the metaphysical spirit of the time, of which the Church had obtained control for her own purposes, visibly became master of political common-sense.

The Crusades were one of the great movements matured by the newly-awakened metaphysical yearning. The same spirit in another, profounder, way, manifested itself in the efforts of religious reform which were being made here and there. "The appearance and spread of heresy has always been the gauge by which the religious life of the individual must be measured," says Büttner very pertinently in his preface to his edition of Eckhart. For the first time since the days of Christ true religious feeling was again quickening the hearts of men; the ecclesiastical dogma, which until then had represented absolute truth, no longer satisfied their need. Soon opposition, timidly at first, made itself felt. Laymen ventured to interfere in the domain of religion. All knowledge—and consequently all tradition and religion—had been for a thousand years the exclusive possession of the clergy; those laymen who had any culture at all knew a little Latin and a few scholastic propositions. All this was changing. Despite reiterated ecclesiastical prohibitions, parts of the Bible were translated into the vulgar tongue and eagerly studied by ignorant folk; everywhere men appeared to whom religion was a matter of vital importance, men who strove to find God in their own souls, instead of blindly accepting the God of foreign doctrine.

The more obvious cause of the growing dislike to ecclesiastical authority was the immorality of the priests. The contrast between the professions of humility, and the greed, vice and tyranny of the clergy was too pronounced. The ecclesiastical offices were publicly sold. Divine forgiveness was cheaper than a new garment; every priest was allowed to keep a mistress if he paid a tax to the bishop. Two poems of the troubadour, Guillem Figueiras, express the state of affairs very bluntly: "Our shepherds have become thievish wolves, plundering and despoiling the fold under the guise of messengers of peace. They gently console their sheep night and day, but once they have them in their power, these false shepherds let their flock perish and die." In the other poem he says of the priest:

He lies in a woman's arms all night,
And wakes—defiled—in the morning light
To proffer the sacred host.

Worse invectives even, no less forcible than those of later reformers, he hurled against Rome. "In the flames and torments of hell is thy place! . . . Thou hast the appearance of an innocent lamb, but inwardly thou art a raging wolf, a crowned snake, begotten by a viper, the friend of the devil!" Even the good-natured German minnesinger, Walter von der Vogelweide, found bitter words against Rome: "They point our way to God and go to hell themselves." Bernard of Clairvaux, the supporter of the Church, sharply criticised the abuses of pope and clergy in his book, *De Consideratione*: "The property of the poor is sown before the door of the rich, the gold glitters in the gutter, the people come hurrying up from all sides; but not to the neediest is it given, but to the strongest and to him who is first on the spot." He accused the pope of extravagance and luxury: "Was Peter clothed in robes of silk, covered with gold and precious stones? Was he carried in a litter surrounded by soldiers and vassals?" And he uttered a word which to this day is a historical truth: "In all thy splendour thou art the successor of Constantine rather than the successor of Peter."

Dissatisfaction with the life of the clergy and the tyranny of Rome was the more external reason which, although it vexed even those who were indifferent to religion, did not question the sacred tradition; the other reason was more a matter of principle; it was rooted in the desire for a religious revival and openly attacked perverted truths. The dreaded, hated, and cruelly persecuted heretics were fearless men, sturdily fighting for their convictions. The fundamental ideal of these reformers was the suppression of the outward pomp of the Church and the return to the simplicity of the gospels. Their fates varied. The gentle St. Francis of Assisi was canonised; the illumined Eckhart, on the other hand, was tortured; most of them, like the ardent Arnold of Brescia, were burnt at the stake. This conduct of the hierarchy towards the truly religious men is easily explained. The Church was faced by a problem; on the one hand, the genuine and profound piety of these men was unmistakable, but on the other, the contrast of their teaching with Church tradition was too obvious, and by many of them too strongly emphasised to be silently ignored.

The Provençal heretic, Peter of Bruis, seems to have been the first reformer who preached against iconolatry and even objected to the images of the Crucified. He ordered churches to be razed to the ground because he acknowledged only the invisible community of the saints. He was burnt at St. Giles' by an infuriated mob. More powerful, and far more numerous than his followers, the Peterbrusians, were the Cathari and the Waldenses (founded by Peter Valdez A.D. 1177) who soon spread to Northern Italy and amalgamated with the sect of the Lombards. The Cathari advocated a simple and ascetic life, in accordance with the teaching of primitive Christianity, refrained from all ecclesiastical ceremonies and despised the sacraments, particularly baptism. More radical than later reformers, they rejected the doctrine of transubstantiation, and saw in the eucharist only a symbol of the union of God and the soul. This made their name synonymous with heresy. But by far the most famous of heretical sects was the sect of the Waldenses or Albigenses. It numbered amongst its adherents—if not publicly, at any rate secretly—many of the great Provençal lords, and there can be no doubt that this community was permeated by the spirit of a renewed Christianity, the Christianity of St. Francis and the German mystics. The Albigenses believed that not Christ, but His semblance only, had been crucified; they rejected the God of the Old Testament and their doctrine of the two creators,—the devil who created the objective world, and the true God who created the spiritual world—is reminiscent of the loftiest Parseeism and the profoundest gnosticism. They regarded man as placed between good and evil; the choice lay in his own hand. An extraordinary poem by Peire Cardinal—not by any means a heretic—breathes this spirit. He confronts God not with the customary humility, but as one power confronts the other. "I will write a new poem, and on the day of the Last Judgment I will read it to Him who has created me from nothing. If He should condemn me to everlasting damnation, I will say to Him: Lord, have mercy on me, for I have always striven against the wicked world," (the troubadour here alludes to his many polemic poems) "and save me from the torments of hell. The heavenly host will marvel at my speech. And I shall say to God that He sins against His creatures if he delivers them into the hands of the devil. Rather let Him drive away the devils, for then He will win more souls and all the world will be blessed. . . I will not despair of Thee and therefore Thou must forgive my sins and save my soul and my heart. If I had not been born I should not have sinned. It would be a great wrong and a sin if Thou didst condemn me to burn in hell everlastingly, for truly I may accuse Thee of having sent me a thousand evils for one blessing."

Most terrible was the punishment inflicted upon Provence by Innocent III. That highly intellectual pope realised that he was faced by a revival of the true religious instinct from which the authority of the Church had far more to fear than from all sultans and emirs put together. The system of absolute, immutable values was threatened with destruction. In the year 1208 the Spanish nobleman Dominicus Guzman founded the order of the Dominicans and the Inquisition, which invaded Provence together with the papal army supported by France for political reasons. Half a million men were butchered in order to crush the spirit understood by a few hundreds at most; one stake was kindled by the other; in the memory of man no greater sacrifice to tradition and dogma had ever been made. Simon de Montfort, the head of the expedition, sent the following laconic report to the pope: "We spared neither sex nor age nor name, but slew all with the edge of the sword."

THE TROUBADOURS BEWAILED THE DESOLATE country, the beauty that was no more. Montanhagol, although greatly intimidated by the Inquisition, wrote a long poem on the subject, and the otherwise unknown Bernard Sicard de Marvajols laments:

> *Oh! Toulouse and Provence,*
> *And thou, land of Agence,*
> *Carcassonne and Beziers!*
> *As once I beheld you—as I behold you to-day!*

Jacob of Vitry, a cultured French prelate, took a different view. He inveighed against the "foolish poems, the lies of the poets, the sing-song of the women, the coarse innuendoes of the jesters." "Such vermin flourishes on the stream of temporal abundance; it literally crawls over all food, for, as a rule, the meal is followed by a deluge of idle talk." A reconciliation of the two worlds was impossible.

While the Waldenses flourished in Provence, various heretical sects arose in the west of Germany and in the Netherlands; prominent among them were the Apostolics, who took the Gospels literally, and introduced communism and polygamy, and the communities of the Beghards and Beguines, which roused little public attention, and did not aim at reform, but advocated a life of contemplation. They found supporters in all ranks of the community, and were connected with the later German mystics. An indictment preserved for us proves the religious originality of one of those sects, "The Brethren of the Free Spirit," who upheld the heretical view that it were better that one man should attain to spiritual perfection than that a hundred monasteries should be founded. At the same time the inspired seer and hysterical nun, Hildegarde of Bingen, wrote wild letters to the popes, denouncing the vice existing in the Church and the degradation of religion. "But thou, oh Rome, who art well-nigh at the point of death, thou wilt be shaken so that the strength of thy feet shall forsake thee, because thou hast not loved the royal maiden righteousness with an ardent love, but with the torpor of sleep, and thou hast become a stranger to her. Therefore she will desert thee if thou do not call her back." Pope Adrian IV replied, almost humbly: "We long to hear words of warning from you, because men say that you are endowed with the spirit of the divine miracles." St. Bernard craved Hildegarde's prayer, two emperors, popes, bishops and abbots corresponded with her, requesting her prayer and advice, and the interpretation of difficult passages of the Scriptures. Hildegarde replied in an obscure, apocalyptical language: "In the mysteries of the true wisdom have I seen and heard this."

Prophets predicting the revival of the Gospel of Christ and the regeneration of the world appeared in the north and south. The Italian monk and fanatic, Joachim of Floris (about A.D. 1200), preached that this regeneration was predestined to happen. A precursor of Hegel, he taught three eras: the dominion of the Father, or the first era, characterised by fear and the severity of the law; the dominion of the Son, or the era of faith and compassion; and the dominion of the Holy Ghost, or the era of love. This last era was beginning to dawn, and in many places Joachim's words were regarded as the prophecies of a seer. Thus the monk, Gerhard of Borgo San Domino, claimed for the dawning third era the preaching of a new gospel of the Holy Ghost, an unmistakable proof that the spirit of heresy was the outcome of religious enthusiasm.

The people despised the clergy, and were favourably disposed to every reformer; at the same time they were entirely under the sway of a superstitious awe of the administrators of mysterious magic which, by appropriate practices, or by means of presents, could be turned to advantage. The fetichism of relics flourished everywhere; a sufficient number of pieces of the Cross of Christ were sold and worshipped to furnish trees for a big forest—to say nothing of the bones of numerous saints with which many monasteries, more especially French monasteries, did a lucrative trade. Even at the time this traffic repelled the finer intellects; in A.D. 1200, Guibert, the abbot of Novigentum, preached against the cult of the saints and the worship of relics, adducing all the well-known arguments which to this day, however, have proved insufficient to overcome the evil. In Guibert's words, "It was an abominable nuisance that certain limbs should be detached from the body, thereby defying the law that all bodies must turn to dust. How can the bones of any man be worth framing in gold and silver," he asked, "when the body of the Son of God was laid beneath a miserable stone?" He exhorted the people to turn from the visible and obvious to the invisible. He maintained that the worship of relics was opposed to true religion because "not until the disciples were bereaved of the bodily presence of Christ could the Holy Ghost descend upon them." He even rejected the prevalent, entirely materialistic, view of a life after death, and dared to suggest that the torments of hell should be interpreted spiritually. "The eternal contemplation of the Lord is the supreme bliss of the righteous; who could dare to deny that the misery of the damned consists in the eternal bereavement of the face of the Lord?"

Religion had been lost; what should have been a vital force had become as far as the most learned were concerned a knowledge of historical events. Many saw in a return to evangelical simplicity and love the only remedy; but it was the life, not the preaching of a man, which once again was vouchsafed to the world as a great example. "Nobody has shown me what I should do; but the Most High Himself has commanded me to live according to the Gospels." Francis of Assisi accepted the accounts of the life of Christ with the utmost naïveté; he neither searched for an allegorical meaning (as the theologians did), nor did he subordinate the man Jesus to the divine principle of the *logos* (in the manner of the great mystics). To him the imitation of Christ meant a ministry of love; he did not conceive religion as dogma and the political power of a hierarchy, but as a state of the heart. This is a characteristic which he shares with Eckhart, the great recreator of European religion, although he was fundamentally alien to him. St. Francis never uttered a single hostile word against tradition or the clergy; he never inveighed against the corruption of morals and religious indifference, as other reformers did; he exerted a reformatory influence solely by his life, for he possessed the secret of the great love. During his whole life he was averse to laying down rules for his followers, although continually urged to do so by popes and bishops.

His importance does not lie in the foundation of an order with certain regulations and a specific object, but in the fact that he was a vital force. He broke the norms of the Church whenever it seemed right to him to do so, for he was absolutely sure of himself; without being ordained he preached to the people in his own tongue, probably the first man (after the Provençal Peter Valdez) who did so; without possessing the slightest authority he consecrated his friend Clara as a nun. Innocent III, who made the suppression of heresy the task of his life, showed great intelligence and wisdom in sanctioning St. Francis' sermons to the people and acknowledging his unecclesiastical brotherhood. This probably transformed a dangerous revolutionary into a faithful servant of the Church. Maybe the Church was indebted to St. Francis for being saved from a great early reformation; signs of it were not wanting, and another Arnold of Brescia might have arisen and brought about her overthrow. It is doubtful whether the Church would have come out of a Franciscan crusade as victoriously as she came out of her struggle with Provence.

St. Francis regarded science with indifference. "Every demon," he said, "has more scientific knowledge than all men on earth put together. But there is something a demon is incapable of, and in it lies the glory of man. A man can be faithful to God." With those words he had inwardly overcome tradition and theology, and direct knowledge of the divine had dawned in his soul. He even forbade his brethren to own copies of the Scriptures. God in the heart—that was the core of his doctrine. With all his wonderful intuition he was absolutely innocent of the pride of ignorance; he really felt himself smaller than the smallest of men—unlike the bishops and popes who called themselves the servants of the servants of God, without attaching the least meaning to it. How characteristic of his simple mind was his passionate insistence on the respectful handling of the vessels used at holy Mass, because they were destined to receive the body of the Lord. And yet he hardly knew anything of the symbolic transmutation of bread and wine—he accepted the miracle without a thought, like a child.

In the year 1219, St. Francis took part in a Crusade. While the battle of Damietta was raging, he went into the camp of the Saracens and preached before the Sultan, who received him with respect and sent him back unharmed. According to the legend, he then went to Bethlehem and Jerusalem, where the Sultan, touched by his personality, gave him access to the sacred shrines. To Francis this pilgrimage to the

Holy Land had a profound meaning, for to him Christianity meant the imitation of Christ.

Although he lived on bread himself, and poverty was his chosen lady, he regarded the asceticism of the early Middle Ages as futile and rejected it. The fire of life burned in him so ardently that he gave no thought to the morrow, and literally followed the admonition of the Gospels: "So likewise, whosoever he be of you that forsaketh not all that he hath, he cannot be My disciple." We read in the *Fioretti* (perhaps the oldest popular collection of poems in existence) that he expressly prohibited asceticism as a principle; an idea too foreign to the spirit of the age to have been an invention. He also disapproved of the secluded monastic life, then the universal ideal of the *vita contemplativa*, and insisted on his followers living in the world, radiating love and sustaining life by the charity of their fellow-men.

There is an anecdote contained in the *Fioretti*, reflecting the great superiority and lucidity of his mind. On a cold winter's day he and Brother Leo were tramping through the deep snow. "Brother Leo," said St. Francis, "if we could restore sight to all blind men, heal all cripples, expel evil spirits and recall the dead to life—it would not be perfect joy." And after a while: "And if we knew all the secrets of science, the course of the stars, the ways of the beasts—it would not be perfect joy—and if by our preaching we could convert all infidels to the true faith—even that would not be perfect joy." "Tell me then, Father," said Brother Leo, "what would be perfect joy?" "If we now knocked at the convent gates, cold and wet and faint with hunger, and the porter sent us away with harsh words, so that we should have to stand in the snow until the evening; if we thus waited, bearing all things patiently without murmuring—that would be perfect joy: the mercy of self-control."

"He met death singing," says his biographer, Thomas of Celano, the author of the magnificent *Dies irae, dies illa*. On his deathbed St. Francis composed and sang without interruption the Hymn to the Sun, that lofty song of praise in which the sum total of his noble life, love for all created things,—is comprised and transfigured. It expresses a new form of devotion, composed of the ecstasy of love and perfect humility. He embraced in his heart his brother Sun, his sister Moon, the dear Stars; his brother Wind, his sister and mother Earth; and on the day of his death this *brother seraphicus* added to it a powerful and touching song of praise of his "brother Death." The legend has it that a flock of singing-birds descended on the roof of the cottage in which he lay dying; the songs of his "little sisters" accompanied him to the world beyond the grave.

We are justified in comparing this death, which was sustained by the fundamental forces of that era, soul and emotion, to that other, more famous, death of antiquity. Socrates died without in the least succumbing to any personal feeling, supported by the purely logical consideration that it was expedient to obey the laws of the State. His death was the application of a universal proposition to an individual case, and because no one could accuse Socrates of a dialectical error, the conclusion, his death, had to take place.

Francis and some of his successors realised in their lives the simple, religious, fundamental emotion of love in a way which the people could clearly understand. "God's minstrels" was the name given to his followers, because they spoke and sang of the love of God without ecclesiastical ceremony. Jacopone da Todi (1236–1306), probably next to Dante and Guinicelli the greatest poet which Italy has produced, praised the transcendent love of God in ecstatic verses. He was the religious counterpart of the troubadours; his passionate devotion to the child Jesus, the Madonna and the Crucified, eclipses their most ardent lyrics. These southerners could not forgo the visible emblems of their religion; the infinitely simple principle that only he who calls nothing his own, and desires no earthly goods, is perfectly free, and can never fall foul of his neighbour, was, if not lived up to, at any rate understood and respected. The grateful hearts of the people surrounded the name of St. Francis with legends; the study of his life inspired Giotto, the father of the new art, to the study of plant and animal life. The story of St. Francis is written on the walls of the cathedral at Assisi, the first monumental work of Italian art.

St. Francis re-lived the terrestrial life of Jesus; in one direction he excelled his model, for though the love of Christ embraced all mankind, the heart of St. Francis went out to all things, beasts and plants and stars. He applied the words, "Whatsoever ye do to the least of my brethren, ye have done unto me," to *Brother Bear* and *his sisters the little birds*. He was one of the first men, since the Greek era, who saw nature in its true aspect and not as a hieroglyphic of the divine word. Men had realised with a feeling of helplessness the dangers of the elements, without perceiving their magnificence; they had speculated on and attempted to decipher the secret language of the terrestrial and celestial phenomena. The discovery of the beauty of nature, and with it the revival of aesthetics, was an essential part of the new-born civilisation. This fact was accomplished—in an almost sentimental way—by the troubadours and minnesingers. But the relationship of St. Francis to nature was something very different. The co-ordination of man and beast—in his sermon to the birds, for instance—cannot be called anything but frankly pagan. St. Francis said to his disciples: "Tarry a little while in the road while I go and preach to my little sisters, the birds." And he went into the fields and began to preach to the birds which sat on the ground; and straightway all the others flew down from the trees and flocked round him, and did not fly away until he had blessed them; and when he touched them, they did not move. And these were the words which he spoke to them: "My brothers and sisters, little birds, praise God and thank Him that He has given you wings with which to fly and clothed you with a garment of feathers. That he admitted your kind into Noah's ark so that your race should not disappear from the earth. Be grateful to Him that He has given you the air for your kingdom; you sow not, neither do you reap, but your Heavenly Father gives you abundance of food. He gave you the rivers and fountains; He gave you the mountains and valleys as a refuge, and the high trees so that you may build your nests in safety. And because you can neither spin nor cook, God clothed you and your little ones. Behold the greatness of the love of your Creator! Beware of the sin of ingratitude and diligently praise God all day!" And when he had thus spoken, the birds opened their beaks, beat their wings and bowed to the ground.

More than a hundred years later (1300–1365), a man was living in Swabia whose soul was kindred to the soul of St. Francis: Suso, who is, as a rule, classed with the mystics. He had a profound, typically German love of meadow and forest, and expressed it more exquisitely than the best among the minnesingers. "Look above you and around you and behold the vastness of heaven and the speed of its revolutions. The Lord has emblazoned it with seven planets, each of which—not only the sun—is far larger than the earth; he has adorned it with myriads of radiant stars. See how serenely the glorious sun is riding in the cloudless sky, giving to the earth abundance of fruit! Behold the verdure of the meadow! The trees are bursting into leaf and the grass is springing up; behold the smiling flowers and listen to glen and dale re-echoing with the sweet song of the nightingales and little singing birds; the beasts which the bitter winter drove into nooks and crannies, and into the dark ground, are emerging from their hiding-places to rejoice in the sun and seek a mate. Young and old are glad with an exceeding joy. Oh! Thou gentle God, how fair art Thou in Thy creatures! Oh! fields and meadows, how surpassing is your beauty!" Or: "My dear brethren, what more shall I say to you than that my eyes have seen many gladsome sights. I walked across the flowering meadows and listened to the heavenly harps of the little birds praising their gentle and loving Creator so that the woods echoed with their songs." And, more compassionate even than St. Francis: "I will say nothing of the children of man; but the misery and sorrow of all the beasts and little birds, and all created things, is well-nigh breaking my heart; and having no power to help them, I sighed, and prayed to the Most High, Most Merciful Lord, that He would deliver them." His description of a paradisean meadow sounds like the description of a picture by Fra Angelico: "Now behold with your own eyes the heavenly meadow! Lo! What summer joy! Behold the kingdom of sweet May, the valley of all true joy! Glad eyes are gazing into glad eyes! Hark to the harps and fiddles, the singing and laughter! Young men and maidens are leading the dance! Love without sorrow shall reign for ever. . ." etc. There is a picture, drawn by this same Suso, representing the journey of man through life, his departure from God and his return. In this picture the path of humanity is renunciation and asceticism; death flourishes his scythe above the heads of a dancing couple, and underneath is written: "This is earthly love; its end is sorrow"; to such an extent was this sincere and sensitive man under the influence of the traditional hatred of the world which Eckhart, his great master, had completely overcome.

Provençals and Italians sang the delight of spring, and the German minnesingers greeted it as the deliverer from all the hardships of the severe winter; with the latter it was more a childish delight in the open-air life which had again become possible, after the long imprisonment of winter, than pure joy in beauty. But some of the German epic poems, "Tristan and Isolde," for instance, contain genuine, sincere descriptions of sylvan beauty. The student of art, especially the German art of the Renascence, cannot help being struck by the extraordinary love with which quite insignificant objects of nature, such as a bird, or a flower, are treated. The familiar things of every-day life were in this way brought into connection with solemn biblico-historical subjects.

There is no doubt that at all times a certain keen perception of the beauty of nature has been inherent in some favoured individuals; but the universally accepted opinion that only the supernal was really beautiful, and that terrestrial beauty was merely its reflected glory, was too strong even for them. Thus we have seen Suso translating the beauty of the earthly spring to the kingdom of heaven.

At the same time men were beginning to travel to distant countries for the sole purpose of seeing new scenes and acquiring fresh knowledge. The famous Venetian, Marco Polo, was the first European who (in 1300) visited Central Asia, crossed China and Thibet, and brought news to Europe of the fairyland of Japan. Sight-seeing as an end in itself was discovered. Long sea-voyages for commercial purposes were no novelty, but no human foot had ever trod the summits of the Lower Alps, unless it had been the foot of a peasant whose cattle had strayed. Petrarch was the first man (in 1336) to climb a barren mountain, the Mont Ventoux in Provence, voluntarily undergoing a certain amount of fatigue for sheer delight in the beauty of nature. This was a great, an immortal deed, greater than all his sonnets and treatises put together. In a long letter which has been preserved to us, he describes with much spirit and erudition this extraordinary ascent, before whose profound significance all the Alpine exploits of our time shrink into paltry gymnastic exercises.

The beauty of nature discovered and appreciated, interest began to be evinced in the relationship existing between the various phenomena and there arose a desire to obtain ocular proof of what was written in the venerable books—perhaps even make new discoveries. The first man of any importance in this direction was the German Albrecht Bollstädt (Albertus Magnus), who, although he contributed more than any other man to the promulgation of Aristotelian philosophy, wrote a book on natural history founded on personal observation; his great English contemporary, however, Roger Bacon, is the true father of modern experimental science. It was he who coined the expression "scientia experimentalis," and framed the principle that all research must be based on the study of nature. He maintained that experience was the "mistress of all sciences," and said: "I respect Aristotle and account him the prince of philosophers, but I do not always share his opinion. Aristotle and the other philosophers have planted the tree of science, but the latter has not by any means put forth all its branches or matured all its fruit." This thought, though it seems to us self-evident, was of great moment in the age of scholasticism. Bacon spent ten years in prison; but in spite of everything, he was so much under the influence of scholasticism that he considered it the task of philosophy to adduce evidence for the truth of the Christian dogma.

Here it is essential roughly to sketch the essence of the philosophical thought of that period, and point out the way which led from the Christianity of the Fathers of the Church and scholasticism to the religion of unhistorical Christianity, the so-called mysticism. Scholasticism had reached its climax in the thirteenth century; universities were founded in Paris, Oxford and Padua, and he who aspired to the full dignity of learning had to take his degrees there; even Eckhart did not neglect to obtain his scholastic education in Paris.

Scholasticism was an imposing and yet strangely grotesque system of the world, built up—before a background of blazing stakes—of scriptural passages and ecclesiastical tradition, lofty, pure thought and antique-mediaeval superstition. Its fundamental problem, the determination of the border line between faith and knowledge, was purely philosophical. While the older scholasticism, based on Platonic traditions, endeavoured to bring these into harmony with Christianity, that is to say, prove the revelations by dialectics, Albertus Magnus and, authoritatively, his pupil, Thomas Aquinas (1226–1274), strictly distinguished, by the use of Aristotelian weapons, the rational or perceptive truths from the supernatural verities or the subjects of faith. This distinction, made in order to safeguard dogma, quickly revealed its double-face. The handmaiden philosophy rebelled against her mistress theology, and asked her for her credentials. According to the classic and dogmatic doctrine of Thomas, the natural verities alone could be grasped by human understanding; the supernatural or revealed truths (the dogmas) were beyond proof and scientific cognition. To submit them to research was not only an impossible task, but Thomas stigmatised every effort in this direction as heresy, fondly believing that he had once and for all safeguarded the position of faith. But more resolute and profound thinkers, although not in so many words attacking the authority of the Scriptures, and leaving Thomas' border-line unquestioned, found the unfathomable truths not in ecclesiastical tradition but in their own souls, thus investing "faith" with a new meaning, unassailable by criticism.

The idea of drawing a line between perceivable or rational truths and imperceivable or divine truths, is fraught with the burning question as to the limits of human knowledge, a question which to this day remains unanswered. In the course of time the limits were extended in favour of imperfect knowledge (but the character of the unknowable was problematised and questioned). While Thomas was still convinced of the possibility of proving the existence of a God by the power of the human intellect, Duns Scotus removed the problem of the existence of a God and the immortality of the soul from the domain of science, and made both propositions a matter of faith. William of Occam, more uncompromising than Duns Scotus, maintained the absolute impossibility of acquiring knowledge of supernatural things, and taught—on this point, too, anticipating Kant—that objective knowledge acquired through the senses should precede abstract knowledge. The last conclusion of nominalism was thus arrived at, the existence of universal conceptions, or universals, supposed to exist outside material things—the curse of the Platonic inheritance—declared to be impossible, and reality conceded to the individual only. Roscellinus, the founder of this doctrine, had still been content to deny the existence of the conception of "deity," leaving the individual persons, Father, Son and Holy Ghost, as real individuals, untouched.

We see from the foregoing that the universally derided scholasticism travelled along the whole line of modern thought: from the "realism" of Thomas, which leaves the universals as yet unassailed by doubt and occupying the very heart of knowledge, past the first and, to our view, very modest doubts of the nominalists, to the agnosticism of Bacon, Duns and Occam.

With the new position of decided nominalism the foundation was prepared for the experimental sciences on the one hand, and mysticism on the other. For the conclusion that things supernatural are a closed book to us may have two results: on the one hand, the rejection of the transcendental and the victory of science; on the other, the need to descend into the profoundest depths of the universe and the soul, and grasp by intuition what common sense does not see.

The time was ripe and the consummators came: Dante in the south, Eckhart in the countries north of the Alps. With regard to Dante, I will say one thing only; he gathered together all the achievements of the new art and transcended them in a work which has never been surpassed. The profoundly symbolical words, "The new life is beginning," are written at the commencement of his *Vita Nuova*, and with his *Divine Comedy* the art of Europe had attained perfection.

It is necessary to give a more detailed account of Eckhart. He had been almost forgotten in favour of his pupils, Tauler and Suso, and the unknown author of the *Theologica Germanica* (to which Luther wrote a preface), but to-day a faint idea of the great importance of this man is beginning to dawn upon the world. Eckhart was the greatest creative religious genius since Jesus, and I believe that in time his writings will be considered equal to the Gospel of St. John. He grasped the spirit of religion with unparalleled depth; everything produced by the highly religious later mediaeval era pales before his illumination. Compared to him, St. Augustine, St. Bernard, and even St. Francis dwindle into insignificance; all the later reformers are small beside the greatness of his soul. Every one of his sermons contains profound passages, such as "God must become I and I must become God." "The soul as a separate entity must be so completely annihilated that nothing remains except God, yea, that it becomes more glorious than God, as the sun is more glorious than the moon." "The Scriptures were written and God created the world solely that He may be born in the soul and the soul again in Him." "The essence of all grain is wheat, of all metal gold, and of all creatures man. Thus spoke a great man: 'There is no beast, but it is in some way a semblance of man.'" "The least faculty of my soul is more infinite than the boundless heavens." "Again we understand by the kingdom of God the soul; for the soul and the Deity are one." "The soul is the universe and the kingdom of God." "God dwells so much within the soul that all His divinity depends on it." "Man shall be free and master of all his deeds, undestroyed and unsubdued."

Eckhart was the first man who thought consecutively in the German vernacular, and who made this philosophically still virginal language a medium for expressing profound thought. In addition he wrote Latin treatises which were discovered a short time ago; I have not read them, but I have no doubt that his profoundest convictions were expressed in the German tongue. The Latin language has at all times fettered the spirit far more successfully than the still untainted and living German.

The religious genius of a single individual had created Christianity. But from the very beginning it was misunderstood; the salvation of the world was linked to the person of a man who had aspired to be an example to the whole race. The term, "Son of God," was understood in the sense of the hero-cult of antiquity; possibly the Jewish faith in a Messiah, the politico-national hope of the Children of Israel, was a good deal to blame for this. A historical event was translated into metaphysic. The only truly religious man was made the centre of a new mythology and naïvely worshipped. It may sound like a paradox, but it is a fact that the whole of the first millenary was inwardly irreligious;

it concealed its want of metaphysical intuition behind the falsification of historical events. The entire mediaeval (and a large proportion of the Protestant) theology laboured to obtain an intellectual grasp of the doctrine of a unique historical salvation of humanity and frame it into a dogma. And thus occurred that unparalleled misunderstanding (a misunderstanding which never clouded the mind of India) which based religion, the timeless metaphysical treasure of the soul, on the historical record of an event which had happened in Asia Minor, and had come down to us in a more or less garbled—some say entirely falsified—version. This was the great sin of Christianity: It regarded a historical event, revealing the very essence of religion, and consequently capable of being formulated, as a divine intervention for the purpose of bringing about the salvation of the world, instead of recognising in the sublime figure of the founder of the Christian religion a great, perhaps even perfect, incarnation of the eternally new relationship between God and the soul. It promulgated the strange thought that only the one soul, the soul of the founder, was divine, and instead of teaching the divinity of humanity, it taught the divinity of this one man only—Jesus became a God who could no longer be looked upon as the perfect specimen and prototype of the race, but before whom it behoved man to kneel and pray for salvation. Perhaps it was not possible to understand the new doctrine in any other way; before men can conceive the idea of their divinity, they must have become conscious of their souls.

This complete misunderstanding and externalising of religion which took place in the first millenary, and which can never now be retrieved, is fundamentally pagan, antique. The record of the salvation of the world, achieved by a hero once and for all time, the historification of the divine spark which is daily re-born in the soul, entirely corresponds to the Greek myths of gods and demi-gods which before their new, symbolical interpretation, were taken quite literally. I am not now concerned with the problem of how far the antique heroes and Eastern mysteries directly influenced the conception of the figure of Christ; I only wish to emphasise the profound contrast between true religion which springs up in the soul of the individual, and historical tradition. If there is such a thing as religion, it must exist equally for all men, for those who accidentally received a report of a certain historical event, as well as for those who remained in ignorance of the fact. All heretical demonstrations were rooted in a vague realisation of this contrast. But Eckhart accomplished the unparalleled deed of once more building a bridge between the soul and the deity; of relegating to the background all the ineradicable historical misrepresentations or, if there was no alternative, of unhesitatingly proclaiming them as erroneous, or interpreting them symbolically. "St. Paul's words," he says, for instance, "are nothing but the words of Paul; it is not true that he spoke them in a state of grace." He did not regard the Scriptures as the bourne of truth, but as subsequent proof of the directly experienced truth of the divine event. With this conception Christianity had reached its highest stage. Henceforth the origin of all truths and values was no longer sought in doctrine and authority, but in the soul of man; God was neither to be found in the heavens nor in history, but in the soul; the soul must become divine and creative; it had found its task: the recreation of the world. It was true, St. Augustine had said: "*Non Christianised, Christi sumus*," but this saying had never been understood, and very probably St. Augustine had not meant it in its literal sense. At last the fundamental consciousness of Christianity had triumphed: the principle of the "Son-of-Godship" inspired the soul of the mystics; in future religion must emanate from the soul and find its goal in God; written documents and—in the case of the profoundest thinkers— examples were no longer needed. The heretical sects had been content to reject post-evangelical tradition, in order to lay greater stress on the words of Christ. They were genuine reformers, but they were as much constrained by the historical facts as the Roman Catholic Church, and their standpoint has to this day remained the standpoint of the Protestant professions of faith.

The fact of this new conception attaching no importance to the historical Jesus of Nazareth (had he never lived it would have made no difference) made of it a new religion. By putting aside this external and accidental moment, it placed the metaphysical and purely spiritual core of Christianity, the fundamental conviction of the divinity of the soul, and the will to eternal life, within the centre of religious consciousness, and by so doing put itself beyond the reach of historical criticism and scepticism, Eckhart, more than any other teacher, was profoundly convinced of the freedom and eternal value of the soul. "I, as the Son, am the same as my Heavenly Father." He taught that Christ is born in the soul, that the divine spark is continuously re-kindled in the soul: "It is the quality of eternity that life and youth are one," and that man must become more and more divine, more and more free from all that is unessential and accidental until he no longer differs from

God. It is only a logical conclusion to say that a perfect man, mystically speaking, is God; his being and his will are in nothing differentiated from absolute, universal, divine will—German mysticism agrees in this with the Upanishads. Kant would have said that the principles of such a man would become cosmic laws; sin would be the estrangement from God, the will to draw away from God.

The profound and only mission of religion is the endowment of man in this hurly-burly of life with the consciousness of eternity. Religion places our transient life under the aspect of eternity, and therefore it must, in its essence, remain a stranger to things temporal. Only that moment in the life of a man can be called religious which lifts him beyond himself, out of his petty, narrow existence, conditioned by and subject to accidents, into timeless, universal life; which gives him the certainty that historical events can never be regarded as definite and ultimate—that moment which has the power to set free, to deliver, to save. Thus it is irreligious to regard an event which occurred on the temporal plane—and were it the greatest event which ever befell on earth—as the pivot of metaphysical value for all men; to link the salvation of the world to an occurrence which was relatively accidental, to base the consciousness of eternity on the knowledge of a fact. This would be a victory of time over eternity, a victory of irreligion over religion.

I regard it as the greatest achievement of that great time that spontaneous religion again became possible. Eckhart rediscovered the divine nature of man; never has the consciousness of timeless eternity been expressed as he expressed it in his tract, *On Solitude*. Doubtless there have been men before him who possessed direct religious intuitions, and now and then gave timid utterance to them; but the authority of tradition has always been too great, and they never did more than compromise between the historical events on which the Christian religion is based and the genuinely religious experience of their own souls. Eckhart, too, was careful not to offend against the letter, and his pupils, after suspicion had fallen on them, made many a concession in terms, and perhaps even in thought. St. Augustine already had steered a middle course between the historical and the religious conception, in his phrase: *Per Christum hominem at Christum deum*, and Suso (in his *Booklet of Eternal Wisdom*) followed his lead. "Thus speaks the eternal wisdom: If ye will behold me in my eternal divinity ye must know and love me in my suffering humanity. For this is the quickest road to eternal salvation." The brutality of the tenet which maintains that all those are eternally lost who, without their own fault, have no knowledge of the salvation of the world (especially therefore, those who died before the event), was a stumbling-block to many thoughtful minds. The patriarchs of the Old Testament were looked upon as saved—to some extent—by the fact of their being the ancestors or prophets of Christ; but pagans and Greeks, including Aristotle, were condemned even by the great Dante. At the conclusion of his *Divine Comedy* Dante proved himself a truly inspired mystic, for he gave to us the profoundest vision of the divinity which has ever been vouchsafed to man. But his genius was directed and restricted by the dogmas of the Church; his religious standpoint was the standpoint of the early Middle Ages and dogmatic Catholicism. As poet and lover he was the inaugurator of a new world; here he represents the culmination and conclusion of the condemned world-system. He was the iron landmark of the ages—Eckhart, the creator of eternal values.

The foremost of the precursors of Eckhart was Bernard of Clairvaux (1091–1153). He was the exponent of the love of God which he placed above knowledge; in one of his letters he calls love "the existence of God Himself," basing his definition on the passage in the Gospel of St. John, "God is Love." "Love is the eternal law which created and preserves the universe; the whole world is governed by love; but although love is the law to which all creation is subject, it is not itself without law, but it is a law unto itself. Serfs and mercenaries are ruled by laws which are not from God, but which they made themselves; some because they do not love God, others because they love the things of this world better than God. . . They made their own laws and subordinated the universal and eternal laws to their own will. But those (who live righteously) are in the world as God is: neither serfs nor mercenaries, but the children of God and, like God Himself, they live only by the law of love." "His greatest happiness is complete absorption in the vision of the divine and forgetfulness of self." "All love is an emanation of that one love. It is the eternally creative and governing law of the universe." "To be penetrated by such emotion is to become deified. As a drop of water in a cup of wine is completely dissolved and takes the taste and colour of the wine, so also, in an indescribable manner, is the human will absorbed in the divine will, and transformed into the will of God. For how could God become all in all if anything human were left in man?" "They are completely immersed (the martyrs) in the infinite ocean of eternal light, in radiant eternity. . ."

The entranced soul "shall lose all knowledge of itself and become completely absorbed in God; it shall become unlike itself in the measure as it has received the gift of becoming divine." Sensuous metaphors from the Song of Songs and the Psalms are again and again intermingled with these lofty thoughts. But in spite of his divine emotion, in spite of his anticipations of the German mystics, Bernard took the standpoint of ecclesiastical orthodoxy whenever he was not in the ecstatic state; his contemplative mind was unable to grasp the importance of independent thought, a fact amply proved by his inglorious quarrel with Abélard, the greatest thinker of his time. This quarrel was a typical illustration of the difference between the believer and the thinker. Bernard forgot all about love, and did not hesitate to stir up unpleasantness whenever he could do so. So he wrote to Pope Innocent II: "Peter Abélard is striving to destroy the Christian faith, and imagines that his human intellect can penetrate the depths of the divine mind. . . Nothing is hidden from him, neither in the earth below, nor in the heavens above; his intellectual pride exceeds all limits; he attacks the doctrines of faith, and ponders problems far above his intellectual capacity; he is an inventor of heresies. . . ," etc. Thanks to his machinations, Abélard was compelled to recant at the Council of Sens, and was condemned by the Pope to eternal silence. Berengar of Poitier took Abélard's part, and in a satirical treatise ventured to criticise St. Bernard's conduct: "Thus philosophise the old women at the looms. Of course, when Bernard tells us that we must love God, he speaks a true and venerable word; but he need not have opened his lips to do so, for it is a self-evident truth." As a matter of fact, these words branded and contradicted the merely subjective emotional mysticism; to the emotional mystic salvation lies in the "absorption in God," in shapeless, thoughtless contemplation. Richard of St. Victor, founding his theories on St. Bernard, established six stages of meditation. The Franciscan monk, Bonaventura, the famous author of the *Biblia Pauperum*, added a seventh, a complete rest in God—"like the Sabbath after the six days of labour." To Bonaventura, as later on to Dante, the world was a ladder leading up to God.

If we turn from these thinkers of the Neo-Latin race, who in spite of their undeniable mysticism were completely under the dominion of the Church—to German mysticism, we find above and beyond mysticism, we find above and beyond love, a new principle: The soul of man is the starting-point of religious consciousness and the content of the religious consciousness is the soul's road to God. The nativity of Christ ceased to be regarded as a historical event, and became the birth of the divine principle in the soul of man. In passing I will mention a German nun, Mechthild of Magdeburg (1212–1277), who anticipated some of the great thoughts of Eckhart, although she was incapable of grasping their mutual connection. "The Holy Trinity and everything in heaven and earth must be subject to me" (the soul), were words in the true spirit of Eckhart, leaving St. Bernard far behind. Mechthild found metaphors of true poetical grandeur when she spoke of the union of the soul with God. "The dominion of the fire has yet to come. That is Jesus Christ in Whose hands the Heavenly Father has laid the salvation of the world and the Last Judgment. On the Day of Judgment He shall fashion cups of wondrous beauty out of the crackling sparks; therein the Father will drink on His festival all the holiness which through His dear Son He has poured into human souls."

Emotional mysticism was the prevailing form of mysticism in those days; even Eckhart's pupil, Suso, belonged to this class of mystics. This vague sentimentalism saved many a mind from the rigid dogmas of the Church, and as its vagueness could be interpreted in more than one way, it caused very little offence; but these visions and ecstasies, which are so often mistaken for true mysticism, have done much to bring the latter into contempt with the seriously minded. Eckhart did not acknowledge it as genuine mysticism and directly condemned it in many of his writings; and as he rejected mystic sentimentalism, clearly divining its pathological cause, so he also rejected asceticism and all religious ceremonies. The evangelical poverty of the Franciscan monks was an object of loathing to him. St. Francis (and thirty years before him Peter Valdez) had naïvely interpreted the imitation of Christ as a life of absolute poverty, and had been relentless in his denunciation of worldly wealth, which every monk of his order had to renounce. He himself never touched money, seeing in it the source of all evil. His transcendent treasure was "Holy Poverty"; Jacopone wrote an ardent hymn to "Queen Poverty," and even Thomas, the representative of Dominican erudition, theoretically took up the cudgels on its behalf. But even in the primitive Church the principle of worldly and spiritual poverty was widely spread and encouraged. In the defence of poverty, which was practically nearly always synonymous with idleness and begging, and therefore roused much hostility among the people, Bonaventura pointed out (in his treatise, *De Paupertate Christi*) that Jesus Himself had never done any manual work. The universal preference for a contemplative life encouraged the tendency, and the extreme charitableness of the Middle Ages made its realisation possible. Work was frequently looked upon as a punishment—a view which could easily be upheld by reference to Adam's expulsion from Paradise—and inflicted upon the monks for offences against the rules. Dante's friend, Guido Cavalcanti, expressed the natural sentiment that poverty is a distressing condition, in a canzone which bristles with insults hurled at the Queen of the Franciscans:

> *Yea, rightly art thou hated worse than death,*
> *For he, at length, is longed for in the breast.*
>
> *But not with thee, wild beast,*
> *Was ever aught found beautiful or good;*
> *For life is all that man can lose by death,*
> *Not fame and the fair summits of applause;*
> *His glory shall not pause*
> *But live in men's perpetual gratitude.*
> *While he who on thy naked sill has stood*
> *He shall be counted low, etc.*

D.G. Rossetti

The concept of the German mystics was infinitely more profound than the concept of the merely external poverty of the Franciscans, which in the case of St. Francis and Jacopone was an inherent characteristic and pure, but in the case of the others more or less vicious. "Man cannot live in this world without labour," says Eckhart, "but labour is man's portion; therefore he must learn to have God in his heart, although surrounded by the things of this world, and not let his business or his surroundings be a barrier." There is a passage in the book of an unknown author, entitled *The Imitation of Christ's Poverty* (formerly ascribed to Tauler), which reads as follows: "Poverty is equality with God, a mind turned away from all creatures; poverty clings to nothing and nothing clings to it; a man who is poor clings to nothing which is beneath him, but to that alone which is greater than all things. And that is the loftiest virtue of poverty that it clings only to that which is sublime and takes no heed of the things which are base, so far as it is possible." "The soul while it is burdened with temporal and transient things is not free. Before it can aspire to freedom and nobility it must cast away all the things of the world." "Nobody can be really poor unless God make him so; but God makes no man poor unless he be in his inmost heart; then all things will be taken from him which are not God's. The more spiritual a man is, the poorer will he be, for spirituality and poverty are one. . ." Pseudo-Tauler even affirms that a man "can possess abundant wealth and yet be poor in spirit." The meaning of this is clear: He whose heart is not wrapped up in the things of the world, will find his way to God; a soul which is without desire is rich.

But there was a still greater contrast between the naïve religion represented by St. Francis of Assisi and the religion of Eckhart. The former lived entirely in the obvious and visible; the love of all creatures filled his heart and shaped his life. The heart of the mystic too, was filled with love, but it was love transcending the love of the individual, love of the primary cause. In the last sense Eckhart taught, contrary to traditional Christianity, and in conformity with Indian wisdom, that the soul must be absorbed into the absolute and that everything transient and individual must cease to exist. "The highest freedom is that the soul should rise above itself and flow into the fathomless abyss of its archetype, of God Himself."

Even St. Bernard was not quite free from this mystical heresy (*cf.* the previously quoted passages). "When he has reached the highest degree of perfection, man is in a state of complete forgetfulness of self, and having entirely ceased to belong to himself, becomes one with God, released from everything not divine." Even compassion must cease in this state, for there is nothing left but justice and perfection.

We recognise here a characteristic of all those who are greatest among men: of Goethe, for instance, of Bach, or Kant: namely, the correspondence of intense personality and the most highly developed objectivity; for the greatest personality ceases in the end to distinguish between itself and the world, has eradicated everything paltry, selfish and subjective and has become entirely objective, impersonal, divine. St. Francis knew nothing of this consciousness. "God has chosen me because among all men He could find no one more lowly, and because through my instrumentality He purposed to confound nobility, greatness, strength, beauty and the wisdom of the world." He was the disciple of the earthly Jesus, Who went through life the compassionate consoler of all those who were sorrowful. But Eckhart aspired "to the shapeless nature of God." "We will follow Him, but not in all things," he said of the historical Jesus. "He did many things which He meant us to understand spiritually, not literally. . . we must always follow Him in the profounder sense." Compared to the religion of Eckhart, the religion of St. Francis is the faith of a little child, picturing God as a benevolent old man. Such a religion is equally true and sincere, but it represents an earlier stage on the road of humanity. If Christianity were—as we are occasionally assured—the religion of Jesus, then the great mystics cannot be called Christians. And yet St. Augustine's: "We are not Christians, but Christs," was fulfilled in them.

The profoundest depth of European religion, of which Eckhart was the exponent, and which found artistic expression in Gothic art, was not sounded by music until very much later. Bach, more emphatically in the High Mass and the Magnificat, but also in his purely instrumental music, brought the universal feeling of mysticism to absolute artistic perfection. The deep religious sentiment which pervades the High Mass is so far above all cults, that it has no real connection with any historical faith—it is pure consciousness of the divine.

The peculiar state of the soul, called mysticism, could never become popular, or exert any very great influence. A few men, such as Tauler, Suso, Merswin, and the unknown author of the *Theologica Germanica* handed on—not by any means always unadulterated—the doctrine they had received from Eckhart—which at all times appealed to a few thinkers—but the real influence on the world and on history was reserved for the reformers. The reformer, in his inmost nature, is related to the people; his soul is agitated by formulas and ceremonies, to which the mystic is indifferent; they are to him obstacles to his faith and he strains every nerve to destroy them. He has every appearance of the truly free spirit, but he is secretly dependent on that against which he is fighting. He suffers under its inefficiency; his deed is the final reaction against his environment; salvation seems to him to lie in the improvement of existing conditions, and not until he has succeeded in accomplishing his purpose can he hope for religious peace. The mystic is possible in all states of civilisation. He is not dependent on external circumstances; his whole consciousness is filled with one problem only, before which everything else pales: the relationship of the soul to God. But the reformer is possible only under certain circumstances. He, too, starts from an inner religious consciousness, but his problem is soon solved, and he devotes all his energy to the world. The mystic is not even aware of the difference between his own conception of God and traditional religion; he is under the impression that he is still an orthodox believer, long after he has broken fresh ground; for he has taken from the traditional doctrine everything which he can re-animate. The remainder is dead as far as he is concerned. To accuse him of heresy appears to him as a monstrous misunderstanding.

Thus mystic and reformer drink from the same well of direct religious consciousness. But while in the case of the mystic the well is fathomless, it is much more shallow in the case of the reformer. Certain of himself, he directs his energy to the conversion and reformation of the world. He resembles in some respects the public orator and agitator; he has a grasp of social conditions, strives to influence his surroundings by word and deed, and is ready to sacrifice his life to his convictions. The mystic remains solitary and misunderstood. Luther, who was to some extent influenced by German mysticism, fought, at his best, against the dogma of historical salvation.

It is the tragic fate of all religions that they must crystallise into a system. A reflection of the enthusiasm which animated their founders still falls on their disciples: Follow me! But the second generation already demands proofs, tradition and clumsy miracles; reports are drawn up and looked upon as sacred—religion has become a glimpse into the past. Most people never have any direct religious experience, their salvation lies in the dogmas, the universally accepted doctrines. The founder of a new religion is always regarded by his contemporaries as abnormal, and is persecuted accordingly; not in malice, but of necessity. Arnold of Brescia died at the stake; St. Francis was no more than a heretic tolerated by the Church, and Eckhart escaped the tribunal of the Inquisition only through his death.

I have attempted to show in diverse domains of the higher spiritual and psychical life, how powerfully *the Christian principle of the individual soul, the real fundamental value of the European civilisation*, manifested itself at the time of the Crusades, and everywhere became the germ of new things. The deepest thinkers teach the deification of man as the culmination of existence, the ultimate purpose of this earthly life, and claim immortality for the soul. This position, which may roughly be conceived as the raising of the individual into the ideal, has determined the European ideal of culture and differentiated it from all Orientalism, including even the loftiest Indian philosophy. Every attempt to substitute for this fundamental concept and its emotional content something else—whether it be pantheism, Buddhism, or naturalism—will always remain a failure.

Side by side with the splendid achievement of the German mysticism, the Teutonic race has always been apt to give practical proof of its individualism by endless petty quarrels and by splittings into numerous cliques. But even before this race began to play a part in history, at the beginning of the third century, the principle of the individual soul was outwardly carried to extremes. While it was the ideal of the man of antiquity to serve the higher community of the State with body and soul, nascent Christianity cared solely for the salvation of the individual soul, and frequently proved this by quite external evidence, by living a hermit's life in the desert, for instance. Children left their parents, husband and wife separated, dignitaries forsook their office to seek solitude and prepare their souls for the world beyond the grave. The first convents—the outcome of Christian individualism and asceticism— were founded; and the anti-social extreme of this individualism acquired such ominous proportions that the Emperor Valens in the year of grace 365, was forced to legislate against the monastic life.

This hatred of the world, which was quite in harmony with the spirit of Christianity, was only overcome by the profounder concepts of German mysticism, for in the primitive dualistic view of the first millenary the renunciation of the world was the only possibility of avoiding sin. The Emperor Justinian decreed that any man who induced a consecrated nun to marry him should be punished by death. The thought that personal greatness did not consist in renouncing the world but in living in it and overcoming it, had not yet been conceived.

The delight in the human form, characteristic of antiquity, was extinguished, a crude dualism denied all antique values. The body must be hated, so that the soul could flourish. But as the Hellenic period was preceded by vague, unindividualised, material life, so the impersonal, chaotic, spiritual life of the first thousand years of Christianity matured the individual soul. It found its climax in Dante and Eckhart, the greatest poet of the Neo-Latin race, and the most illumined religious genius of Germany. These two men, who were contemporaries (Dante died in 1321 and Eckhart in 1329), finally revealed the character of two kindred nations, completing and fructifying each other. In Dante the great artistic power of the Neo-Latin race appeared for the first time in its full intensity; it took possession of the whole visible universe, and poured new beauty into the traditional myths of Christendom. Eckhart experienced and recreated the shapeless depths of the soul, the regions of the blending of the soul with God. With these two men Europe definitely severed herself from antiquity and barbarism, henceforth to follow her own star.

The new world had come into existence! Renascence, the lucky heir, gathered the ripe fruit from the tree of art which had blossomed so marvellously. God was no longer sought in the depth of the soul, all emotion was projected into the world of sense. Churches were built, not from an irresistible impulse, but as store-houses of the pictures which were painted with amazing rapidity. The fundamental principle of personality was externalised in the Renascence. Vanity and boasting, traces of which frequently appeared in the age of chivalry, grew exuberantly. No less manifest than the incomparable genius and *esprit* of the heyday of the Renascence—although far less frequently commented on—was the desire to be conspicuous, to shine, to display wealth and learning. The essence of personality, instead of being sought in the soul, was sought in outward magnificence. As a matter of fact, the much extolled Renascence only perfected the various branches of art and poetry, which had sprung up in the period of the Crusades. The latter was the time of the planting of the tree of European culture; all that followed was merely its growth and ramification. Only exact science had its origin in the Renascence, and this fact, in historical perspective, must be regarded as the supreme glory of this period. However paradoxical it may sound—the "impersonal" science is the perfection of the European system of individualism, its most potent weapon for taking spiritual possession of the world and all that the world contains. The consciousness of personality had to permeate the whole soul before it could recover its external function: organic existence justified by itself. While art borrows from nature and mankind all that we ourselves deem beautiful, perfect, valuable, and imposes on the world a man-made law—science strives to understand all things and all creatures according to the law which dominates them; it strives to comprehend nature and humanity—even where they are foreign and hostile—not according to human values, but according to their inherent nature—and this is only possible when the individuality of all things is respected. The method of science has slowly become the perfect weapon by whose aid Europe has attained the mastery of the world; it rests on the fundamental feeling for the material, and is capable of confronting the "I" with the whole system of natural phenomena, the "not-I," and expresses the final victory of comprehending spirit over matter.

II

The Deification of Woman
(The First Form of
Metaphysical Eroticism)

(a) The Love of the Troubadours

IN THE LONG CHAPTER ON the Birth of Europe, I have attempted to bring corroborative evidence from all sides in support of my contention that the twelfth and thirteenth centuries witnessed the birth and gradual development of a new value of the highest importance: the value of individuality, impersonated by the citizen of Europe. We are now prepared to realise the psychological importance and the importance for progress of one of the greatest results of this new development—the spiritual love of man for woman. From this subject, the specific subject of my book, I shall not again digress.

We are aware that the man of antiquity (and also the Eastern nations of to-day) recognised between man and woman only the sexual bond, uninfluenced by personal and psychological motives, and leading in Greece to the institution of monogamy on purely economical and political grounds. In addition to this bond there existed a very distinct spiritual love, evolved by Plato and his circle and projected by one man on another member of his own sex. In the true Hellenic spirit this love aspired to guide the individual to the ideal of perfection, the beauty and wisdom of the friend serving as stepping-stones in the upward climb. In Christianity the spiritual love of the divine became the greatest value and the pivot on which the emotions turned. The primitive Christian scorned the body, his own as well as that of his fellow; he despised beauty of form, and regarded only the divine as worthy of love. Woman was disparaged and suspected; all thinkers, down to Thomas and Anselm, looking upon her merely as a snare and a pitfall. The period discussed in detail in the foregoing chapter ushered in a new and, until then, unknown feeling. In crude and conscious contrast to sexuality, deprecated alike by classical Greece and primitive Christianity, spiritual love of man for woman came into existence. It was composed of three clearly distinguishable elements: the Platonic thought, maintaining that the greatest virtue lies in the striving for absolute perfection; the entirely spiritual love of the divine, sufficient in itself, and representing the final purpose of life, as developed by Christianity; and the dawning knowledge of the value of personality. From these three elements: the noblest inheritance of antiquity, the central creation of Christianity, and the pivot of the new-born European spirit, sprang the new value which is the subject of the second stage of eroticism. The position of woman had changed; she was no longer the medium for the satisfaction of the male impulse, or the rearing of children, as in antiquity; no longer the silent drudge or devout sister of the first Christian millenary; no longer the she-devil of monkish conception; transcending humanity, she had been exalted to the heavens and had become a goddess. She was loved and adored with a devotion not of this earth, a devotion which was the sole source of all things lofty and good; she had become the saviour of humanity and queen of the universe.

The rejection of sensuality is an inherent part of the Christian religion; only he who had overcome his sinful desires was a hero. Spiritual love was as yet unknown, only the sexual impulse was realised, and that was looked upon as a sin; there was but one way of escape: renunciation. This view is very clearly expressed in the legends of Alexius, and in Barlaam and Josaphat (which although of Indian origin, had found a German interpreter and were known all over Europe). The latter legend tells how Prince Josaphat, a devout Christian, married a beautiful princess. On his wedding night he had a vision of the celestial paradise, the dominion of chastity, and the earthly pool of sin. Recognising in his bride a devil who had come to tempt him, he left her and fled into the desert. Many legends illustrate the incapacity of the first millenary to realise the relationship between the sexes in any other sense. Woman was evil; the struggle against her a laudable effort.

Very probably the stigmatising of all eroticism during that long spell of a thousand years was necessary. Only the unnatural condemnation of love in its widest sense, a hatred of sex and woman such as was felt by Tertullian and Origen, could result in the reverse of sexuality— purely spiritual love with its logical climax, the deification and worship of woman. There can be no doubt that the Christian ideal of chastity was largely responsible for the evolution of the ideal of spiritual love. The identity of love and chastity was propounded—in sharp contrast to sexuality and—more particularly amongst the later troubadours, such as Montanhagol, Sordello, and the poets of the "sweet new style" in Italy—with a distinct leaning towards religious ecstasy.

Infinite tenderness pervaded the nascent cult of woman. It seemed as if man were eager to compensate her for the indignity which he had heaped upon her for a thousand years. His instinctive need to worship had found an incomparable being on earth before whom he prostrated himself. She was the climax of earthly perfection; no word, no metaphor was sufficiently ecstatic to express the full fervour of his adoration; a new religion was created, and she was the presiding divinity. "What were the world if beauteous woman were not?" sang Johannes Hadlaub, a German poet.

Once more I must revert to personality, the fundamental value of the European. In antiquity, even in Greece and Rome, personality in its higher sense did not exist. The hero was the epitome of all the energies of the nation, a term for the striving of the community; the statesman was the incarnate political will of the people; even the poet's ideal was the representation of the Hellenic type in all its aspects. Agamemnon was no more than the intelligent ruler, Achilles the headstrong hero, Odysseus the cunning adventurer. The individual was a member and servant of the tribe, the town, the state; each man knew that his fellow did not essentially differ from him; and even at the period when Hellas was at its meridian the individuals were, compared to modern men, but slightly differentiated. But the Greek differed from the Oriental, the barbarian, inasmuch as he felt himself no longer a component part of nature, but realised his distinct individuality.

We find the first germs of the new creative principle of personality in the Platonic figure of Socrates who, first of all, conceived the idea of a higher spiritual love, blended it with the love of ideas and separated it sharply from base desire. Though his conception was not yet personal love in the true sense, it was nevertheless a spiritual divine love. The Greek State could not tolerate him, and sentenced him to death. But this same Socrates also said (in "Crito") that man was indebted to the State for his existence. "Did not thy father, in obedience to the law, take thy mother to wife and beget thee?" This sentiment was as antique as it could well be, and the death of Socrates—as related by Plato—was the most magnificent confirmation of the Greek idea that the individual, even the wisest, was entirely subordinate to the community.

The civilisations of China and Japan are impersonal even to a greater extent than the civilisation of ancient Greece. Percival Lowell maintains that the diverse manifestations of the spirit of those countries can only be understood if regarded from the standpoint of absolute impersonality.

He sees in a "pronounced impersonality the most striking characteristic of the Far East", "the foundation on which the Oriental character is built up." It is very instructive to observe how it determines the individual's conception of birth and marriage, thoughts and acts, life and death. It is carried to so great an extreme that special terms for "I," "you," "he," do not even exist in the Japanese language, and have to be replaced by objective circumlocutions. Not content with the fact of having been born impersonal, it is the ambition of the inhabitant of the Far East to become more and more so as his life unfolds itself. Witness the heroic exploits of Japanese soldiers during the last war: individual soldiers frequently went to their death for the sake of a small advantage to their group. We Europeans regard this in the light of heroism—and it would be heroism in the case of a European. But with the sacrifice of his individual life in the interest of the community, the Japanese instinctively yields the smaller value. In the same way Greeks and Romans did not attach very much importance to life; suicide was very common, and frequently committed without any special motive. As true love is based on personality, it is impossible for the modern East-Asiatic to know love in our sense. Lowell agrees with this: "Love, as we understand it, is an unknown feeling in the East." He reports that Japanese women will appear before strangers entirely nude, without the least trace of embarrassment—as would Greek women!—because they are innocent of that other aspect of personality—the feeling of shame. To be ashamed implies the desire of concealing something individual and intimate; where this is not the case, there can be no feeling of shame. Finally, I should like to point out that the perversity and sexual refinement peculiar to China and Japan are attributable simply to the fact that the limits of sexuality cannot be overstepped, and that sexuality is therefore dependent on vice and perversity to satisfy its craving for variety.

The first manifestation of overwhelming personality appears in Jesus, and he created the religion of love. In him personality and love were convertible forces, one might even say they were identical. He, first of all, revealed their mysterious intimate connection, and clearly showed that love can only be experienced by a distinct personality, because it is an emanation of the soul and not a natural instinct.

It was, again, personality which, in the twelfth century, produced a new force: spiritual love projected not only on God and nature, but also on woman. Now only had personality acquired its true significance; it no longer meant—as it did in the mature Greek world—the individual

EMIL LUCKA

separated from his environment, the individual with a conscious beginning and a conscious end, but the principle of the synthesis, a higher entity above the mere individual, the source of all values and virtue.

Personality is the self-conscious, individual soul, producing out of its own wealth the universal ideal values, and re-absorbing and assimilating these ideal values in their higher form. It admits of the fusion of the subjective with the universal and eternal, with the religious and artistic, the moral and scientific values of civilisation. "Personality is the blending of the universal and the individual," said Kierkegaard, expressing, if not exactly my meaning, something very near it.

I shall endeavour to depict the spiritual love of man for woman— the position cannot be reversed—from its inception to its climax. I shall submit abundant evidence to make the great unbroken stream of emotion clearly apparent, and indicate all its tributaries. I do not pretend that I have exhausted the subject—that would be impossible. The works from which I have drawn may be safely regarded as the direct outpouring of emotion; those purely lyric poets were entirely subjective and ever intent upon their own feelings; there hardly exists one Provençal, old-Italian, or mediæval love-song without the "I."

Spiritual love first appeared as a naïve sentiment—unconscious of its own peculiar characteristics—in the poems of the earlier troubadours of Provence. There is a poem in which the Provençals claim the fathership of the cult of woman; their opponents do not deny it, but add that it was an invention which "could fill no man's stomach." These words express the great and insurmountable barrier between pure spiritual love and pleasure. The Christian dualism: soul-body, spirit-matter, had invaded the domain of love.

Spontaneous, genuine love, untainted by speculations and metaphysics, is found in the songs of the earlier troubadours. The greatest among all of them, Bernart of Ventadour, was the first to praise chaste love. If any champion of civilisation deserves a monument, it is this poet.

> *Dead is the man who knows not love,*
> *A sweet tremor in the heart.*
>
> *Love's rapture fills my heart*
> *With laughter and sighs.*
> *Grief slays me a hundred times,*
> *Joy bids me rise.*

> *Sweet is love's happiness,*
> *Sweeter love's pain.*
> *Joy brings back grief to me,*
> *Grief, joy again.*

Guillem Augier Novella expressed the feeling of being "elated with exaltation and grieved to death" as follows:

> *Lady, often flow my tears,*
> *Glad songs in my mem'ry ring,*
> *For the love that makes my blood*
> *Dance and sing.*
> *I am yours with heart and soul,*
> *If it please you, lady, slay me. . .*

Aimeril de Peguilhan is of opinion that the pain of love is no less sweet than the joy of love:

> *For he who loves with all his heart would fain*
> *Be sick with love, such rapture is his pain.*

And Bernart again:

> *God keep my lady fair from grief and woe,*
> *I'm close to her, however far I go;*
> *If God will be her shelter and her shield,*
> *Then all my heart's desire is fulfilled.*

And:

> *My mind was erring in a maze,*
> *That hour I was no longer I,*
> *When in your eyes I met my gaze*
> *As in a mirror strange and shy.*
> *Oh, mirror sweet, reflecting me,*
> *Sighing I fell beneath your spell;*
> *I perished in you utterly*
> *As did Narcissus in the well.*

In the same poem he goes on to say that he will ask for no reward, but finally concludes:

> *My fervent kisses her sweet lips should cover,*
> *For weeks they'd show the traces of her lover.*

The German minnesinger, Heinrich of Morungen, called woman "a mirror of all the delights of the world," and sang:

> *Blessed be the tender hour,*
> *Blest the time, the precious day,*
> *When my brimming heart welled over,*
> *When my secret open lay.*
> *I was startled with great gladness,*
> *And bewildered so with love,*
> *I can hardly sing thereof.*

The sensuous element still dominated Bernart and his contemporaries to some extent. In their poems, all of which are genuine and sincere, the longing for kisses, sometimes for more, is frankly expressed, but the tendency towards the not sensuous and super-sensuous is already apparent. The lover loves one woman only, and would rather love in vain, patiently enduring every pang she causes him, than receive favours from another woman, were she beautiful as Venus her self.

Bernart says:

> *My sorrow is a sweet distress*
> *To which no alien bliss compares,*
> *And if my pain such sweetness bears,*
> *How sweet would be my happiness!*

Elias of Barjols:

> *Full of joy I am and sorrow*
> *When I stand before her face.*

Bonifacio Calvo:

There is no treasure-trove on earth
Which I would barter for my pain;
I love my grief, but spite and wrath
Run riot in my heart; my brain
Is reeling—and I laugh and cry.
Jubilant and desperate,
Exultant, I bewail my fate.
Quarter! Lady, ere I die.

The earlier troubadours were still ignorant of the later dogma which made chaste love the sole fountain of virtue and the road to perfection— the beloved woman can make of her admirer what she wills—a saint or a sinner.

Thus Guillem of Poitiers says:

Love heals the sick
And a grave does it delve
For the strong; mars the beauty of beauty itself,
Makes a fool of the sage with its magic,
A clown of the courteous knight,
And a king of the lowliest wight.

The equally early Cercamon:

False can I be or true for her,
Sincere or full of lies,
A perfect knight or worthless cur,
Serene or grave, stupid or wise.

Raimon of Toulouse:

In the kingdom of love
Folly rules and not sense.

It was typical of this enthusiastic love that the social rank of the beloved, the mistress, was invariably above the rank of the lover. The latter was fond of calling himself her vassal and serf, proclaiming that she had invested him with all his goods; even kings and German emperors composed love-songs, although in all probability they would have achieved their purpose far more quickly by other means; but in all cases we find the characteristic attitude of the humble lover, looking up to his mistress. The underlying thought is obvious: Love, the loftiest value in all the world, is the great leveller of all social differences, a force before which wealth is as dust. "I would rather win a kind glance from my lady's eyes than the royal crown of France," was a favourite profession of the poets. Montanhagol, for instance, in a rhymed meditation, stated that a lady was wise in choosing a lover of a lower social rank, because not only could she always count on his gratitude and devotion, but she would also have more influence over him, a fact which in the case of a social equal or superior was, to say the least, a little doubtful. This supreme reverence for love soon became an accepted doctrine. We constantly meet the thought that chaste love alone can make a man noble, good and wise. I will select a few illustrations from a wealth of instances:

Miraval:

Noble is every deed whose root is love.

Peire Rogier:

Full well I know that right and good
Is all I do for love of her.

Guirot Riquier:

The man who loves not is not noble-minded,
For love is fruit and blossom of the highest.

And:

Thus love transfigures ev'ry deed we do,
And love gives everything a deeper sense.
Love is the teaching of all genuine worth.
So base is no man's heart on this wide earth,
Love could not guide it to great excellence.

Giraut of Calenso said of the City of Love that no base or ignorant man could enter it, and the Italian Lapo Gianni sang:

> *The youthful maiden who appeared to me*
> *So filled my soul with pure and lofty thoughts,*
> *That henceforth all ignoble things I scorn.*

Dante in the *Vita Nuova* calls Beatrice "the destroyer of all evil and the queen of all virtues."

The very thought of the beloved makes a good man of the lover:

> *"I cannot sin when I am in her thoughts."*

asserts the sincere Guirot Riquier, and he prays Christ to teach him the true love of woman.

While it was a generally accepted theory that love was the source of man's perfection, I know of only one passage (by Raimon of Miraval) contending that woman, also, was perfected by love; everywhere else we meet the universal and silently accepted opinion that the essence of womanhood is something unearthly, unfathomable and divine. Perhaps the most classical formulation of the new doctrine, to wit, that spiritual love is the begetter of all virtue and the mother of chastity, outside which there is nothing divine, is to be found in the poems of the somewhat pedantic Montanhagol:

> *The lover who loves not the highest love,*
> *Is like a fool polluting precious wine.*
> *Let loftiest love alone within thee move,*
> *And purity and virtue will be thine.*

Guirot Riquier expressed a similar sentiment:

> *For chaste and pure my love has always been,*
> *From my "sweet bliss" I've never asked a boon;*
> *If I may humbly serve her night and noon,*
> *My life be her inalienable lien.*

Walter von der Vogelweide says: "Love is a treasure heaped up of all virtues."

As time went on the barrier erected between true spiritual love and insidious sensuality became more and more clearly defined; the former pervaded the erotic emotion of the whole period. Parallel with chaste love, sensuality continued to exist as something contemptible, unworthy of a noble mind; and it must be admitted that according to the contemporary "Fabliaux," later German comedies and Italian and French novels, the sexual manifestations of the period, were of incredible coarseness. As against these, spiritual love was not merely an artistic and theoretic concept, but the profound emotion of the cultured minds, and remained a powerful and creative force even in later centuries. Spiritual love and sexuality were irreconcilable contradistinctions; the man who thought otherwise was looked upon as a libertine. The following passages from the poems of the troubadours and their heirs, the Italian poets of the *dolce stil nuovo*, will prove the historical reality of this relationship, the ideal of the declining Middle Ages. We need take no account of the German minnesingers, for although they shared the same ideal, they did not influence principle in the same way as the neo-Latin poets.

Bernart of Ventadour:

> *Lady, I ask no other meed*
> *Than that you suffer me to serve;*
> *My faith and love shall never swerve,*
> *I'm yours whatever you decreed.*

Peire Rogier:

> *Mine is her smile and mine her jest,*
> *And foolish were I more to ask*
> *And not to think me wholly blest.*
> *'Tis no deceit,*
> *To gaze at her is all I need,*
> *The sight of her is my reward.*

Gaucelm Faidit:

> *Of all the ways of love I chose the best,*
> *I love you, love, with ardour infinite,*
> *Yours is my life, do as you will with it.*
> *Nor kiss I ask, nor sweet embraces, lest*
> *I were blaspheming. . .*

The most enthusiastic champions of pure love were Montanhagol, Sordello and Guirot Riqiuer. The former maintained that a lover who asked for favours incompatible with his lady's honour, neither loved her nor deserved to be loved.—"Love begets purity, and he who knows the meaning of love can never forsake virtue."

There is a controversy between Peire Guillem of Toulouse and Sordello, which contains the following passages:

> Of all mankind I never saw
> A man like you, Sordell', I wis,
> For he who woman does adore
> Will never flout her love and kiss.
> And what to others is a prize
> You surely don't mean to despise?
>
> Honour and joy I crave from her,
> And if a little rose she bind
> Into the wreath, Sir Guillem Peire,
> From mercy, not from duty, mind,
> That would be happiness indeed,
> Oh! that such bliss should be my meed!
>
> A humble lover such as you,
> Sordell', in faith, I never knew.
>
> Sir Peire, methinks what you express
> Is lacking much in seemliness.

In another poem the talented Sordello says:

> My love for her is so profound
> I'd serve her, spurn and scorn despite
> Ere with another I'd be found—
> Yet I'd not serve without requite,

and in another, after stating that he loves his lady so much that he would thank her even if she killed him, he continues:

> Thus, lady, I commend to thee
> My fate and life, thy faithful squire

I'd rather die in misery
Than have thee stoop to my desire.

The knight who truly loves his dame
Not only loves her comely face,
Dearer to him is her fair fame
Undimmed, unsullied by disgrace.

How grievously I should offend
Thy virtue, if I spoke of passion;
But if I did—which God forfend!
Sweet lady, stoop not to compassion.

Although Sordello appeared so extremely modest, yet he was grieved to death because his lady did not return his love. There is a poem in which he compares himself to a drowning man whom the beloved alone could save.

This spiritual love (then as now) puzzled the commonplace, and was misunderstood and regarded with scepticism. Bertran d'Alaman taunted Sordello with his "hypocritical happiness" and "the whole deception of his love," and Granet, in a satirical poem, cast doubt upon his sincerity.

It is very significant to find that Sordello, that typical champion of chaste love, kept up a number of questionable liaisons with all sorts of women. Bertran reproached him with having changed his lady at least a hundred times, and he himself shamelessly confesses:

The jealousies of husbands ne'er amaze me,
For in the art of love I do excel,
And there's no wife, however chaste she may be
Who can resist me if I woo her well.
And if her husband hate me I'll not grumble,
Because his wife receives me in the night,
If mine her kiss, if mine sweet love's delight,
His pain and wrath my spirit shall not humble.
No husband e'er shall rob me of my pleasure,
None can resist me, what I wish I gain,
All do I love and never will refrain
Spite husbands' wrath to rob them of their treasure.

It may seem strange at first sight that this enthusiastic exponent of pure love should have led such a double life. But Sordello's conduct is not in the least paradoxical; in accordance with the tendency of the period, he carefully distinguished in his own heart between sexuality and love; before the one he lay prostrate, unable to find words enough in self-depreciation, so that he might the more exalt his mistress; but with respect to all other women he was a mere sensualist. We read that although he was "an expert in the treatment of women" in her presence his voice forsook him and he lost all self-control. Petrarch, who—while living with a very earthly woman—extolled all his life long a lofty being whom he called Laura, was akin to Sordello, although he was a far less brutal character. The latter approached the type of the seeker of love, the Don Juan.

In a tenzone between Peirol and the Dauphin of Auvergne, the former maintains that love must die at the moment of its consummation. "I cannot believe," he says, "that a true lover can continue to love after he has received the last favour." (Otto Weininger agrees with this.) But Peirol winds up with the subtle suggestion that though love be dead, a man should always continue to behave as if he were still in love.

The troubadours never weary of drawing a line between *drudaria* and *luxuria*, pure love and base desire. *Mezura*, seemliness, is contrasted with *dezmezura*, licentiousness. Pure love is regarded as the creator of all high values, luxuriousness as their destroyer. In the same way the German minnesingers distinguished between "low" love and "high" love.

As both cultured minds and the upper classes, contemning sexuality, acknowledged spiritual love only, it follows as a matter of course that the avowal of such sentiments became good form; the motif that the honour of the beloved must be carefully shielded, and that no desire must dim her purity, occurs again and again. But it should not be forgotten that a poet may love a sentiment for its own sake, without being in the least influenced by it. Many a troubadour drew inspiration from an emotion which all praised as the supreme value; even if he had no earthly mistress, he adored the sublime sentiment. Not infrequently it happened that a troubadour who had been loud in praise of high love and denunciation of base desire—a trick of his trade—suddenly came to himself and changed his mind. Folquet of Marseilles, for instance, after more than ten years of vain sighing, came to the conclusion that he had been a fool.

> *Deceitful love beguiles the simple fool*
> *And binds with magic thongs the hapless wight;*

That like a moth lured by the candle-light,
He hovers, helpless, round the heartless ghoul.

I cast thee out and follow other stars
Full evil was my meed and recompense—
New courage steels my fainting heart, and hence
I kneel at shrines which passion never mars.

In an interesting poem Garin the Red implores *Mezura* to teach him the way to love purely and nobly; but he is anything but pleased with his instructress, and comes to the conclusion that her whole wisdom is "just good form" and nothing else.

But by my merry mood impelled
I kiss and dally night and morn
And do the things I feel compelled
To do—or else, with tonsure shorn,
I'd seek a cloister. . .

Elias of Barjols, finding that his love will never be returned, and having no mind to sigh all his life in vain, renounces love altogether. "I should be a fool if I served love any longer!"

"All you lovers are fools!" exclaimed another. "Do you think you can change the nature of women?" This is one of the very rare criticisms of woman; as a rule we hear only of her angelic perfection, wisdom, beauty and aloofness.

The distinguished poet Marcabru was a woman-hater, and enemy of love from the very beginning. He said of himself that he had never loved a woman and that no woman had ever loved him.

The love which is always a lie
And deceiver of men, I decry
And denounce; I had more than enough.
Can you count all the evil it wrought?
When I think of it I am distraught.
What a madman I was to believe,
To sigh, to rejoice and to grieve;
But no longer I'll squander my days,
We have come to the parting of the ways. Etc.

He was indefatigable in abusing the tender passion, and had a great deal to say about the immorality of women. But it is characteristic of the strong public opinion of the time that even this misogynist (who, perhaps, after all was only a disappointed man) praised "high love."

The subject also found its theorists, prominent among whom was the court-chaplain Andreas, who wrote a very learned book on love in Latin. He expressed in propositions and conclusions what the contemporary poets expressed in verse, proving thereby that spiritual love was not merely a poetic fiction but the profoundest belief of the period, supported by the full complement of its philosophical weapons. "In the whole world there is no good and no courtliness outside the fountain of love. Therefore love is the beginning and foundation of all good." He also proved that a noble-minded man must be a lover, for if he were not, he could not have attained virtue. "Love disregards all barriers, and makes the man of low origin the equal and superior of the nobleman."

This conception of spiritual nobility, which was later on perfected in the theory of the *cor gentil*, only existed in Provence and in Italy; it remained unknown in France and Germany.

Andreas drew a distinction between base love, the *amor mixtus sive communis*, and pure love, the *amor purus*. "Love," he maintained, fully agreeing with the poets, "gives to a man the strength of chastity, for he whose heart is brimming over with the love of a woman, cannot think of dallying with another, however beautiful she may be." He proved from substance and form that a man cannot love two women. In the *Leys d'Amors*, a voluminous fourteenth-century Provençal treatise, largely a text-book of grammar and prosody, we read: "And now lovers must be taught how to love; passionate lovers must be restrained, so that they may come to realise their evil and dishonourable desires. No good troubadour, who is at the same time an honest lover, has ever abandoned himself to base sensuality and ignoble desires." The same author opined that a troubadour who asked his lady for a kiss, was committing an act of indecency. On the other hand, Andreas was very broad-minded in drawing the line between both kinds of love, allowing kisses, and even more, in the case of true love. (The best troubadours disagree with him in this respect.)

A scholasticism of love, modelled on ecclesiastical scholasticism and substituting the beloved woman for the Deity, was gradually evolved. Love, veneration, humility, hope, etc., were the sacrifices offered at her shrine. She was full of grace and compassion, and was believed in as fervently as was God. Some of the poets were animated by a curious ambition "to prove" their feelings with scholastic erudition, and more especially by the later, Italian, school, *amore, cor gentil, valore*, were conceived as substances, attributes, inherent qualities, etc. The allegories of *amore* played a prominent part, and spoiled many a masterpiece. The German poets steered clear of these absurdities, which even Dante did not escape.

At the famous courts of love, presided over by princesses, the most extraordinary questions relating to love were discussed and decided with a ceremonial closely following the ceremonial of the petty courts of law. Andreas preserved for us a number of these judgments, some of which prove the really quite obvious fact that love and marriage are two very different things, for if spiritual love be considered the supreme value, matrimony can only be regarded as an inferior condition. And it was a fact that in the higher ranks of society,—the only ones with which we are concerned,—a marriage was nothing but a contract made for political and economical reasons. The baron desired to enlarge his estate, obtain a dowry, or marry into an influential family; no one dreamed of consulting the future bride, whom marriage alone could bring into contact with people outside her own family. To her marriage meant the permission to shine and be adored by a man who was not her husband. "It is an undeniable fact," propounded Andreas as *regula amoris*, "that there is no room for love between husband and wife," and Fauriel translated a passage as follows: "A husband who proposed to behave to his wife as a knight would to his lady, would propose to do something contrary to the canons of honour; such a proceeding could neither increase his virtue nor the virtue of his lady, and nothing could come of it but what already properly exists."—Another judgment maintained "that a lady lost her admirer as soon as the latter became her husband; and that she was therefore entitled to take a new lover." At the court of love of the Viscountess Ermengarde, of Narbonne, the problem whether the love between husband and wife or the love between lovers were the greater, was decided as follows: "The affection between a married couple and the tender love which unites two lovers are emotions which differ fundamentally and according to custom. It would be folly to attempt a comparison between two subjects which neither resemble each other, nor have any connection." A husband declared: "It is true, I have a beautiful wife, and I love her with conjugal love. But because true love is impossible between husband and wife, and because everything good which happens in this world has its origin in love, I am of opinion that I should seek an alliance of love outside my married life." All this was not frivolity, but the only logical conclusion of dualistic eroticism, incapable of blending sensuality and love. It was equally logical that love between divorced persons was not only regarded as not immoral, but as perfectly right and justifiable; it was even decided that "a new marriage could never become a drawback to old love." In the old novel, *Gérard of Roussillon*, the princess, beloved by Gérard, is married to the emperor Charles Martel, and compelled to part from her knight. At their last meeting, before a number of witnesses, she called on the name of Christ and said: "Know ye all that I give my love to Sir Gérard with this ring and this flower from my chaplet. I love him more than father and husband, and now I must weep tears of bitter sorrow." After this they parted, but their love continued undiminished though there was nothing between them but tender wishes and secret thoughts.

Matrimony had no advantage over the love-alliance, not even the sanction of the Church. A love-alliance was frequently accompanied by a ceremony in which a priest officiated. Fauriel describes—without mentioning his source—such a ceremony as follows: "Kneeling before his lady, with his folded hands between hers, he dedicated himself to her service, vowing to be faithful to her until death, and to shield her from all harm and insults as far as lay within his power. The lady, on her side, declared her willingness to accept his service, promised to devote her loftiest feelings to him, and as a rule gave him a ring as a symbol of their union. Then she raised and kissed him, always for the first, usually for the last time." The parting of the lovers, too, was a solemn act, resembling in many ways the dissolution of a marriage.

> *So that our solemn plighted troth*
> *When love is dead, we shall not break,*
> *We'll to the priest ourselves betake.*
> *You set me free, as I do you,*
> *A perfect right then shall we both*
> *Enjoy to choose a love anew,*

wrote Peire of Barjac.

It was far more easy to dissolve a marriage than a true love-alliance; the husband had only to state that his wife was a distant relation of his, and the Church was ready to annul the contract. But the love-alliance—so Sordello maintained, in a long poem—should be more binding than any marriage.

Only one love a woman can
Prefer. So let her choose her man
With care. To him she must be true,
For choosing once she ne'er may rue.
More binding than the wedding-tie
Is love; for a diversity
Of causes wedlock may divide,
By death alone be love untied.

The idea that marriage and love cannot be combined is therefore only the logical conclusion of the fundamental feeling that love and desire cannot together be projected on one woman.

If matrimonial love had not been questioned, the choice would have lain between two alternatives: the canonisation of matrimony—an expedient chosen by the Church—or a fusion of love and sexuality in our modern sense. The first was a stage which humanity had left behind, for the ideal of absolutely perfect and pure love had already been evolved, and the world was not ripe for the second. The tendency of the rarest minds was in the direction of a further idealisation of love, of freeing it from all earthly shackles and bringing it nearer and nearer to heaven. One of the early troubadours, Jaufre Rudel, Prince of Blaya, gave a practical illustration to this feeling by falling in love with a lady whom he had never seen. The story of his love was famous for centuries. He loved a Countess of Tripoli, a Christian princess, and his whole soul was filled with his imaginary picture of her. The *Provençal Biography* relates that "he worshipped her for all the good the pilgrims had narrated of her." In order to see her, he took the cross and journeyed across the sea; he fell ill on the ship and was carried ashore in a dying condition. The countess, on hearing of his great love, hastened to the inn where he lay. As she entered his room, Jaufre regained consciousness; he knew her at once and died happily in her arms. She was so touched by his love that she henceforth renounced the world.—This story is no fairy tale; it is well attested and universally accounted genuine to-day. Jaufre's love, expressed in touching poems, was no *amour de tête*, as it is sometimes called, but a genuine *amour de coeur*, a purely spiritual love which asked nothing of the beloved woman but permission to love her.

There are other instances, and even in later times it is not an infrequent occurrence in the case of imaginative people (I need only mention Bürger and Klopstock).

We men of the present age look upon this eccentric woman-worship with uncomprehending eyes. Perhaps we shall feel a little less bewildered when we meet it, stripped of courtly theories and mediaeval fashions, in some of the great men who are closely connected with our own period; in Michelangelo, in Goethe, and in Beethoven.

The Church, dualistic and ascetic from its inception, waged war against sensuality as the evil of evils. "As fire and water will not mix," wrote St. Bernard, "so spiritual and carnal delights cannot be experienced together." The toleration of matrimony was never more than a compromise; we require no proof that as far as the Church was concerned, chastity was the only real value. Even Luther took up that position, and to this day Christianity and sexuality remain unreconciled. But both the Catholic and the Protestant professions of faith regarded matrimony as the lesser evil, a concession made to the enemy, in order to render existence possible. It is very interesting to observe the position taken up by the Church in connection with the new woman-worship which, although it sprang from the most genuine Christian dualism, had for its object not God, but mortal woman. The logical attitude of the Church would have been one of welcome, for the chaste worship of woman which regarded matrimony as an inferior state, was her natural ally. Two clerics, the court-chaplain Andreas, and the prolific rhymester Matfre Ermengau, actually elaborated the theory of spiritual love contrary to the spirit of the Church, but both men hastened to utter a timely recantation and recommendation of orthodoxy as the only means of salvation. After establishing all the desirable details of love according to substance and accidents, Andreas deduced that every love not dedicated to God was bound to offend Him, and advanced eighteen points against the love of woman, starting with the well-known argument that woman was naturally of a base disposition, covetous, envious, greedy, fickle, garrulous, stubborn, proud, vain, sensual, deceitful, etc. "He who serves love, cannot serve God," he declared, "and God will punish every man who, apart from matrimony, serves Venus. What good could come from acting against the will of God?" Here we are face to face with a grotesque position: the official Church favouring sexuality, that is matrimony, as against the newer and higher standard of ascetic, spiritual love. This attitude was quite logical, if not in the spirit of religion and in contradiction to the principle of asceticism, yet in the spirit of orthodoxy; for "whatever was not for her, was against her." The brave, Janus-headed abbé was spokesman for the whole clergy, which branded love not projected on God as *fornicatio*. In his recantation Andreas upheld the previously-despised matrimonial state at the expense of love; "love," he maintained, "destroys matrimony." Matfre did exactly the same thing; after recapitulating in his *Breviari d'Amor* all the splendid achievements rooted in the cult of woman, he suddenly veered round (at the 27,445th verse):

> *And Satan blows on their desire,*
> *In monstrous flames leaps up the fire,*
> *And maddened by the raging fiend,*
> *From love of God and honour weaned,*
> *They turn from their Creator's shrine*
> *And call their mistresses divine.*
> *With soul and body, mind and sense,*
> *They worship woman's excellence.*
> *Abandoned in her beauty revel,*
> *And unawares adore the devil.*

Three hundred years later the fanatical Savanorola stormed: "You clothe and adorn the Mother of God as you clothe and adorn your courtesans, and you give her the features of your mistresses!" which, as we shall presently see, was literally true.

The clergy resisted all counsels of the *cortezia* and *cavalaria* with the sure instinct desiring the continuance of existing conditions rather than the victory of the higher conception. Some writers aver that it was partly due to this fact that later on the cult of woman developed into the cult of Mary. Again we are confronted by a process which in the course of time has been repeated more than once: the spiritual-mystical principle of Christianity entered upon a new stage, and took possession of a new and important domain; but the Church, rigid and unyielding, preferred clinging to a past lower stage rather than tolerating any change. Had she been absolutely consistent, her greatest poet would be on the index to-day, for, following his own intuition and ignoring her rigid dogma, he introduced his beloved Beatrice into the Catholic heaven.

The new spiritual love was not without its caricatures. Famous in Provence for many strange exploits, committed in order to please his lady, was the talented Peire Vidal. On one occasion he caused himself to be sewn into a wolfskin and ran about the fields; but he was set upon by dogs and so badly mangled that he nearly succumbed to his wounds. He was an insufferable braggart, but never had any success in love. The prince of caricatures, however, was the German knight and minnesinger, Ulrich of Lichtenstein. He is responsible for a novel in prose, entitled *The Service of Woman*, which is faintly reminiscent of Goethe's *Werther*. As a page he commenced his glorious career by drinking the water in which his lady had washed her hands; later on he caused his upper lip to be amputated because it displeased his mistress, for "whatever she dislikes in me, I, too, hate." On another occasion he cut off one of his fingers and used it, set in gold, as a clasp for a volume of his poems which he sent to her. One of his most famous exploits was a journey through nearly the whole of Austria, disguised as Venus, jousting, dressed in women's clothes, with every knight he met. But in spite of his eccentricities, the tendency of his mind was not at all metaphysical; he craved very obvious favours, but as a rule contented himself with a kind, or even an unkind word. Incidentally, we learn that he was married; but he devoted his whole life to "deeds of heroism" in honour of his lady. Not the great book of Cervantes, as is commonly believed, held up mediaeval court life to ridicule and destroyed it as an ideal, but the life and exploits of this knight and minnesinger. The same spirit animated Guilhem of Balaun. At the command of his lady he had a finger-nail extracted and sent to her, after which he was re-admitted to her favour.

Spiritual love was discovered by the Provençals, but the greater and profounder Italian poets developed it and brought it to perfection. What had been a naïve sentiment with the troubadours, became in Dante's circle a system of the universe and a religion. The Italian poet, Sordello, who wrote in Provençal, may be regarded as the connecting link, and the forerunner of the great Italians. He died in the year of grace 1270, and Dante, who was almost a contemporary, immortalised his name in the *Divine Comedy*. The doctrine on which the *dolce stil nuovo* was based pointed to the love of a noble heart as the source of all perfection in heaven and earth. Purely spiritual woman-worship was regarded as an absolute virtue. The words of the last of the Provençal troubadours, Guirot Riquier, "Love is the doctrine of all sublime things"—was developed into a philosophy. I will quote a few characteristic verses, omitting Dante for the present. One of the finest lyric poems of all tongues and ages, written by Guido Guinicelli, begins as follows:

> *Within the gentle heart love shelters him,*
> *As birds within the green shades of the grove;*
> *Before the gentle heart in nature's scheme*
> *Love was not, or the gentle heart ere love.*

(*Transl. by* D.G. ROSSETTI)

Cino da Pistoia says in epigrammatic brevity:

> *You want to know the inmost core of love?*
> *'Tis art and guerdon of a noble heart.*

A wonderful canzone by Guinicelli contains the following verses:

> *A song she seems among the rest and these*
> *Have all their beauties in her splendour drowned.*
> *In her is ev'ry grace,—*
> *Simplicity of wisdom, noble speech,*
> *Accomplished loveliness;*
> *All earthly beauty is her diadem.*
> *This truth my song must teach—*
> *My lady is of ladies chosen gem.*

(*Transl. by* D.G. ROSSETTI)

And Cavalcanti sings:

> *What's she whose coming rivets all men's eyes,*
> *Who makes the air so tremble with delight,*
> *And thrills so every heart that no man might*
> *Find tongue for words but vents his soul in sighs?*

(*Transl. by* SIR THEODORE MARTIN)

The sentiment which pervades these verses has lifted us into the higher sphere which will henceforth be our main theme. The beloved was more and more extolled; in her presence the lover became more and more convinced of his insignificance; she was worshipped, deified. The overwhelming emotion, the longing for metaphysical values which dominated the whole epoch, had reached its highest characteristic, had reached perfection. It proved the eternal quality of human emotion: the impossibility of finding satisfaction, the striving towards the infinite; it soared above its apparent object and sought its consummation in metaphysic. The love of woman and the mystical love of God were blended in a profounder devotion; love had become the sole giver of the eternal value and consolation, yearned for by mortal man. Christianity had taught man to look up; now his upward gaze lost its rigidity and beheld living beauty—metaphysical eroticism had been evolved—the canonisation and deification of woman. The ideal of the troubadours to love the adored mistress chastely and devoutly from a distance in the hope of receiving a word of greeting, no longer satisfied the lover; she must become a divine being, must be enthroned above human joy and sorrow, queen of the world. Traditional religion was transformed so that a place might be found in it for a woman.

The reason for the recognition of spiritual love from the moment of its inception as something supernatural and divine, is obvious. The heart of man was filled with an emotion hitherto unknown, an emotion which pointed direct to heaven. The soul, the core of profound Christian consciousness, had received a new, glad content, rousing a feeling of such intensity that it could only be compared to the religious ecstasy of the mystic; man divined that it was the mother of new and great things— was it not fitting to regard it as divine and proclaim it the supreme value? The troubadours had known it. Bernart of Ventadour had sung:

> *I stand in my lady's sight*
> *In deep devotion;*
> *Approach her with folded hands*
> *In sweet emotion;*
> *Dumbly adoring her,*
> *Humbly imploring her.*

Peire Raimon of Toulouse:

> *I would approach thee on my knees,*
> *Lowly and meek,*

I would fare far o'er lands and seas
Thy ruth to seek.

And come to thee—a slave to his lord—
I'd pay thee homage with eyes that mourn,
Until thy mercy I'd implored,
Heedless of laughter, heedless of scorn.

Raimon of Miraval had said, "I am no lover, I am a worshipper," and Cavalcanti:

My lady's virtue has my blindness riven,
A secret sighing thrills my humbled heart:
When favoured with a sight of her thou art,
Thy soul will spread its wings and soar to heaven.

Peire Vidal:

God called the women close to Him,
Because he saw all good in them.

And:

The God of righteousness endowed
So well thy body and thy mind
That His own radiancy grew blind.
And many a soul that has not bowed
To Him for years in sin enmeshed,
Is by thy grace and charm refreshed.

The beauty of the adored was divine. Bernart of Ventadour wrote:

Her glorious beauty sheds a brilliant ray
On darkest night and dims the brightest day.

Guilhem of Cabestaing:

God has created her without a blemish
Of His own beauty.

Gaucelm Faidit:

> *The beauty which is God Himself*
> *He poured into a single being.*

And Montanhagol, anticipating Dante:

> *Wherefore I tell you, and my words are true,*
> *From heaven came her beauty, rare and tender,*
> *Her loveliness was wrought in Paradise,*
> *Men's dazzled eyes can scarce support her splendour.*

Folquet of Romans:

> *When I behold her beauty rare,*
> *I'm so confused and startled by her worth,*
> *I ween I am no longer on this earth.*

A canzone which has been attributed to Cavalcanti, Cino da Pistoia and Dante, reads as follows:

> *My lady comes and ev'ry lip is silent;*
> *So perfect is her beauty's high estate*
> *That mortal spirit swoons and falls prostrate*
> *Before her glory. And she is so noble:*
> *If I uplift to her my inward eye,*
> *My soul is startled as if death were nigh.*

Cavalcanti says:

> *Round you are flowers, is the tender green,*
> *The sun is not as bright as your dear face,*
> *All nature in her glorious summer-sheen*
> *Has not so fair and beautiful a place,*
> *It pales beside you. Earth has never seen*
> *A thing so full of loveliness and grace.*

The perfection which the mere presence of the beloved was supposed to bestow on the lover, is here conceived more broadly and freely; not only the lover, but all men are touched and transfigured by her appearance. The sentiment of the lover aspired to become objective truth. This was an important stage on the road from the spiritual to the deifying love, which I have called metaphysical eroticism. Another rung of the ladder of evolution had been climbed—the mistress had become queen of the world and goddess, a being enthroned by the side of God. I will again quote Guinicelli:

> *Ever as she walks she has a sober grace,*
> *Making bold men abashed and good men glad,*
> *If she delight thee not, thy heart must err,*
> *No man dare look on her, his thoughts being base;*
> *Nay, let me say even more than I have said,*
> *No man could think base thoughts who looked on her.*

(D.G. Rossetti.)

The same poet in his canzone, *Al Cor Gentil* says:

> *"She shines on us as God shines on His angels."*

When madonna dies the angels receive her, rejoicing that she has joined them. The Provençal, Pons of Capduelh, anticipated Dante:

> *And now we know that the celestial choir*
> *Sings songs of jubilee at her release*
> *From this dull earth; I heard and am at rest;*
> *Who praise His hosts, praise the Eternal Sire.*
> *I know she is in Heaven with the blest,*
> *'Midst flow'rs whose glory time can never dim*
> *Singing God's praise, and blest by seraphim.*
> *Nought but the truth from my glad lips shall fall,*
> *In Heaven she is, enthroned above all.*

Folquet of Romans wrote a letter to his beloved, in which he said amongst other things:

> *Kneeling in church before God's face,*
> *—A sinner to beseech His grace,—*
> *And for my sins to make amends,—*
> *'Twas you to whom I raised my hands;*

Your loveliness alone was there,
My soul knew only of one pray'r.
I fancied "Our Father" framed
My trembling lips, when they exclaimed
Exultant at His sacred shrine:
Oh! Lady! All my soul is thine!

Lady, you have bewitched me with your beauty,
That God I have forgotten and myself.

Cino da Pistoia wrote the following commendatory prayer:

Into thy hands, sweet lady of my soul,
The spirit that is dying I commend;
And which departs so sorrowful that Love
Views it with pity, while dismissing it.

By you to His dominion it was bound,
So firmly, that it since hath had no power
To call on Him but thus: Oh, mighty Lord,
Whate'er thou wilt of me, Thy will is mine.

(Transl. by C. LYELL)

Lancelot, one of the great mediaeval lovers, possessed a lock of Guinevere's hair, which he prized above all the relics of the saints. When he parted from his mistress (whom he had loved not only spiritually) he fell on his knees before the door of her chamber and prayed as if "he were kneeling before the altar."

Spiritual love was obviously acquiring a religious tinge. The mistress took the place of God; her grace was the source of all joy and consolation; she led the souls of the dying to eternal life. God had yielded His position to her, she had stepped to His side, nay, above Him. With the curse of the Church still clinging to her, she had been remoulded by man's emotion into a perfect, a celestial being. The God of Christianity was in danger—would the new religion of cultured minds, the religion of woman (unwilling to tolerate any other God beside her) replace the religion of the masses? Was a reformation imminent? Would the traditional religion be transformed into metaphysical eroticism,

EMIL LUCKA

dethroning God, enthroning a goddess? It is impossible to say in what direction the spiritual history of Europe would have developed if Dante had been merely a metaphysical lover, and not also an orthodox theologian; if instead of penetrating to the vision of the divine secret, he had fainted before the face of Beatrice. . .

The religion of woman and the dominant religion came to terms. This compromise was possible because the Christian pantheon included a female deity who, although she had not hitherto played a prominent part, held an exceptional position: this was Mary, the Mother of the Redeemer. From A.D. 400 to A.D. 1200, her rank had been on a level with the rank of the antique goddesses; now the new emotion enveloped and revivified her. The rigid, soulless image with the golden circle round the head slowly melted into sweet womanhood. In Italy this sentiment inspired wonderful paintings of the Madonna, and was responsible for the development of portraiture in general. The hold of the overwhelming tradition was broken. Rejecting the universal conviction that the historical Mary had resembled the Mary of Byzantine art, the artist, under the dominion of his woman-worship—which surpassed and re-valued all things—drew his inspiration from the fulness of life. I do not agree with Thode that we are indebted to the legend of St. Francis for the modern soulful and highly individualised art. Its source must have been the strongest feeling of the most cultured minds, and that was undoubtedly spiritual love. The Jesuit Beissel wrote with deep regret: "Every master almost formed his own conception of Mary, but in such a way that the hieratic severity of earlier times disappeared but slowly." And he continued: "It is true, the artists' models were the noble ladies of their period; not only on account of their kindly smiling faces, but also on account of the charming coquetry with which their hands drew their cloaks across the bosom." And the art-historian, Male, says: "It is a remarkable fact that in the thirteenth century the legend, or the story, of the Virgin Mary was depicted on the doors of all our (i.e., French) cathedrals."

The difference between the Catholic and the Protestant world-principles is strongly marked in this connection. Catholicism with its striving for absolute uniformity, acknowledging no individual differences, but eager to shape all life and all doctrines in harmony with one definite ideal, very consistently pronounced one single, historical woman to be divine, and made her the object of universal worship. This dogma had to be rigid, immutable, and almost meaningless. Again, the historic and pagan principle of Catholicism was maintained; a unique event in the history of the world was immortalised and systematised and all new religious conceptions were excluded. Catholicism invariably places all really important events in the past, even in a quite definite period of the past, a period unassailable by historical criticism. But with the commencement of individual intellectual life the uniform, ecclesiastical image of the Madonna gradually gained life and individuality. Just as according to Protestant teaching every soul must establish its individual relationship with God (which is subject to change because individuality is not excluded as it is in Catholicism), so the imaginative emotionalist created his own Queen of Heaven. Frequently he was still under the impression—this was especially the case with monks—that he was worshipping the ecclesiastical deity, when he had long been praying to a metaphysical conception of his own. The great Italian art since the fourteenth century, as well as the Neo-Latin and German cults of the Virgin Mary were, though apparently still orthodox, in their innermost essence the outcome of a personal desire for love, and had therefore abandoned the teaching of the Church and become Protestant. The fact that the so-called Protestant Church looked askance at Mary, and that the rather coarse-minded Luther said, in his annoyance: "Popery has made a goddess of Mary, and is therefore guilty of idolatry," does not contradict my statement. The true Queen of Heaven was a conception of the artist and lover, incomprehensible to those who were only thinkers and moralists.

Through the legitimation of a divine woman open enmity between the religion of woman and the religion of the Church was avoided. A woman had stepped between God and humanity as mediator, intercessor and redeemer. Every metaphysically-loving soul could conceive her as it pleased, could love her and pray to her without being a heretic and worshipper of the devil. Matfre had complained that men

Abandoned in her beauty revel
And unawares adore the devil.—

but now a means had been found to adore the beloved, and yet remain faithful to God. Once in a way it was remembered that the adored, strictly speaking, was the Mother of God—if for no other reason, for fear of the Inquisition which the Dominicans had founded and placed under the special patronage of Mary—her bodyguard as it were, defending her from the onslaught of minds all too worldly. Very rarely the adored earthly woman was identified with the official Queen of Heaven—(this may have been done occasionally by monks); sometimes as in the case of Michelangelo and Guinicelli, the beloved was the sole goddess; other poets, among whom we may include Dante and Goethe, conceived her as enthroned by the side of Mary.

At this point I must interrupt my argument, and briefly sketch the position occupied by Mary in the western world from the dawn of Christianity.

(b) The Queen of Heaven

DURING THE FIRST TWO HUNDRED years Mary did not occupy a prominent place in the Christian communities; even in the fourth century she was still regarded as a human woman and denied divinity by St. Chrysostom, who reproached her with vainglory. But in proportion as Christ transcended humanity, and was more dogmatically and formally interpreted by the Church—more especially the Greek Church—the desire for a mediator between the wrathful Deity and sinful humanity grew more pronounced, a mediator who, although a human being, could be endowed after the manner of the ancient demi-gods with super-human virtues. The Mother of the Saviour gradually assumed this position. She had been an earthly woman, born of earthly parents, and would be able to understand human needs and wishes, and she had become the Mother of God. Would not her intercession have weight with the Son of God? Simultaneously with the growing recognition of asceticism, the doctrine of the immaculate conception gained ground; in the course of time this moment was more and more emphasised, and virginity was set up as an ideal.

St. Athanasius (fourth century) had written: "What God did to Mary is the glory of all virgins; for they are attached as virginal saplings to her who is the root." At the close of the fourth century a long and bitter controversy arose over the question as to whether Mary had remained a virgin after the birth of Jesus. St. Ambrose, St. Jerome and St. Augustine were in favour of this new doctrine. St. Ambrose, the founder of Western music, was the first to praise her perfection in the Latin tongue, and St. Augustine in his treatise *De Natura et Gratia*, maintained that she was the only human being born without original sin. This was the first important step towards the stripping of the Saviour's mother of her humanity, and establishing her as a divine being. St. Irenaeus contrasted Eve, the bringer of sin, with Mary, the second Eve, the bringer of salvation, and St. Ambrose said: "From Eve we inherited damnation through the fruit of the tree; but Mary has brought us salvation through the gift of the tree, for Christ too, hung on the tree like a fruit."

Hitherto Mary had not been worshipped; all prayers had been addressed to God and to Christ. The idea of approaching her in prayer appeared for the first time in a pamphlet entitled "On the Death of Mary," written about the end of the fourth century, and Gregory of Nazianz pictured Mary in Heaven, caring for the welfare of humanity. The fourth and fifth centuries produced the first hymns to the Virgin, written in Syriac; but orthodox bishops objected to her deification; St. Epiphanus (end of fourth century) said: "Let us honour Mary by all means, but let us worship only the Father, the Son and the Holy Ghost."

This was the position of the evangelical and historical Mary before the famous and decisive Council of Ephesus.

There is a very important fact which must not be overlooked. All the nations dwelling on the shores of the Mediterranean, Semites, and Egyptians, as well as Greeks and Romans, had been accustomed to the worship of female deities. In the minds of the ancient peoples, woman, the symbol of sex, had always been endowed with qualities of magic and mystery. There was something supernatural in her power of bringing forth a living specimen of the race, and in all cults the maternal woman occupied a very important position. Had Christianity suddenly destroyed this ancient and natural need? We know that the Church had assimilated a great number of antique superstitions; nor were the female deities sacrificed. The great Asiatic Mothers had not been forgotten; the very ancient Babylonian Istar (Astarte), Rhea Kybele of Asia Minor, and above all the Egyptian Isis, still lived in the heart of man,—subconsciously, probably—as lofty, sacred memories, but nevertheless influencing his life. The Egyptian Isis with Horus in her lap is the direct model of the Madonna with the Child. She represented earth, bringing forth fruit without fertilisation. "This religious custom (the worship of Isis)," says Flinders Petrie, "exerted a powerful influence on nascent Christianity. It is not too much to say that without the Egyptians we should have had no Madonna in our creed. The cult of Isis was widely spread at the time of the first emperors, when it was fashionable all over the Roman Empire; when later on it merged into that other great religious movement, and fashion and conviction could be combined, its triumph was assured."

Advancing Christianity had depopulated the national pantheon. There must have been a great sense of loss, especially among the lower classes, and it does not require much psychological insight to realise that it was the lack of female deities which more especially roused a feeling of anxiety and distress. The masses were yearning for a goddess, and it was at Ephesus, the classical seat of the hundred-breasted Diana, that the stolen divinity was restored to them. The theologians were divided into three camps. While some of them regarded Mary merely as "the mother of man" others acknowledged her as the "Mother of God," and Nestorius suggested as a compromise the title "Mother of Christ." At the synod of Alexandria, in the year of grace 430, and at the council of Ephesus in 431, Nestorius was found guilty of blasphemy and deprived of his bishopric. Henceforth Mary was, the "Mother of God," and her worship was sanctioned by the Church. "Through Thee the Holy Trinity has been glorified," exclaimed Cyril joyfully, "through Thee the Cross of the Saviour has been raised! Through Thee the angels triumphed, the devils were driven back; the tempter was beaten and human nature uplifted to Heaven; through Thee all intelligent creatures who were committing idolatry, have learned the truth!" Loud rejoicing filled the streets of Ephesus. When the judgment passed on Nestorius was announced, the people exclaimed: "The enemy of the Holy Virgin has been overcome; glory be to the great, the divine Mother of God!" The highest authority in the land had re-established the public worship of the great goddess, who had for many years been worshipped in secrecy. The ancient paganism had triumphed over the spiritual intuition of the loftier minds. According to ancient custom sacrifices were offered at Mary's shrine; the second epoch of her history had begun.

In the East the worship of female divinities was older and more spontaneous than in the Western world, and thus the cult of Mary existed in the Orient long before it penetrated to Italy and thence into the newly Christianised countries. The Virgin, who for the first few hundred years had held a clearly defined position in evangelical history, had become an independent object of worship. Festivals were held in her honour; churches were dedicated to her; the will of the people triumphed in the litany; art took possession of the grateful subject. The tendency to make Mary the equal of Christ grew steadily. Metaphors originally intended for Christ alone were used indifferently for either. We constantly find her addressed as the "archetype, the light of the world, the vine, the mediator, the source of eternal life, etc." Finally she ceased being regarded as a passive participator in the work of salvation, as the Mother of the Saviour, and was accredited with independent saving power. John of Damascus (eighth century) first called Mary, and soon after she was styled "Saviour of the World" in the Occident also. With this the cult of Mary had reached its third stage, the stage which interests us; she had become the object of metaphysical love. But before dealing with this third stage, we must glance, in passing, at the ancient Teutonic tribes. They, too, worshipped goddesses and sacred women; virginity, a virtue not appreciated by the Orientals, here stood in high repute. According to Tacitus and others, the Teutons looked upon the Virgin as a mysterious being, approaching divinity more closely than all others. Thus there was here, perhaps, more than on the shores of the Mediterranean, a favourable soil for the cult of Mary. The characteristics of Holda and Freya, as well as their perfect beauty, were transferred to Mary, and Mary's name was substituted for the names of the old auxiliary goddesses. In the oldest German evangelical poems Mary does not yet rank as a divinity, she is merely extolled as the most perfect of all earth-born women. In the "Heliand" (about A.D. 830) she is called "the most beautiful of all women, the loveliest of all maidens"; and the monk Otfried, of Weissenburg (860), calls her, "Of all women to God the most pleasing, the white jewel, the radiant maid."

Mary had now taken her place by the side of God, and was commonly addressed as divine. Anselm of Canterbury explains: "God is the Father of all created things, Mary the Mother of all things recreated. . . God begat the creator of the world, Mary gave birth to its Saviour." Peter of Blois declared that the Virgin was the only mediatress between Christ and humanity. "We were sinners and afraid of the wrath of the Father, for He is terrible; but we have the Virgin, in whom there is nothing terrible, for in her is the fulness of mercy and purity." The twelfth century produced the *Ave Maria*, the angelic salutation, the principal prayer to Mary, which was introduced into all churches. The Italian Franciscan monk, Bonaventura, and Peter Damiani, were above all others instrumental in spreading the worship of the Virgin, and Damiani said of her: "To Thee has been given all power in heaven and on earth." The fresco of the Camposanto at Pisa, ascribed to Orcagna, shows the transfigured Virgin sitting by the side of Christ, not below Him. The numerous legends in which Mary, often regardless of justice and propriety, delivers her faithful worshippers from all manner of dangers, were written during the same period. One of the most famous of these is the legend of Theophilus, the forerunner of Faust. In a German version (by Brun of Schönebeck) dating from the thirteenth century, Theophilus abjures God and all things divine, with the sole exception of Mary, wherefore she saves him from eternal damnation. This poem therefore shows us Mary as absolutely opposed to God.

We have now arrived at the third stage of the cult of Mary; the new, spiritual love, translated into metaphysics, was projected on her; she was approached by her worshippers with the ardent love which hitherto had been the prerogative of earthly women. The two currents, the one arising in ecclesiastical tradition, and the other in the soul of the metaphysical lover, had met; the genuine spiritual cult of Mary was the creation of the great metaphysical lovers, who existed not only in the twelfth and thirteenth centuries, but are met not infrequently later on; man's irresistible need to raise woman above him and worship her, created the true Madonna, for whose sake romantic souls of all times have "returned home" into the fold of the Church, the true Madonna who at heart is alien to the principles of the Church, but is re-born daily in the soul of the metaphysical lover. The hierarchy knew how to take advantage of and control this adoring love; the metaphysical lover raised his mistress above humanity and prayed before her shrine; religion said: "The celestial woman whom you may lovingly adore is here, with me. All you have to do is to call her by the name I have given her, and the kingdom of Heaven will be yours."

But on the other hand Mary represents to-day, and doubtless will do for a long time to come, a dogmatically acknowledged deity, recognised by the spirit of Protestantism as a remnant of Paganism, and duly detested; the masses in Italy and Spain pray to-day to her image, as in bygone days the masses prayed to the images in Greek and Roman temples. This goddess is unchanging, and from the point of view of the psychologist uninteresting.

It is not difficult to understand why the two conceptions of Mary (more especially in the souls of the monks) were so often inextricably intermingled; circumstances frequently demanded a complete fusion. As late as in the nineteenth century, a romantic poet, Zacharias Werner, said:

> *Oh, sov'reign lady, mistress of my fortune,*
> *And thou, the Queen and ruler of the heavens,*
> *(I cannot keep you sundered and apart.)*

I shall endeavour to keep them sundered and apart as far as possible, for I am only concerned with man's metaphysical emotion of love and its creation, womanhood deified, and not with Catholic dogmas. With this object in view, I will return to the poets previously quoted, and continue the unfolding of the process of deification. As a rule the metaphysical lovers were content with immortalising their feelings in, very often, excellent verses, raising the beloved mistress above the earth and worshipping her as the culmination of beauty and perfection. The quite unusual craving to give her a place in the eternal structure of the cosmos animated only one poet, Dante, who, combining the Catholic striving for unity with spontaneous, magnificent woman-worship, created a masterpiece which is unique in literature.

Typical among the later Provençals was Guirot Riquier. Several of his poems which have been preserved to us make it impossible to say whether they are addressed to an earthly woman or to the Queen of Heaven; these poems mark, in a sense, a period of transition. They are exceedingly vague, and it is not worth while to translate them; but as they are dated it is interesting to watch the poet's love growing more and more spiritual and religious, to see him gradually deserting his earthly love for the Lady of Heaven. In one poem he prays to his lady "who is worshipped by all true lovers," to teach him the right way of loving. In the next he repents his all too earthly passion:

> *I often thought I was of true love singing,*
> *And knew not that to love my heart was blind,*
> *And folly was as love itself enshrined.*
> *But now such love in all my soul is ringing,*
> *That though to love and praise her I aspire*
> *As is her meed—in vain is my desire.*

Henceforth her love alone shall be my guide
And my new hope in that great love abide.

For her great love the uttermost shall proffer
Of honour, wealth, and earthly joy and bliss,
With her to love, my heart will never miss
Those who no gifts like her gifts have to offer.
She the fulfilment is of my desire,
Therefore I vow myself her true esquire;
She'll love me in return—my splendid meed—
If I but love aright in word and deed.

and one of his rather more religious songs ends as follows:

Without true love there is on earth no peace,
Love gives us wisdom, faith which will not swerve,
A noble mind and willingness to serve.
How rare a thing on earth in perfect ease!
To Thee, oh Virgin! Mother of all love,
I dedicate this song; if thou deniest
Me not, thou shall be my "sweet bliss." With Christ
I pray Thee, intercede for me above.

In this song, then, he calls Mary "his sweet bliss" (*bel deport*), a name which he had previously given to a certain countess with whom he had been in love. In the next poem, in which earthly love and love of the Madonna are again brought into juxta-position, he commends himself "to the Virgin, the sublime mother of love, on whom all my happiness depends." One of his poems which begins in quite an earthly strain, ends thus:

I feel no jealousy; for he whose soul
Is filled with yearning for his heavenly love,
Has purest happiness; he is her serf,
And he has all things that his heart can crave.

But long before this, in one of his very worldly poems there is a sudden outburst, addressed to the Madonna: "He who does not serve the Mother of God, knows not the meaning of love." Excellent proof of this intimate connection between earthly and Madonna love is found in the poems of the trouvere Ruteboeuf, who calls Mary his "very sweet lady."

Lanfranc Cigala wrote genuine love-songs to the Virgin. The following are two stanzas from one of his poems:

> *I worship a celestial maid,*
> *Serene and wondrously adorned;*
> *And all she does is well; arrayed*
> *In noble love and gentleness.*
> *Her smile is bliss to all who mourn,*
> *Her tender love is happiness,*
> *And for her kiss the world I scorn.*
> *Lady of Heaven, Thy heart incline*
> *To me, and untold bliss is mine.*
> *By day and night my only thought*
> *Art, Mary, Thou. I am distraught*
> *Say many men, for few can gauge*
> *The ardour which consumes my soul.*
> *I care not that they say bereft*
> *I am of sense; the world I've left,*
> *To worship Thee, love's spring and goal.*

But other poems written by Cigala are unmistakably addressed to the celestial Madonna; some of them seem to be written in a penitential mood; he almost seems to repent of his former passionate adoration. The same poet, in his love-songs, uses all the metaphors which are commonly used for Mary (or for Christ), "root and climax, flower, fruit and seed of all goodness."

A little older is an erotic hymn to Mary by Peire Guillem of Luserna; I quote a few stanzas:

> *Thy praise is happiness unmarred,*
> *For he who praises Thee, proclaims the truth,*
> *Thou art the flower of beauty, love and ruth,*
> *Full of compassion, with all grace bedight,*
> *From Thy white hands we gather all delight.*

The love of Mary had usurped the peculiar property of the love of woman: it had become the source of poetic and artistic inspiration.

The songs of Aimeric of Peguilhan resemble those of Cigala; the former bewails the decline of the service of woman; he sings of the "root and crown of all noble things," but it is not quite clear whether he is addressing an earthly or a heavenly lady. "Suffer my love, which asks for no reward!" The terms, "friends" and "lovers" (*amans*) of the Virgin are with these poets convertible terms, and the Virgin is styled "the true friend" (*i.e.*, the beloved).

Guilhem of Autpol wrote a fine poem to the Queen of Heaven, beginning:

> *Thou hope of all sad hearts who yearn for love,*
> *Thou stream of loveliness, thou well of grace,*
> *Thou dove of peace in fret and restlessness,*
> *Thou ray of light to those who, lightless, grope.*
> *Thou house of God, thou garden of sweet shades,*
> *Rest without ceasing, refuge of the sad,*
> *Bliss without mourning, flow'r that never fades,*
> *Alien to death, and shelter in the mad*
> *Whirlpool of life, to all who seek thy port.*
> *Lady of Heaven, in whom all hearts rejoice,*
> *Thou roseate dawn and light of Paradise!*

Perdigon, among many worldly songs, wrote one to the *regina d'auteza e de senhoria*, which might be translated thus:

> *Supreme ruler of the world,*
> *Thy grace sustains*
> *And maintains*
> *The world.*
> *Thou fragrant rose, thou fruitful vine,*
> *Thou wert the chosen vessel of*
> *Mercy divine.*

Unsurpassed in the fusion of his earthly and his celestial lady was Folquet de Lunel. Some of his poems cannot be classed with any certainty.

The first poem which obtained a prize at the Academy of Mastersingers of Toulouse was a hymn to Mary.

This very genuine sentimentalism appears strange to us; we cannot enter into the feelings of that period. A modern philologist, Karl Appel, regards Jaufre Rudel's pathetic songs, addressed by him to the Countess of Tripoli:

> *Oh, love in lands so far away,*
> *My heart is yearning, yearning. . .*

as songs to the Madonna; but it is a matter of indifference to the lover whether his heart's impulse, translated into metaphysic, is projected on an unknown Countess of Tripoli, or a still more unknown Lady of Heaven. It is not the loved woman who is of importance—what do we know of the ladies who inspired the exquisite mediaeval poetry? They have long been dust, and we may be sure that their perfection was no greater than is the perfection of their grand-daughters. But the love of the poets is alive to-day, an eternal document of the human heart, representing one of the great phases through which the relationship between man and woman has passed.

The following are a few stanzas by the German minnesinger, Steinmar, which were later on adapted to the Holy Virgin:

> *In summer-time how glad am I*
> *When over lea or down*
> *A country lass mine eyes espy,*
> *Of maidens all the crown.*
>
> *Oh! Paradise! How glad am I*
> *When o'er the heavenly down*
> *God and God's Mother I espy,*
> *Of women all the crown.*

The Italian poets, far more profound than the Provençals, saw a goddess in the beloved (whom they always addressed as Madonna), and humbled themselves before her. Social differences, which played such a prominent part in the North, are here ignored. The impecunious poet no longer extols the princess, the wife of his lord and master. There is no question of such a relationship; the poet is a free citizen of the town, subject only to the emotion of the heart, and his song carries its own reward. It has ceased to be the married woman's privilege to be lauded and extolled; the maiden of unaristocratic origin, who to the poets represents more strongly the ideas of purity and perfection, has usurped her place. We know that Lapo Gianni, Dino Frescobaldi, Guinicelli and Dante worshipped a maiden untouched by as much as a sensuous thought, and Frescobaldi decided the question whether it were better to love a married woman or a maiden, in favour of the latter. The feeling of those lovers was pure and lofty, and they had the power of giving it perfect expression.

In a canzone, the authorship of which is ascribed to both Cavalcanti and Cino da Pistoia, it is said of the beloved dead that God needed her presence to perfect Heaven, and that all the saints now worship her. She was a miracle of perfection while she was yet on earth, but now:

> *Look thou into the pleasure wherein dwells*
> *Thy lovely lady, who is in heaven crowned,*
> *Who is herself thy hope in heaven, the while*
> *To make thy mem'ry hallowed she prevails.*
>
> *Of thee she entertains the blessed throngs,*
> *And says to them, while yet my body thrave*
> *On earth, I gat much honour which he gave,*
> *Commending me in his commended songs.*

(*Transl. by* D.G. ROSSETTI)

At the conclusion of his finest poem, "Al Cor Gentil," Guinicelli, next to Dante doubtless the greatest poet of the Middle Ages, says: "God will ask me after my death: 'How could'st thou have loved aught but Me?' And I will reply: 'She came from Thy realm and bore the semblance of an angel. Therefore in loving her, I was not unfaithful to Thee!'" Here we have the perfection of metaphysical eroticism: the beloved woman is God; he who loves her, loves God in her.

Cavalcanti maintained in a poem that an image of the Madonna actually bore the features of his lady.

> *Guido, an image of my lady dwells*
> *At San Michele, in Orto, consecrate,*
> *And daily worshipped. Fair, in holy state,*
> *She listens to the tale each sinner tells.*
> *And among them who come to her, who ails*
> *The most, on him the most does blessing fall;*

She bids the fiend men's bodies abdicate;
Over the curse of blindness she prevails,
And heals sick languors in the public squares. . .

(*Transl. by* D.G. Rossetti)

And Guido Orlandi replies to him from the ecclesiastical standpoint, as to a lost man: "Had'st thou been speaking of Mary, thou would'st have spoken the truth. But now I must bewail thy errors."

A complete blending of sensuality and Mary-worship was achieved in an Italian poem of the fifteenth century. The author of this poem addressed Mary as "queen of my heart," and "blossom of loveliness," and goes on to say: "I can tell by your gestures and your face that you respond to my love; when you look at me, you smile, and when you sigh, your eyes are full of tenderness. . . Sometimes, in the evening, I stand below your balcony; you hear my sighs, but you make no reply. . . When I gaze at your beauty, I burn with love, but when I think of your cruelty, I call on death to release me." In this poem we have a caricature of metaphysical eroticism.

In the sonnets of Petrarch, metaphysical love has become stereotyped. Adoration has become a phrase (as Cupid has become a phrase with the earlier poets). It is obvious that he loves Laura because the play on the word Laura and *lauro* (laurel) caught his fancy. I can find no spontaneous feeling in the famous Canzoniero; all I see is erudition and perfection of form. But among the few sincere specimens there is one beautiful poem addressed to Mary: "*Vergine bella che di sol vestida!*" which is not without erotic warmth. But the singer and humanist expresses himself judiciously:

Oh, Thou, the Queen of Heaven and our goddess
(If it be fitting such a phrase to use).

So far we have observed the current which, emanating from the beloved woman, lifted her into supernal regions and endowed her with perfection—the mistress is stripped of everything earthly, the longing which can never be stilled on earth, soars heavenward. Now we will examine the opposite current; the current which emanates from the Madonna of dogma, the Lady of Heaven who is the same to all men, in her last stage, that is to say when she is finally enthroned by the side of

God. Many a monk—earthly love being denied to him—was driven to a purely spiritual, metaphysical love by the fact of his being permitted to love the Lady of Heaven without hesitation or remorse. She was the fairest of women, and he was at liberty to interpret the meaning of "the fairest" in any sense he chose.

The climax of the emotional worship of the ecclesiastical Mary was reached by St. Bernard, the *Doctor Marianus* mentioned on a previous occasion. He was the author of sermons and homilies in honour of Mary, and has been instrumental in dogmatising her worship by placing her side by side with the Saviour. "It was more fitting that both sexes should take part in the renewal of mankind," he says, "because both were instrumental in bringing about the fall. . ." "Man who fell through woman, can be raised only by her." "Humanity kneels at Thy feet, for the comfort of the wretched, the release of the prisoners, the delivery of the condemned, the salvation of the countless sons of Adam depend on a word from Thy lips. Oh! Virgin, hasten to reply! Speak the word for which the earth, the nethermost hell, and the heavens even, are waiting; yea, the King and Ruler of the universe, greatly as He desires Thy loveliness, awaits Thy consent, in which He has laid the salvation of the world." Basing his description on the Revelation of St. John the Divine, he draws her picture as follows: "Brilliant and white and dazzling are the garments of the Virgin. She is so full of light and radiance that there is not the least darkness about her, and no part of her may be described as less brilliant, or not glowing with intense light." And with increasingly pronounced erotic emphasis, passing from the Church dogma of salvation to passionate fervour, he goes on to say: "A garden of sacred delight art Thou, oh, Mary! In it we gather flowers of manifold joys as often as we reflect on the fulness of sweetness which through Thee was poured out on the world. . . Right lovely art Thou, oh, perfect One! A bed of heavenly spices and precious flowers of all virtues, filling the house of the Lord with sweet perfume! Oh! Mary, Thou violet of humility! Thou lily of chastity! Thou rose of love!" etc.

St. Bernard inaugurated that extraordinary blending of eroticism with half-crazy, inconceivable allegories and fantasies, which lasted for centuries. Here, again, we perceive the ideal of metaphysical eroticism, which in the case of a loyal son of the Church could only refer to the official Queen of Heaven, and consisted partly of the genuine emotion of love, partly of allegorically constructed connections with the Church dogma.

St. Bernard's emotional outbursts were comprehended and admired. His authority was sufficient to override all scruples that might have stood in the way of this downright description of Mary's charms. He became the model for all her later worshippers; Suso, for instance, often quotes him, and Brother Hans called him *the harpist and fiddler of her praise*.

The great ecstatic poet, Jacopone da Todi, sang Mary's praise as follows:

Hail, purest of virgins,
Mother and maid,
Gentle as moonlight,
Lady of Aid!

I greet thee, life's fountain,
Fruitladen vine!
Infinite mercy
Thou sheddest on thine!

Hope's fairest sunshine,
Balm's well serene!
I claim a dance with thee,
All the world's Queen!

Gate of beatitude!
—All sins forgiven,—
Lead us to paradise,
Sweet breeze of heaven!

Thou pointest us upward
Where angels adore,
White lily of gentleness
Thy grace I implore.

Mirror of Cherubim!
Seraphim laud thy grace,
All things in heaven and earth
Ring with thy praise!

The spiritual love of Mary especially appealed to the German temper. Among the adoring monks Suso deserves particular mention.

He laid great stress on the difference between *high* love and *low* love. "Low love begins with rapture and ends with pain, but high love begins with grief, and is transformed into ecstasy, until finally the lovers are united in eternity." He was keenly conscious of the older motive of the cult of Mary, namely, the need of a gentle mediator between man and the inaccessible Deity. "Oh, thou! God's chosen delight, thou dulcet, golden song of the Eternal Wisdom, suffer me, a poor sinner, to tell thee a little of my sufferings. My soul prostrates itself before thee with timorous eyes, shamefaced. Oh! thou Mother of all mercies, I ween that neither my soul nor the soul of any other poor sinner needs a mediator, or permission to come to thy throne, for thou, thyself, art the intercessor for all sinners." Compared to his forerunner, St. Bernard, Suso exhibits a marked degree of intimacy in his relationship with Mary. He describes heaven as a kind of flowered meadow, and Mary keeping court, like any earthly princess. "Now go and behold the sweet Queen of Heaven, whom you love so profoundly, leading the procession of the celestial throng in great gladness and stateliness, inclining to her lover with roses and lilies! Behold her wonderful beauty shedding light and joy on the heavenly hosts! Eya! Look up to her who giveth gladness to heart and mind; behold the Mother of Mercy resting her eyes, her tender, pitiful eyes, on you and all sinners, powerfully protecting her beloved child." The whole sixteenth chapter of the *Booklet of Eternal Wisdom* is an ardent hymn to the Madonna, almost comparable to St. Bernard's prayer to Mary in Dante's *Divine Comedy*. It was written about the time of Dante's death, not very long, therefore, after the composition of the last chapters of the *Paradise*.

The Life of Suso (the first German biography ever written) evidences his adoration for the Lady of Heaven: "It was customary in his country, Swabia, for the young men to go to their sweethearts' houses on New Year's Eve, singing songs until they received from the maidens a chaplet in return. This custom so pleased his young and ardent heart that he, too, went on the eve of the New Year to his eternal love, to beg her for a gift. Before daybreak he repaired to the statue which represented the Virginal Mother pressing her tender child, the beautiful Eternal Wisdom, to her bosom, and kneeling down before her, with a sweet, low singing of his soul, he chanted a sequence to her, imploring her to let him win a chaplet from her Child. . ." "He then said to the Eternal Wisdom" (and it is uncertain whether he is addressing the mother or the child): "Thou art my love, my glad Easter day, the summer-joy of my heart, my sweet hour; thou art the love which my young heart alone worships, and for the sake of which it has scorned earthly love. Give me a guerdon, then, my heart's delight, and let me not go away from thee empty-handed."

With a sweet, low singing of his soul, this worshipper approached the statue of the Queen of Heaven. This is love of woman undisguised, it merely has a religious undertone. Other secular merry-makings were adapted by Suso to his celestial mistress, as, for instance, the planting of the may-tree, and he repeatedly makes use of similes and metaphors borrowed from the chivalrous service of woman. He frequently alludes to himself as "the servant of the Eternal Wisdom"; the meaning of this expression is apparently intentionally obscured, but it has a savour of the feminine. Suso pictured himself, after the manner of lovers, with a chaplet of roses on his brow. In his *Life* there is a passage unsurpassed by the best of the minnesingers: "In the golden summer-time when all the tender little flowers had opened their buds, he gathered none until he had dedicated the first blossoms to his spiritual love, the gentle, flower-like, rosy maiden and Mother of God; when it seemed to him that the time had come, he culled the flowers with many loving thoughts, carried them into his cell and wove them into a garland; and after he had done so, he went into the choir, or into Our Lady's Chapel, prostrated himself before his dear lady, and placed the sweet garland on her head, hoping that she would not scorn her servant's offering, as she was the most wondrous flower herself, and the summer-joy of his heart."

Doubtless we here have an analogy to the religious feeling of the mystics. The metaphysical lover is still under the impression that he is worshipping the Mary of the Catholic Church; but as in the case of the mystic the Christ of dogma is transformed into the divine spark in his own soul, so the love of Mary has become undogmatic and pure woman-worship, the ideal of the great lovers of that age.

Another prominent Madonna-worshipper was Conrad of Würzburg (died 1278). He began his career as a minnesinger, but later on entered a monastery. He was the author of a very extensive, and in part, poetical collection of songs in praise of the Queen of Heaven. "The Golden Smithy" is an interesting instance of the mingling of genuine metaphysical eroticism and traditional Church doctrines. Conrad inextricably mingles all the Biblical allegories more or less applicable to Mary, the stories of the Gospels, the doctrine of the Immaculate Conception, etc., with his own emotions, and thus creates a world of feeling which, though in many respects exaggerated, still represents in its quaint unity something entirely novel and unique:

> *Thy glorious form,*
> *Though by beauty all envested,*
> *Never passion has suggested*
> *Nor has lit unholy fire*
> *In man's heart, that gross desire*
> *From thy purity should spring.*

He, too, describes the celestial Paradise as a lovely garden, in which Mary walks as queen, and he says of her celestial maidens, (perhaps a reminiscence of the mythological German swan-maidens):

> *Thy white hand with blossoms*
> *Their chaplets enhances,*
> *Thou show'st them the dances*
> *Of God's Paradise.*
> *'Mid radiant skies*
> *Thou gather'st heavenly roses.*

The Italian Franciscan monk Giacomo of Verona also wrote poems to the "Queen of the Heavenly Meadows". "On the right hand of Christ sits Mary, more lovely than the flowers in the meadows and the half-opened rose-buds. Before her face stand the heavenly hosts singing jubilant songs in her praise, but she adorns her knights with garlands and gives them roses." Just as Pons of Capduelh describes the transfiguration of his earthly mistress, Jacopone describes Mary's ascent into Heaven, where she is received by the angels singing songs of jubilee, their *sanctus, sanctus, sanctus*, replaced by a joyful *sancta, sancta, sancta*—a goddess has been received in the place of God.

Gottfried of Strassburg, the author of the sensuous and passionate epic poem "Tristan and Isolde," composed a long poem in honour of Mary couched in the well-known terms of the loving worshipper:

> *Thou vale of roses,—violet-dell,*
> *Thou joy that makest hearts to swell,*
> *Eternal well*
> *Of valour; Queen of Heaven!*

Thou rosy dawn, thou morning-red,
Thou steadfast friend when hope has fled,
The living bread,
Oh! Lady, hast thou given.

Thou sheen of flow'rs with love alight,
Thou bridal crown, all maids' delight,
Thou art bedight
With heaven's golden splendour!

Thou of all sweetness sweetest shine,
Thou sweeter than the sweetest wine,
The sweetness thine,
Is my salvation ever.
Thou art a potion sweet of love,
Sweetly pervading heaven above,
To sailors rough
Sang syrens sweeter never.

Thou enterest through eye and ear,
Senses and soul pervading,
Thou givest to the heart great cheer,
A guerdon dear,
A glory never fading.

The poet who wrote of Isolde's love potion here calls the Queen of Heaven a *potion sweet of love*, a strange metaphor to use in connection with the Mary of dogma. Another characteristic frequently alluded to is her *sweet perfume*, an attribute which we to-day do not look upon as exclusively celestial.

Quaintly delicate and tender are the love-songs of Brother Hans, an otherwise unknown monk of the fourteenth century. He himself tells us that he deserted his earthly mistress for the Queen of Heaven. Perhaps the dualism between earthly and transcendent love has never been expressed more clearly than by him; for in his case the worshipping love did not gradually lead up to Mary, the essence of womanhood, but an earthly love had to be killed so that the pure heavenly love could live.

> *Mary! Gentle mistress mine!*
> *I humbly kneel before you;*
> *All my heart and soul are thine.*

And:

> *Oh, Mary! Secret fountain,*
> *Closed garden of delight,*
> *The Prince of Heaven mirrors*
> *Him in thy beauty bright.*

But after describing all the joys of heaven, Brother Hans comes to the conclusion that a man knows about as much of celestial matters as an ox knows of discant singing.

His relationship to Mary is tender, intimate and familiar:

> *Within my heart concealed*
> *There is a secret cell;*
> *At nightfall and at daybreak*
> *My lady there does dwell.*
> *The mistress of the house is she,*
> *I feel her love and care about.*
> *If she denies herself to me,*
> *Methinks the mistress has gone out.*

In another poem he prays to Mary to allow him to tear off a small piece of her robe, so that he may keep himself warm with it in the winter.

Like Cino da Pistoia, who commended his dying soul not to God but to his loved one, Brother Hans commends himself to Mary:

> *Thus I commend my soul into thy hands,*
> *When it must journey to those unknown lands,*
> *Where roads and paths are new and strange to it.*

And:

> *Oh, come to me, thou Bride of God,*
> *When my faint soul departs from me!*

There remains one more motif to consider, a motif which in a way completes the picture of the celestial lady: As men love and desire the women of the earth, so God loves the Lady of Heaven. St. Bernard first expressed this naïve idea, which makes God the Father resemble a little the ancient Jupiter. "She attracted the eyes of the heavenly hosts, even the heart of the King went out to her." "He Himself, the supreme King and Ruler, so much desires thy beauty, that He is awaiting thy consent, upon which He has decided to save the world. And Him Whom thou delightest in thy silence, thou wilt delight even more by thy speech, for He called to thee from Heaven: 'Oh! fairest among women! Let me hear thy voice!'" etc. Here we have St. Bernard, the rock of orthodoxy, representing God as Mary's languishing admirer! Suso is irreproachable in this respect, but Conrad says that the colour of Mary's face was so bright and made it so lovely,

> *That even the Eternal Sire*
> *Was filled with sacred fire,*
> *And all the heavenly princes. . .*

Thus, at the turn of the fourteenth century the great celestial change was complete: By the side of God, nay, even in the place of God, a woman was enthroned. "The Virgin became the God of the Universe," says Michelet, a thorough, though rather imaginative expert on the Middle Ages. The people primitively worshipped idols. The clergy, headed by the Dominican and Franciscan monks, introduced Lady Days into the calendar and invented the rosary to facilitate the recital of the *Aves*; secular orders of knighthood placed themselves under the Virgin's protection (La Chevalerie de Sainte Marie), but the rarest minds, sublimating the beloved, raised her into Heaven and worshipped her as divine. The established religion was compelled to enter into partnership with the great emotion of the time, metaphysical love, lest it ran the risk of losing its sway over humanity.

And a feeling was born then which to this day constitutes one of the striking differences between the Eastern and the Western worlds: the respect for womanhood. It is based on the woman-worship of secular, and the Madonna-worship of ecclesiastical circles. It is true that Jesus, anticipating the intuition of Europe, had taught the divinity of the human soul and recognised woman—in this respect—as on an equality with man, but the instincts of Greece and the Eastern nations had proved to be stronger than his teaching; for twelve hundred years woman was despised, and more than once the question as to whether or no she had a soul—in other words, as to whether or no she was a human being—had come under discussion. The crude and primitively dualistic minds of the period realised in her sex merely an embodiment of their own sensuality, the enemy against whom they fought, and to whom they knew themselves subject. The strongest argument in her favour which the first millenary could adduce, was the fact that the Saviour of the world had been borne by a woman, and that consequently her sex had a share in the work of salvation; the idea that through the "other Eve" a part of the sin of the first Eve was expiated. But genuine appreciation and respect were only possible after base sensuality had been contrasted with spiritual love, whose vehicle again was woman. Now the "eternal-feminine"—contrasted with the "earthly-feminine"—drew the lovers upwards, and this new emotion threw such a glamour over the whole sex, that it never entirely died away; if to-day women are respected and their efforts at emancipation supported, they are not indebted, as they are sometimes told, to Christian ethics, but rather to the mundane culture which had its origin at the courts of the Provençal lords, whose ideals ultimately became the controlling ideals of Europe, and whose inmost essence still influences the world.

The evolution of love had obviously arrived at a stage when respect was considered due to women—though not perhaps to all women. I will not go to the courts of the great for evidence, but merely relate an episode from the life of the Dominican friar Suso: "In crossing a field, Suso met on a narrow path a poor, respectable woman. When he was close to her, he stepped off the dry path and stood in the mud, waiting for her to pass. The woman, who knew him, was astonished. 'How is it, Sir,' she said, 'that you, a venerable priest, are humbly standing aside to allow me, a poor woman, to pass, when it were far more meet that I should stand aside and make room for you?' 'Why, my good woman,' replied Suso, 'I like to honour all women for the sake of the gentle Mother of God in Heaven.'"

It may seem extraordinary, but this absolutely unphilosophical, and really paradoxical emotion, found an appreciator in the German philosopher Ludwig Feuerbach, the enemy of Christianity. In his *Essence of Christianity*, as well as in his treatise *On the Cult of Mary*, he refers to it more than once. "The holy Virgin," he says, "the Mother of God, is the only divine and positive, that is to say, the only lovable and poetical figure of Christian mythology, and the only one worthy of worship; for Mary is the goddess of beauty, the goddess of love, the goddess of humanity, the goddess of nature, the goddess of freedom from dogma." Feuerbach is right. The Lady of Heaven stands for the delivery from dogma, because she had her origin in spontaneous emotion, clothed with but a few rags of dogma. "The monks vowed the vow of chastity," he continues in his great work; "they suppressed the sexual impulse, but in exchange they had the personification of womanhood, of love, in the Virgin in Heaven. The more their ideal, fictitious representative of her sex became an object of spontaneous love, the more easily could they dispense with the women of flesh and blood. The more they emphasised in their lives the complete suppression of sexuality, the more prominent became the part which the Virgin played in their emotions; she usurped in many cases, the place of Christ, and even the place of God." Feuerbach then explains the need of man to project his noblest sentiments on Heaven, and lays much stress on the necessity of believing in the Mother of God, because the love of a child for its mother is the first strong feeling of man. "Where the faith in the Mother of God declines, the faith in the Son of God, and in God the Father, declines also."

I WILL NOW LEAVE THE region of the historical and examine the emotion whose reality and influence I have substantiated, from a timeless standpoint, for my principal point is the psychical, and more particularly the metaphysical consummation of the emotion of love. The sole object of the abundant evidence I have been compelled to adduce is my desire to prove the existence and significance of all the emotions which stir the soul, and in the later Middle Ages strove so powerfully to express themselves. My thesis that sexuality and love are opposed principles will no doubt be rejected, for, under the strong influence of the theory of evolution, all the world is to-day agreed that love is nothing but the refinement of the sexual impulse. I maintain that (as far as man is concerned) they differ very essentially, and I have attempted to prove their incommensurability by submitting historical facts. That they may, and will, ultimately merge, is my unalterable conviction. My assertion that something so fundamental as the personal love of man and woman did not exist from the beginning, but came into existence in the course of history, at a not very remote period, may seem even more strange. My only reply is that instead of advancing opinions I have brought forward facts and allowed them to speak for themselves. Moreover, to my mind the realisation of the intimate connection of love and evolving personality is a far more magnificent proof of the soundness of the evolutionary theory than the reflection that we have received all things ready-made from the hands of nature. Has it not been proved to us that the religious consciousness of the divinity of the human soul was also evolved in historical time, and has never again disappeared?

Every strong love which finds no response is fraught with the possibility of an infinite unfolding; it may powerfully seize the whole soul and make life a tragedy. But this tragedy is not of the very essence of tragedy, inasmuch as here we have merely love confronted by an unsurmountable obstacle, meeting and overwhelming it; the discord is not inherent. Many a lover suffering from unrequited love, is born with the tendency to become unhappy, with a secret will to the voluptuousness of pain and melancholy; he will enjoy his unhappiness, perhaps become productive through it. Thus, this deliberately unhappy love may be regarded as an analogy to genuine metaphysical eroticism. For the worship of woman is in its essence infinite striving; its object is always unattainable, an illusion. Every earthly love, even if it finds no response at all, may, in principle, be gratified, and is only unhappy if external circumstances intervene. But the love of the Madonna is in itself fraught with the tragic impossibility of requital; its foundation is the recognition, or divination, of the fact that mortal women are too insignificant for a passion which yearns for infinitude. A lover filled with the longing to glorify a woman and worship her as a divine being, has frequently experienced a certain disappointment. The beloved may have died young—as did Beatrice—without his ever having come into close contact with her; instinctively his soul turns heavenward—and imagination has ample scope to transform and transfigure the dead. Or he may have been disappointed in his mistress; it may have been that he, attuned to pure, spiritual love, has found her all too human. He flees from reality into the world of dreams, and envelops her with the veil of mysteriousness and divinity. Purely spiritual love is an intense emotion, and as men and women of flesh and blood cannot always live at high pressure, hours of dejection and disappointment will necessarily have to be experienced. The soul takes refuge in an illusion which becomes more and more an end in itself, and gradually the lover creates an inaccessibly lofty, celestial woman. For purely spiritual love aspires to absolute transcendency; it cannot bear contact with every-day life. The psychologists of the present day tell us that a feeling, in becoming spiritualised, loses strength,—history teaches us that in the case of great souls the opposite is the rule.

These suggestions purpose to explain the inception of an ecstatic love; but the true metaphysical erotic is born and needs no outside stimulus; his heart yearns for the inaccessible from the very beginning. There are certain elements of feeling which must be present in his soul simultaneously: a religious elementary feeling tending to the metaphysical; the need of a sacred—a divine—being, as the foundation of all existing things; a powerful and purely spiritual craving for love, hurt, perhaps unconsciously, in early youth, and finally an imagination endowed with plastic force—artistic tendencies. In the case of the mystic the soul, too, is filled with the consciousness of the divine; he, too, has the capacity for a great love, but with him it is not the love of woman, but of something universal, not individualised, the world, the cosmos, God.

While the mystic attempts to embody the inconceivable Deity in his soul, the worshipper of the Madonna, like the artist, imaginatively creates a being which he sets up for contemplation at the greatest possible distance. The mystic is blind, as it were; he is yearning personified, and he would force God into his soul. The metaphysical lover needs a plastic figure which, in the extremest case, may represent the whole world to him, and this figure must be a woman. It is a historical accident that this woman is frequently connected with a woman of ecclesiastical tradition, an accident strengthened by insufficient creative power on the part of the lover, or lack of courage and self-confidence. He is grateful for the support given to him by tradition. The greatest metaphysical lovers, Dante, Goethe and Michelangelo, freely created the objects of their love; the Protestant Goethe—whom some people even accuse of paganism—clung more closely than either of the others to the Mary of Catholicism (in the final scene of *Faust*). The worship of the Madonna is the love of great solitary souls, and—as is proved by Goethe—of the great souls in the hours of their last solitude.

While there was only unindividualised sexual instinct, the chastity of woman was of no account; we have seen that neither the Eastern nations nor the Greeks attached any value to it. The woman who had best fulfilled her vocation as a mother, was the woman most highly respected. In the East, as well as with Jews and Romans, a woman could be divorced by her husband for sterility. The only women who were, to some extent, appreciated for their own sakes, were the Greek hetaerae. But when asceticism became a moral value, chastity, too, was regarded as a virtue, and personal love between two individuals invested it with a profound significance. Henceforth woman should no longer be regarded as the vehicle for the gratification of male sensuality; it should be her mission to lead the lover to spiritual perfection. The fusion of the older ideal of womanhood, the mother (acknowledged and sanctioned by religion in the mother of the Saviour), with the newer ideal, the Virgin, created the ideal of the late Middle Ages: the virgin with the Child. Here the natural vocation of woman and the fantastic mission laid upon her by man were united in a paradoxical higher intuition, and it is superfluous to point out that the most irreligious minds of the Renascence, as well as those of all later eras, have to this day worshipped this ideal, and never wearied of representing it under new forms.

But the worship of the Virginal Mother contains another element, an element of which man in his contact with woman is deeply conscious: the element of mystery. To a man a young girl, untouched by the faintest breath of sensuality, has a quality of strangeness and mysteriousness (this is probably a result of European sentiment), and at all times the woman who has become a mother has been regarded with a slight feeling of superstitious awe. In the Virginal Mother these two vaguely reverential feelings are blended; she is a strange and awe-inspiring being, and man, divining a mystery, bows down before her.

Otto Weininger was the first to give us a psychology of the cult of the Madonna, and he did it in a manner which proved his entire comprehension of this peculiar sentimental disposition. He realised and pointed out the contrast between sexuality and eroticism (his terms for sexual impulse and love), but in accordance with his extreme mental disposition he left these two principles in irreconcilable conflict, while I regard their antithesis merely in the light of a transient phase which will be followed by a reconciling synthesis. Weininger is, I believe, in conflict with spiritual reality when (guided by ethical, not psychological considerations) he proposes the theory that a man endows the beloved woman with all the lofty values he desires for himself. "He projects his ideal of an absolutely perfect being on another human being, and this and nothing else is the meaning of his love." "To bestow all the qualities one would like to possess, but never can quite possess, on another individual, to make it the representative of all values, that is to love." It is a commonplace experience that genuine love will awaken in the soul new and transcendent emotions, compared to which all previous experience appears petty and insignificant.

The waves of this emotion are able to carry the lover to the infinite, or at least his emotion will help him to divine the infinite. He sees, unexpectedly, his inmost soul revealed to him, he has exceeded the limits upon which he has hitherto looked as a matter of course; the barrier between him and the universe has fallen, the whole world belongs to him; the egoist becomes less selfish, the cruel man gentle, the dullard clairvoyant; every man feels that he has become greater and more human. This is neither illusion nor projection, nor is it a subtle, psychical deception—it is sober reality. Weininger's suspicion of a delusion is nothing but the result of his ascetic solipsism, refusing to accept another being's help in his striving for perfection, a consequence of the one-sided, sterile cult of his individual soul, a noble but puerile pride refusing to be indebted to the world and to his fellow-men, the fanatical, metaphysical dualism which is so often met with in the second stage of eroticism, and to which stage he belongs.

Weininger shrank from the idea that an individual might be made the means to an end, instead of being an end in itself. In my opinion his justification for the translation of this formula—framed by Kant for pure ethics—to empirical psychology, is doubtful. To use an individual only as a means to an end which is alien to his inmost being, is certainly immoral. But all social life is based on a mutual relationship of means and ends; a man is an end in himself at the same time that he is a means to other individuals and the community. The teacher is a means as far as his pupils are concerned; the poet is a means in respect to all who seek in his writings information or recreation. To carry the stigmatisation of these facts to a logical conclusion, one would have to call it immoral to accept anything from parents or teachers; one would have to reject every good influence—which always comes from outside—and become completely absorbed in the cult of one's own soul. One would even have to object to being born, and would have to create one's self out of nothing. It has always been regarded as the splendid privilege of great men to exert an ennobling influence on others—why, therefore, should the influence of a beloved woman on her lover be objectionable?

Weininger's error in the sphere of eroticism arises from the fact of his imprisoning love in a formula which is by no means applicable to it. In love the mutual relationship of means and ends does not exist, the lover feels that the beloved is always an end in herself in the highest sense; he would find it impossible inwardly to establish such a relationship between himself and her; very frequently himself, his well-being and his life, are of no account to him if he can serve her. Weininger's assertion that at the consummation of love every woman is merely the means of gratifying a man's passion, is simply not true. On the contrary, it is a characteristic of genuine love that the physical embrace is of no great importance, does not even rise to full consciousness. The personality of the beloved is everything, physical sensation nothing. Weininger identifies love with passion and his argument is easily refutable by the experience of many. In love there is neither means nor end; if, however, categoric formulas must be used, one might speak of a reciprocal action. Equally erroneous is his corresponding assertion that the artist loves a woman spiritually, that is, in the sense of deifying her, for the purpose of drawing from her inspiration for his work. If he loves her, then his love is the alpha and omega of his striving, and if love inspires him to achieve a masterpiece, the effect of love on him must be considered great and good, because it is a creative effect.

The extreme individualistic ideal would lead to an absolutely unproductive view of life. Asceticism stands condemned because it is unproductive. I may regard an Indian fakir who has become so godlike that he can sustain life on six grains of rice a day, and draw breath once every quarter of an hour—to say nothing of speech or cleanliness—as a very strange individual; but I see nothing positive or important in him. The road which leads from the individual to the universal cannot be the rejection of the world; it must be its perfection, resulting from productivity of mind, or soul, or deed. He who on principle refuses to be productive, condemns himself to annihilation in the higher sense. I admit that he who works at his own perfection does good work, too; but it is the inexplicable secret of all truly creative labour—in the highest as well as in the lowest sense—that it must ultimately affect the world and eternity. The strongest emotions, the inner illumination of the mystic and the love of the great erotic, have been conceived in the *heart of hearts*; and have ultimately grown beyond their creator, from the individual to the universal. The more intimate and powerful the creative impulse has been, the more retarded and abundant may, perhaps, be the effect. But the chain which links the great soul to humanity cannot be broken, the work will make itself manifest—the work of deed, the work of the mind, the work of love—I do not say to "the public," but to life, to the world. The creative personality alone is the father of the objective values of civilisation.

The great love which led Dante, Goethe and Wagner to the summits of humanity is in the highest sense positive and creative. And he who realises that love is not subject to sexual impulse, who knows it as something purely personal, foreign and even hostile to the genus, must admit that it is one of the very highest of values. A contrary ethic is sterile, Indian, unproductive, not European. I am well aware that Weininger did not explicitly draw this conclusion; but he rejects spiritual love because it endows the lover with new capacities, the capacities of growth and perfection, and he is therefore in the last resort a representative of philosophic nihilism.

(c) Dante and Goethe

THE WORSHIP OF WOMAN FOUND its climax in Dante. Through the work of his youth, the *Vita Nuova* and his masterpiece, *The Divine Comedy*, we can trace step by step the stages of the road, beginning with a glimpse of a young girl in Florence, and ending with the incorporation of a woman into the world-system. We are face to face with an extraordinary process of evolution. The young girl he had seen a few times, and who died in her youth, goes on growing and developing in his soul, until, at last, in him the will to raise woman above time into eternity, the will to make her a member of the divine system, reaches its full realisation. What had been begun by the troubadours and fully comprehended by the poets of the *sweet new style*, reached completion in Dante, and, was henceforth an eternal value for all humanity.

We see that the later troubadours were inclined to blend the lady of their heart with the universal Lady of Heaven; the need of deifying the loved woman was at the root of many dubious growths, and possibly these early poets were also to some extent influenced by their dread of the Inquisition (which never gained much importance in Italy). The new poets deepened this feeling, stripped it of all externalities, and appeared before the adored simply as lovers. They did not require the dogmatic support of the Church, their own feeling was sufficient guarantee. Dante, moreover, was possessed by a craving for an absolutely perfect and consistent world-system, and had, besides, the power to build it up and people it with sublime intelligences. And in this system, the crown and perfection of the mediaeval-Catholic conception of the universe, he assigned to the love of his youth a high and permanent place by the side of the deities. Dante thus raised his individual feeling to a universal dogma, and enriched the Catholic heaven by his personal love. What for two hundred years had been a dream and a desire, had become a matter of faith and truth. Now, and not until now, love and religion were one; the love of a woman had been included in the system of eternal verities, and had become identical with the love of immortality. "Love which moves the sun and all the stars" was acknowledged as a fundamental feeling. The anchoring of the subjective in the eternal was achieved in this metaphysical setting: the deification of the beloved; and no greater gift was ever vouchsafed to man than the creation of metaphysically true beings and values. All that had been done before had merely prepared the ground for this great deed: the enshrinement of the beloved in the heart of the divine secrets.

The *Vita Nuova*, which is at once a glorified historical record and the greatest testimony of metaphysical love, emphasises from the outset the inspiring, purifying influence emanating from the beloved; Beatrice is "the destroyer of all evil and the queen of all virtue." "When I saw her coming towards me and could hope for her salutation, the world held no enemy for me, yea, I was filled with the fire of brotherly love to such an extent, that I was ready to forgive anybody who had ever offended me. And whoever had begged me for a gift, I should have replied: Love! and my face would have been full of humility." Even before his love had been translated to the world beyond, he portrayed spiritual love as hardly any other poet before or after him. The women of Florence ask Dante: "Why doest thou love this lady, seeing that thou canst not even bear her presence? Tell us, for the end of such love must be incomprehensible to men." And he replies: "Ladies, the end and aim of my love is but the salutation of that lady; therein I find that beatitude which is the goal of my desire. And now that it has pleased her to deny me her salutation, my whole happiness is contained in that which can never perish." And the women: "Tell us, then, wherein lies such happiness?" "In the words that praise my lady" (that is to say in the emotion which is an end in itself and in its artistic expression). The lover never exchanged a word with her; had he done so, attempting to establish a reciprocal relationship, Beatrice, bereft of his idealising love, would have had to descend from her pedestal and show herself a girl like all the rest. Not until after her deification has become an established fact, does Beatrice (in the beginning of the *Divine Comedy*) remember her lover and come to save him. In one of his poems Dante says that not every woman could inspire such a love, but only a woman of peculiar nobility of character. It is very apparent that Dante, at first, was not sure of himself, and that he only gradually discovered the new consciousness which was stirring his soul; with every chapter the beloved recedes to a greater distance and becomes more sacred to him.

It is quite in keeping with all this that our knowledge of this girl of eighteen is very vague and uncertain. Some of Dante's commentators believe her to have been a figment of his brain, a woman who never lived, or an allegory of wisdom, virtue, the Church, theology, etc. But at the death of her father Beatrice again behaves like any other earthly maiden. There is a grain of truth in every one of these theories, for Dante was a great scholastic as well as a great poet, and in more advanced years he felt a need somehow to connect the love of his youth with the system of the Church; this could be done in an allegorical way without being inwardly untruthful.

Vague forces, which the lover himself realises as mysterious, run high in the *Vita Nuova* and in the poems; the lover has hallucinations in sleep and sickness. In the third canzone Dante speaks of the impossibility of comprehending what gave him a glimpse of the nature of his mistress. It was a foreboding of new and great things, struggling slowly and gradually to take shape, for the creation of a world-system, one of whose supporting pillars was personal love of an individual, was an unprecedented achievement. "When she speaks a spirit inclines from heaven." The angels implore God to call this "miracle" into their midst, but God wills that they shall have patience until the "Hope of the Blessed" appears.

> *Love says of her can there be mortal thing*
> *At once adorned so richly and so pure?*
> *Then looks on her and silently affirms*
> *That heaven designed in her a creature new.*

(*Transl. by* C. Lyell)

Again and again recurs the motif of her beauty before which the world must fall prostrate. In a sonnet not included in the *Vita Nuova* he says:

> *In heaven itself that lady had her birth,*
> *I think, and is with us for our behoof;*
> *Blessed are they who meet her on the earth.*

(*Transl. by* D.G. Rossetti)

The lover has a foreboding of the fate awaiting him: "I have set my feet into that phase of life from whence there is no return." He divines the sorrow to which love has predestined him. But others, too, divining that this man "expects more, perhaps, of love than others," ask him to explain to them the essence of love, and he answers them with the famous sonnet:

Amor e cor gentil sono una cosa
(Love and the gentle heart are but one thing.)

The death of Beatrice is accompanied by the same phenomena as was the death of Christ: the sun lost its brilliance, stars appeared in the sky, birds fell to the ground, dead, the earth trembled; God visibly intervened in the course of nature.

For from the lamp of her meek lowlihead
Such an exceeding glory went up hence,
That it woke wonder in the Eternal Sire,
Until a sweet desire
Entered Him for that lovely excellence,
So that He bade her to Himself aspire;
Counting this weary and most evil place
Unworthy of a thing so full of grace.

(Transl. by D.G. ROSSETTI)

In the 29th chapter, which we, to-day, do not readily understand, Dante established by a system of symbolical numbers a connection between Beatrice and the Trinity; the deification of the beloved had been achieved in thought and emotion, religion enriched by a new divinity. "Love, weeping, has filled my heart with new knowledge," he says, at the conclusion of the work of his youth. I repeat what I have already said in another place, and supported by passages from the *Divine Comedy*: It was never Dante's intention to write fictitious poems in our meaning of the term, but at every hour of his life he was convinced that he was proclaiming the pure truth; he knew himself to be the chosen vehicle for the interpretation of the eternal system of the world.

At the conclusion of the *Vita Nuova*, Beatrice is a divine being, devoid of all emotion—enthroned in Heaven; in the *Comedy* she becomes her lover's saviour and redeemer, and through him a helper of all humanity. The love of the youth had found no response in the heart of the Florentine maiden, but the soul of the glorified woman was inspired by love of him. She trembles for him, and when Mary's messenger admonishes her: "Why doest thou not help him who has loved thee so much?" she sends Virgil to him as a guide and finally herself leads her redeemed lover to God. Now she responds to his love; she has even wept for him. This ultimately fulfilled, but always chastely hidden longing for love in return, gives the woman-worship of Dante a peculiarly noble charm. At the end of his journey through life he prays to her, who has again disappeared from his sight, and his last confession is: "Into a free man thou transform'st a slave."

Love's greatest miracle has been made manifest in him; it has transfigured and purified him, and made of the slave of the world and its desires, a personality—the fundamental motif of love.

There is a close connection between the metaphysical love of Dante and Goethe's confession in the last scene of *Faust*, which reveals the poet's deepest conviction, his final judgment of life. The confessions of both poets are identical to the smallest detail. The *Divine Comedy* represents the journey of humanity through the kingdoms of the world in a manner unique and representative, applicable alike to all men, in the sense of the Catholic Middle Ages. The fundamental idea of *Faust* is again the desire of man to find the right way through the world. Here also the journey through life is intended to be typical; it is undertaken five hundred years later; the scene is laid for the most part on the surface of the earth, but the ultimate goal of the wayfarer is Heaven. Hell, instead of being a subterraneous region, is embodied in a presence, accompanying and tempting man; modern man has no faithful guide; he must himself seek the way which to the man of the Middle Ages was clearly indicated in the Bible. The love of his youth (which in the case of Dante fills a book in itself) is merely an episode at the beginning of the tragedy—the lover wanders through all the kingdoms of the world, finally to return home to the beloved.

The last scene of *Faust* is an unfolding of metaphysical love into its inherent multiplicity; its summit is the metaphysical love of woman. All human striving is determined and crowned by the saving grace of love. Faust has no longer a specific name; he has dropped everything subjective, and is briefly styled *a lover*; like Dante, he has become representative of humanity. The hour of death revives the memory of the love of his youth, apparently forgotten in the storm and stress of a crowded life, yet never quite extinguished in the heart of his heart. Margaret is present and guides him (as Beatrice guided Dante) upward, to the *Eternal-Feminine*, that is to say, to the metaphysical consummation of all male yearning for love. "The love from on high" saves Faust as it has saved Dante. *The blessed boys* (who, as well as the angels, are present in both poems) singing:

> *Whom ye adore shall ye*
> *See face to face.*[2]

are again referring to the transcendently loving lover. Like Beatrice, Margaret intercedes for him (intercession for her lover has always been woman's profoundest prayer) with the Queen of Heaven:

> *Incline, oh incline,*
> *All others excelling,*
> *In glory aye dwelling,*
> *Unto my bliss thy glance benign;*
> *The loved one ascending,*
> *His long trouble ending,*
> *Comes back, he is mine!*

These words are more intimate and human than the words of Beatrice, but fundamentally they mean the same thing. Dante, meeting Beatrice again, says:

> *And o'er my spirit that so long a time*
> *Had from her presence felt no shuddering dread,*
> *Albeit my eyes discovered her not, there moved*
> *A hidden virtue from her, at whose touch*
> *The power of ancient love was strong within me.*[3]

But when he who has said so much beholds her face to face, he is stricken dumb.

---

2. The quotations from *Faust* are from the translation of Anna Swanwick.
3. The quotations from the *Divine Comedy* are from the translation of Henry Francis Cary.

Beatrice receives Dante from his guide and herself unveils to him the mysteries of life. Similarly Margaret beseeches the Virgin:

> *To guide him, be it given to me*
> *Still dazzles him the new-born day!*

and receives from on high the command which the symbolically burdened Beatrice knows intuitively:

> *Ascend, thine influence feeleth he,*
> *He'll follow on thine upward way.*

As Beatrice approaches, the angels sing:

> *Oh! Turn*
> *Thy saintly eyes to this thy faithful one,*
> *Who to behold thee many a wearisome pace*
> *Hath measured.*

And with the fundamental feeling of Dante's *Divine Comedy* Faust concludes:

> *The ever-womanly*
> *Draws us above.*

The earthly love of his youth is fulfilled in the dream of metaphysical love, in the dream of a divine woman. The genius creates, at the conclusion of his life, the fulfilment of all longing. It may sound paradoxical, but Faust—like Dante and Peer Gynt—unconsciously sought Margaret in the hurly-burly of the world; not the young girl whom he had seduced and deserted, but the *Eternal-Feminine*, the purely spiritual love, which in his youth he divined, but destroyed, bound by the shackles of desire. To Dante, to whom life and poem were one, as well as to Goethe-Faust, the memory of first love remained typical of all genuine, profound feeling; with Dante love and Beatrice are identical. In the soul of these two men metaphysical love, the longing for the eternal in woman, which they did not find on earth, gradually awoke to life. Both place the glorified mistress by the side of another woman, the Catholic Queen of Heaven. In Dante's, as well as in Goethe's Paradise two women, a personal one and a universal one, are loved and adored. The second woman, too, has her exclusive, ecstatic worshipper. St. Bernard, the *Doctor Marianus* of Dante, prostrating himself before her, addresses to her the sublime prayer which begins:

> *Oh, Virgin! Mother! Daughter of thy Son!*

and in *Faust* we meet again the *Doctor Marianus* burning—as the representative of the totality of her worshippers—with the "sacred joy of love" (Dante says

> *The Queen of Heaven for whom my soul*
> *Burns with love's rapture)*

and pronouncing the most beautiful prayer to the Madonna which the world possesses, and which is almost identical with Dante's:

> *Virgin, pure from taint of earth,*
> *Mother, we adore thee,*
> *With the Godhead one by birth,*
> *Queen, we bow before thee!*

And, prostrated before her:

> *Penitents, her saviour-glance*
> *Gratefully beholding,*
> *To beatitude advance,*
> *Still new pow'rs unfolding!*
> *Thine each better thought shall be,*
> *To thy service given!*
> *Holy Virgin, gracious be,*
> *Mother, Queen of Heaven!*

In the Divine Comedy St. Bernard prays:

> *So mighty art thou, Lady, and so great,*
> *That he who grace desireth and comes not*
> *To thee for aidence, fain would have desire*
> *Fly without wings.*

The *Chorus mysticus* could equally well form the conclusion of the *Comedy*. The *inadequate* which to *fulness groweth*, is what the Provençals already, in their time, realised as *folly*, as a paradox: the metaphysical love of woman, for ever remaining dream and longing, always unfulfilled, the eternal-feminine.

As the *Mater Gloriosa* appears, Dante exclaims:

> *Thenceforward what I saw*
> *Was not for words to speak, nor memory's self*
> *To stand against such outrage on her skill.*

And Goethe:

> *In starry wreath is seen*
> *Lofty and tender,*
> *Midmost the heavenly queen,*
> *Known by her splendour.*

Here the "sacred fire of love," metaphysical eroticism, has reached its absolute climax. The universe is represented by a divine woman, and man, abandoning himself to her, worships her. Goethe's *Faust* concludes at this point, but Dante went further, right into the heart of the eternal glory of the Deity, there to lose himself.

I have previously said that the last scene of *Faust* was the final unfolding of the manifold blossom of metaphysical eroticism, and I will proceed to establish my point. Hitherto I have used the term metaphysical eroticism always in its narrow sense of love of woman. Henceforth I shall use it in its broader meaning of mystical love in general, all love that is projected on the transcendental and the divine. Emotion is the specific domain of humanity, its power, its essence. And in the profoundest emotion, in love, a connection between the temporal and the eternal may be divined. Hence the Christian mystery of mysteries, God giving His Son to the world for love of humanity; God unable to approach the world other than as a lover—sacrificing Himself for the sake of love. We cannot conceive the Sublime with any other principal function than that of love; for love is the deepest and profoundest emotion of the human heart, and, in accordance with the first postulate, must therefore be the soul of the universe. On this point all mystics and all metaphysical ecstatics are agreed; "God is love" is written in the Gospel of St. John. "Love which moves the sun and all the stars," stands at the termination of Dante's masterpiece: and in *Faust* the *Pater Profundus* confesses:

> *So love, almighty, all-pervading,*
> *Does all things mould, does all sustain.*

He is still wrestling for divine love; he still has to fight against the temptations of doubt (of thought),

> *Oh, God! My troubled thoughts composing,*
> *My needy heart do thou illume!*

But the true enthusiastic lover of the divine, compelled to annihilate himself so as to become absorbed in God, the lover who no longer knows the difference between pain and delight, is represented by the *Pater Ecstaticus*: The condition of rest is foreign to him, ceaselessly moving up and down, he sings:

> *Joy's everlasting fire,*
> *Love's glow of pure desire,*
> *Pang of the seething breast,*
> *Rapture a hallowed guest!*
> *Darts pierce me through and through,*
> *Lances my flesh subdue,*
> *Clubs me to atoms dash,*
> *Lightnings athwart me flash,*
> *That all the worthless may*
> *Pass like a cloud away,*
> *While shineth from afar,*
> *Love's gem, a deathless star!*

These ejaculations completely exhaust the emotional life of the self-destructive metaphysical erotic—he is conscious of nothing but his passion of love which eclipses all else. With him the second form of metaphysical love, the love-death, is reached. Goethe, in creating this character, must have had in his mind the unique Jacopone da Todi. For this rapturous love was the keynote of Jacopone's character, his whole life was one great ecstasy:

> *My heart was all to broken,*
> *As prostrate I was lying,*
> *With dear love's fiery token*
> *Swift from the archer flying;*
> *Wounded, with sweet pain soaken,*
> *Peace became war—and dying,*
> *My soul with pain was soaken,*
> *Distraught with throes of love.*
>
> *In transports I am dying,*
> *Oh! Love's astounding wonder!—*
> *For love, his fell spear plying,*
> *Has cleft my heart asunder.*
> *Around the blade are lying*
> *Sharp teeth, my life to sunder,*
> *In rapture I am dying,*
> *Distraught with throes of love.*

And:

> *Oh, Love! oh, Love! oh, Jesus, my desire,*
> *Oh, Love! I hold thee clasped in sweet embrace!*
> *Oh, Love! embracing thee, could I expire!*
> *Oh, Love! I'd die to see thee face to face.*
> *Oh, Love! oh, Love! I burn in rapture's fire,*
> *I die, enravished in the soul's embrace.*

The legend has it that the heart of Jacopone broke with the intensity of love. This would have been a love-death of cosmic grandeur.

Before Jacopone St. Bernard, in whom all the radiations of metaphysical eroticism are traceable, was consumed by similar emotions. Some of his Latin poems very much resemble the poems of his successor:

> *Oh, most sweet Jesu, Saviour blest,*
> *My yearning spirit's hope and rest,*

To thee mine inmost nature cries,
And seeks thy face with tears and sighs.

Thou, my heart's joy where'er I rove,
Thou art the perfecting of love;
Thou art my boast—all praise be thine,
Jesu, the world's salvation, mine!

Then his embrace, his holy kiss,
The honeycomb were naught to this!
'Twere bliss fast bound to Christ for aye,
But in these joys is little stay.

This love with ceaseless ardour burns,
How wondrous sweet no stranger learns;
But tasted once, the enraptured wight,
Is filled with ever new delight.

Now I behold what most I sought;
Fulfilled at last my longing thought;
Lovesick, my soul to Jesus turns,
And all my heart within me burns.

(*Transl. by* T.G. CRIPPEN)

We read in his writings: "Blessed and sacred is he to whom it has been given to experience this in his earthly life; even if he have experienced it only once, for the space of a fleeting minute. For to melt away completely, as it were, as if one had ceased to exist, to be emptied of self, dissolved in holy emotion, has not been given to mortal life, but is the state of the blessed."

I shall have to refer to both men in a future chapter, when I shall examine the degenerate growths of metaphysical eroticism; for the ardour of their souls was frequently kindled by sexual imaginings; in the case of emotional mystics it is often difficult to distinguish between sensual conceptions and the pure love of God (a fact which does not, however, justify the superficial opinion that all mysticism is diverted sexuality).

It is obvious that this love of God is not the original creation of the lover, as is the deifying love of woman, but the mystic love whose self-evident object is God or eternity. Jacopone's (and later on Zinzendorf's) love of Jesus, though projected on a historical personality, was fundamentally the same thing. The love of God also—and in this connection I might mention Jacob Boehme, Alphonso da Liguori, Novalis—is metaphysical eroticism; but I have restricted my subject to the metaphysical love of woman, and shall not overstep my limits. I will merely elucidate a little more the last scene of *Faust*.

Pater seraphicus, a title given both to St. Francis and to Bonaventura—requires but a few words: he, too, praises metaphysical love, the essence of the supreme spirits.

> *Thus the spirits' nature stealing*
> *Through the ether's depths profound;*
> *Love eternal, self-revealing,*
> *Sheds beatitude around.*

But even the *more perfect angels* cannot free themselves from the dualism of all things human (body and soul)—an unmistakable confession of metaphysical dualism:

> *Parts them God's love alone,*
> *Their union ending.*

The identity of the last scene of *Faust*, Goethe's masterpiece, and the conclusion of Dante's *Divine Comedy*, is so obvious that I do not think any one could deny it. I have pointed out the thought underlying both works, and could easily advance further proof of their similarity, but I will keep within the limits of the last scene which contains the totality of metaphysico-erotic yearning, and I contend that it is very remarkable that a lifetime after the composition of Margaret, Faust (and with him Goethe) very old, very wise, and a little cold, having had love-affairs with demi-goddesses, and having finally renounced the love of woman, found his mission and his happiness in uninterrupted, productive activity. He has discovered the final value in work. But the long-forgotten heaven opens and the love of his youth comes to meet him. Stripped of everything earthly, a divine being, she still loves him and shows him the way to salvation, presented under the aspect of the *Eternal-Feminine*—exactly as in the *Divine Comedy*. There must be a reason for the uniformity of feeling in the case of the two greatest subjective poets of Europe

(Shakespeare was greater than either, but he was quite impersonal), for the logical possibility that Goethe imitated Dante, and borrowed his supreme values from him, cannot be maintained for a moment. Their mutual characteristic is the longing for metaphysical love. When these great lovers experienced for the first time the sensation of love, their hearts were thrown open to the universe, they had the first powerful experience of eternity, and they became poets. The first love and the cosmic consciousness of genius were simultaneously present, they were one in their inmost soul. (With the philosopher it is a different matter, for to him the love of woman is not fraught with the same tremendous significance.) This experience of first love, awakening the consciousness of eternity, remained to them for all time interwoven with religion and metaphysics—interwoven, that is to say, with all transcendent longing. And though the aged Faust had believed it to be buried in the dark night of forgotten things, it was still alive in his inmost heart, and the dying man's vision of the Divine took colour and shape from it.

The source of both great poems was the poet's will to assimilate the world and recreate it, impregnated with his own soul; the secret motive powers were the mystic love of eternity and the love of woman which had outgrown this world and aspired to the next. To Goethe, thirsting to give a concrete shape to his yearning, God and eternity were too intangible, too remote and incomprehensible—but the woman he loved with religio-erotic intensity was familiar to him. The Eternal-Feminine is thus not fraught with incomprehensibility, but is rather, and this necessarily, the final conclusion. For this conclusion is a profession of metaphysical eroticism, that is to say, the *Eternal-Feminine* in contradistinction to the *Transitory-Feminine*. Both Dante, the devout son of the Middle Ages, and Goethe, the champion of modern culture, demand, in virtue of the inherent right of their genius, the consummation of their mystic yearning for love in another life, and achieve the creation of the divine woman. Precisely because Margaret was nothing but a little provincial, Goethe could sublimate her into a new being, for the greater the tension between reality and the vision of the soul, the greater is the task and the more gigantic the creative power which such a task may develop. It has been said that, in this scene, Goethe revealed leanings towards Catholicism. I do not pretend to deny it offhand, but I must insist on these leanings being understood in the sense of my premises. Goethe took from tradition those elements which were able to materialise his spiritual life and gave them a new interpretation. We are justified in believing that he accepted nothing but what was conformable to his nature; the Madonna represented his profoundest feeling and, like Dante (I attribute the greatest importance to this), he created a new deity, moulded in the shape of his first love, and placed it by the side of the universal Queen of Heaven, the Madonna of the Catholic Church, transformed by love.

The emotional life of both poets agrees fundamentally. They differ not so much in feeling as in thought and in faith. Dante possessed unshakable faith in the reality of his visions; eternal love in the shape of Beatrice was awaiting him; his vision was pure, eternal truth. The vision of Goethe, on the other hand, was poetic longing, tragical, because the vision of the transcendent came to the modern poet only in rare hours. Where Dante possessed, Goethe must seek, strive and err.

The deifying love of woman is, as we have seen, the extreme development of the second stage, in which sexual impulse and spiritual love are strictly separated, in which man despises and fights his natural instinct, or abandons himself to it—which is the same in principle— while his soul, worshipping love, soars heavenward. This dualism of feeling corresponds to the persistent dualism of Christianity and the whole mediaeval period. But as Goethe is frequently looked upon as a *monist*, my proposition that he was a dualist *in eroticis* will possibly be rejected, in spite of the fact that his emotional life is revealed to us with great lucidity. His first important work, his *Werther*, which is also one of the most important monuments of sentimental love, contains the germs of love as we understand it; the love which is no longer content to look upon sexuality and soul as two opposed principles, but strives to blend them in the person of the beloved. I will revert to *Werther* later on. This third stage, love in the modern sense, is programmatically established (as it were) in *Elective Affinities*, but all the rest of the very abundant evidence of his emotional life exhibits the typically dualistic feeling. Many of his early poems evidence sexuality pure and simple; in the *Venetian Epigrams* and in the *Roman Elegies* it is even held up as a positive value. In the third Elegy, for instance, the poet's sensuality is linked directly to the famous lovers of antiquity, and everything which aspires beyond it is rejected. In the same way his *West-Eastern Divan* is characterised by a gay sensuality with homo-sexual tendencies.

The sensual quality of Goethe's eroticism was partly spent in his relationship with Christiane Vulpius. The following passage, which forms an interesting counterpart to Goethe's famous correspondence with Charlotte von Stein, is taken from a letter written to Christiane Vulpius during his absence from home. "The beds everywhere are very wide, and you would have no reason for complaint, as you sometimes have at home. Oh, my sweet heart! There is no such happiness on earth as being together."

If Christiane represented sensuality, unrelieved by any other feeling, Frau von Stein represented the most important object of Goethe's craving for spiritual love. These two liaisons were to some extent contemporaneous; the *Roman Elegies* and the famous letters to Charlotte von Stein were written at the same period. When she reproached him with his love-affair with Christiane, he replied with consistent dualism: "And what sort of an affair is it? Whose interests are suffering by it?" Frau von Stein, his senior by seven years, was thirty-four years old, and mother of seven children when Goethe first met her. According to Schiller she "can never have been beautiful," and in a letter to Koerner the latter says: "They say that their relationship (Goethe's and Charlotte von Stein's) is absolutely pure and irreproachable." It was a great mistake ever to regard this relationship as anything but a purely spiritual one; Goethe never felt any passion for Charlotte; he called her "his sister," the "guide of his soul"; he told her of his little love-affairs and was never jealous of her husband. The following are a few typical passages culled from his letters, arranged chronologically: "My only love whom I can love without torment!" Then, quite in the spirit of the *dolce stil nuovo*: "Your soul, in which thousands believe in order to win happiness," "The purest, truest and most beautiful relationship which (with the exception of my sister) ever existed between me and any woman." "The relationship between us is so strange and sacred, that I strongly felt, on that occasion, that it cannot be expressed in words, that men cannot realise it." The following passage written by Goethe when he was thirty, might have been written by Guinicelli or by Dante: "You appeared to me like the Madonna ascending into heaven; in vain did the abandoned mourner stretch out his arms, in vain did his tearful glance plead for a last return—she was absorbed in the splendour surrounding her, longing only for the crown hovering above her head." "I long to be purified in triple fire so as to be worthy of you." He addresses a prayer to her and says: "On my knees I implore you to complete your work and make a good man of me." "While writing Tasso, I worshipped you." Charlotte knew intuitively what he desired of her, and remained silent and passive like the Madonna. Not a single sensual, or even passionate word, replied to all these utterances.

In the course of time the relationship between the lovers became one of equality; the note of adoration disappeared, and the keynote of his letters became friendship and familiarity. "Farewell, sweet friend and beloved, whose love alone makes me happy." In another letter he said that all the world held no further prize for him, since he had found everything in her. And just as spiritual love approached more and more the mean of a familiar friendship, so was his sexuality concentrated on a single woman, on Christiane, in this connection, too, seeking a mean. But it is an important point that the fundamental dualistic feeling remained unchanged. There was no woman in Goethe's life in regard to whom he arrived at, or even aspired to, the blending of both emotions in a higher intuition.

Even before his friendship with Frau von Stein, at the time of his engagement to Lili Schoenemann, Goethe experienced a spiritual love for a girl he had never seen. He calls Countess Auguste Stolberg "his angel," "his only, only maiden," "his golden child," and says: "I have an intuition that you will save me from great tribulation, and that no other being on earth could do it." These letters also contain the significant passage: "Miserable fate which has denied me a happy mean." And touching the love of his youth, Lotte, Goethe wrote to Kestner: "I really had no idea that all that was in her, for I always loved her far too much to observe her."

The Princess in "Tasso" and "Iphigenia" who delivers Orestes from unrest and insanity, are modelled on Charlotte. Tasso is unmistakably a fantastic woman-worshipper, a fact of which Leonore is fully aware:

> *Now he exalts her to the starry heavens,*
> *In radiant glory, and before that form*
> *Bows down like angels in the realms above.*
> *Then, stealing after her, through silent fields,*
> *He garlands in his wreath each beauteous flower.*

> *He loves not us—forgive me what I say—*
> *His lov'd ideal from the spheres he brings*
> *And does invest it with the name we bear.*
> *He has relinquished passion's fickle sway,*
> *He clings no longer with delusion sweet*

> *To outward form and beauty to atone*
> *For brief excitement by disgust and hate.*[4]

And Tasso says:

> *My very knees*
> *Trembled beneath me and my spirit's strength*
> *Was all required to hold myself erect,*
> *And curb the strong desire to throw myself*
> *Prostrate before her. Scarcely could I quell*
> *The giddy rapture.*

The significant avowal addressed by Dante to Beatrice: "Into a free man thou transform'st a slave," the seal of all great spiritual love, was repeated by Goethe in his letters to Charlotte, and is again repeated in Tasso:

> *Over my spirit's depths there comes a change;*
> *Relieved from dark perplexity I feel,*
> *Free as a god, and all I owe to you.*

Very interesting is also a remark which Goethe made to Eckermann: "Woman is a silver vessel in which we men lay golden apples. I did not deduce my idea of woman from reality, but I was born with it, or I conceived it—God knows how." These notable words, deliberately pronounced, reveal Goethe's feeling very clearly; he knows that there is a little self-deception in his attitude towards woman, but he consciously and lovingly clings to it. His pronouncements are not contradictions; it is natural, almost essential, that in the soul of the highly-gifted and highly-developed representative of a mature civilisation the whole wealth of human emotions should be revivified. He possesses all psychical qualities—at least potentially—and one element after the other regains life and becomes productive. We shall see this with startling clearness when we come to examine the emotional life of Richard Wagner. The intimate connection between the individual and the entire evolutionary process of the race will then become evident.

---

4. The quotations from Tasso are from the translation of Anna Swanwick.

It is remarkable that Dante, too, wrote a poem clearly expressive of the fact that the beloved woman does not actually possess the qualities ascribed to her, but that she has been endowed with them by the imagination of her lover.

I shall discuss the emotional life of only one other poet in detail, and that one is Michelangelo. For the most part the poets whose emotions were akin to that of Dante and Goethe were men who created their ideal woman because reality left them unsatisfied. In passing I will mention Beethoven, and his touching letter to his "immortal love" ("My angel, my all, my I!"), whose name, in spite of all the strenuous attempts to discover it, is to this day not known with any certainty; even if it should ever be discovered, Beethoven's "immortal love" will yet remain a figment of his brain, based on a human woman.

Together with Beethoven, we may notice the other great "old bachelor" Grillparzer, and his eternal fiancée Kathi Fröhlich, and the critical Hebbel, who at the time of composing "Genovefa" wrote in his diary: "All earthly love is merely the road to the heavenly love."

BEFORE CLOSING THIS CHAPTER, I must draw attention to a strange fact in connection with the psychology of races. All nations endowed with fair mental gifts and a sympathetic understanding of nature, have in the period of their youth and anthropomorphistic and animistic thought worshipped light, and its source, the sun, as the supreme deity, the giver of joy and abundance. All the benevolent deities of the Arians were celestial beings, all the malevolent divinities spirits of darkness: Olympian gods and the demons of the netherworld—Aesir and Giants. To the naïve mind of the Indo-Germanic races it appeared a matter of course that the sun, the conqueror of night and winter, the fertilizing, life-giving deity, should be worshipped as the active male principle, and represented as a god, while on the other hand the moon was usually conceived as a female deity. In primitive Christianity Christ, as the bringer of light, was worshipped under the symbol of the sun. Thus we naturally find in the old and new Indo-Germanic languages the designation of the sun—or the sun-god—of the masculine gender. In the following words our word *sun* is easily recognisable:

> *Savar and svari (the oldest Indo-Germanic tongue).*
> *svar and surya (Sanscrit; savitar—the sungod).*
> *saval (the oldest European language).*

savel (Gracco-Italian).
sol (Latin and related languages).

In the Germanic languages and in the Prussian-Lithuanian both genders occur. (Gothic sunnan and Old High-German sunno). *Sol* in the Norse Edda is a female deity, and the Anglo-Saxon *sol* is also feminine. The transition from the male to the female gender was achieved in the Middle-High-German language of the twelfth and thirteenth centuries, and the German language is the only one in which the word *sun* is feminine. As the old Teutonic deities of light were male (Baldur and Sigurd), this change of gender must seem strange. The Germanic tribes at all times observed natural phenomena with the greatest attention, borrowed their ethical symbols from nature and used natural objects to represent their highest values. The change of gender of the supreme symbol of divinity, the sun, can only be explained by the fact that in the period of woman-worship the highest value was no longer felt as male but as female, that secretly a goddess had usurped the place of a god. Very likely the minnesingers finally fixed the female gender when it had become problematical, and worshipped the loved woman under the divine symbol of "Lady Sun."

The great erotic, Heinrich of Morungen, says in one of his poems that his lady is radiant "as the sun at break of day." And also:

> *My lady shines into the heart*
> *As through the glass the sun does shine;*
> *Thus the beloved lady mine*
> *Is sweet as May, full of delight,*
> *Unclouded sunshine, golden light.*

Mary, who had been called *Maris Stella*, the morning star, gradually assumed the symbol of the all-conquering sun. Suso, in one of his poems, still clinging to the older epithet, makes use of a metaphor corresponding to the breaking of the sun through clouds. "When the radiant morning star, Mary, broke through the suffering of thy darkened heart, it was saluted with gladness and with these words: Greeting, beautiful, rising morning star, from the fathomless depths of all loving hearts!" But he also calls Mary: "Thou dazzling mirror of the Eternal Sun!" And his Biography contains the following beautiful passage: "And his eyes were opened and he fell on his knees, saluting the rising morning star, the tender queen of the light of heaven; as the little birds in the summer time salute the day, so he saluted the luminous bringer of the eternal day, and he spoke his salutation not mechanically, but with a sweet low singing of his soul." This is pure and genuine nature-worship mingled with the worship of Mary.

So much for Suso. In Goethe's *Faust*, Doctor Marianus prays:

> *In thy tent of azure blue,*
> *Queen supremely reigning,*
> *Let me now thy secret view,*
> *Vision high obtaining.*

It is obvious that here the Queen of Heaven and the sun are conceived as one. Eichendorff makes use of the metaphor:

> *The sun is smiling languidly*
> *Like to a woman wondrous sweet.*

The typically un-Teutonic modern poet, Alfred Mombert, on the other hand, conceives the sun as a youth, and contrary to all custom, calls a poem: *Der* Sonnengeist (the sun-spirit).

The great Italians, also, were not unaware of this change of the sex of the supreme value; at the conclusion of the *Paradise* there is a passage (in St. Bernard's prayer) which points to a connection in Dante's mind between the sun and the Queen of Heaven:

> *"The love that moves the sun in heaven!"*

(d) Michelangelo

IN MICHELANGELO WE MEET THE spirit of Plato and the plastic genius of Greece raised to a higher plane and lit by the peculiar glory of Christianity—the conception of the soul as an absolute value. Michelangelo was thrilled by a passionate love of beauty; beauty absolute, eternal and immutable. He felt profoundly the need of salvation, and he possessed an unprecedented power of spiritual vision. In the end, added to all these things, came consuming love for a woman, love raised to the pitch of self-destruction, an adoration which entitles us to regard him, next to Dante, as the greatest metaphysical lover of all times.

At the court of the Medici at Florence, Ficinio had founded a Platonic Academy, where Plato's works and the writings of Plotinus—his greatest pupil—were after two thousand years translated and elucidated. Many read and a few understood, but only in Michelangelo did the spirit of Platonic Hellenism revive and become productive; the Platonic ideal of a purely masculine culture, aesthetically and spiritually perfect, illumined his soul; once again the unconditional cult of beauty and the love of the perfect male form, which speaks to us from the *Dialogues*, quickened an imagination, and boyhood and youth were portrayed in a manner which has never since been equalled.

Nearly all Michelangelo's youthful male figures—with the exception, perhaps, of the gigantic David—deviate from the decidedly masculine and approach the mean, the human in the abstract; thus they seem to us imbued with a quality of femininity; they even exhibit decidedly female characteristics. I have in mind first and foremost the youths depicted on the ceiling of the Sistine Chapel (the most soulful adolescent figures in the world), but also Bacchus, St. John, Adonis and the figures in the background of the Holy Family at Florence. Cupid and David Apollo (in the Bargello) are almost hermaphroditic, and even the Adam, and the unfinished Slaves in the Bobili Gardens exhibit female characteristics. Without going further into detail I would draw attention to the breasts and thighs, which positively raise a doubt on the question of sex. (I am referring to the two youths above the Erythrean Sybil.) Seen from a distance they create the impression of female figures, while the youth above Jeremiah is a perfect Hellenic *ephebos*. On the other hand—with the exception of two of his early Madonnas and, perhaps, Eve—he has not given us one glorified female figure; all his women are characterised by something careworn and unlovely; some of his old women—most strikingly the Cumaic Sybil—are depicted with absolutely masculine features, masculine figures and gigantic musculature. His ideal was the Hellenic ideal, was a human form neither man nor woman; all extremes, but also all peculiarities and everything personal, were, if not completely suppressed, at any rate pushed into the background. We regard this ideal, which is alien to our inherent nature, with a feeling akin to contempt, for the modern ideal is male and female, but it nevertheless was of great moment in the obliteration of sex and the accentuation of the purely human. The Platonic (and also Michelangelo's) love of young men was in its essence pure love of humanity, love of the perfect human body and the perfect human soul, whose greatest harmony was achieved in the adolescent. Moreover, the superior mental endowment of the boy made an intelligent conversation—so highly appreciated by Platonists and neo-Platonists—possible, whereas with a girl a man could only jest.

Civilisations and individuals inclining to erotic male friendships are endowed with great plastic talent. Artists and poets whose genius lies in the direction of the plastic arts rather than in music, frequently have homo-sexual leanings. A musical talent, however, is as a rule accompanied by the love of woman. I know of no great musician, or great lyrical poet, inclined to erotic friendships with men. The simple song suggests the love of woman, the artificial metre, let us say the Greek rhythm, the love of man. I am, however, merely pointing out this connection, without drawing any conclusions.

The poems addressed by Michelangelo to Tommaso dei Cavalieri breathe a deep longing for friendship and complete surrender, but above all things for a return of affection; all barriers between the friends must be thrown down, "for one soul is living in two bodies."

These poems are calm and well-balanced, and differ greatly from the rest of his poetry.

> *If each the other love, himself foregoing,*
> *With such delight, such savour and so well*
> *That both to one sole end their wills combine.*

(Transl. by J.A. SYMONDS)

Michelangelo painted "Ganymede" for Tommaso, and even at a ripe old age he addressed poems to Cechino Bracci, who died at the age of seventeen.

His contempt of woman, without which the spirit of classical Greece, too, is unthinkable, formed a parallel to his male friendships.

In the prime of his life the Platonic element was superseded by the other great element which stirred his soul so profoundly. Exceeding the perfection of form of antique statuary, his later works throb with a spiritual and passionate life quite peculiar to him; an inward fire seems to consume his ardent figures. They are not creatures of this earth, a breath of eternity has touched them; they are an embodiment of the Platonic heritage which accounts all earthly things as symbols of eternal beauty, fertilised and glorified by a deep mourning over human destiny and a longing for deliverance. And when his years were already beginning to decline, Vittoria Colonna came into his life, a semblance and symbol of divine perfection. The love which took possession of him transformed his whole life and lifted it into religion. In his tempestuous soul this first love, coming so late in life, far exceeded human limits; it became adoration and religious ecstasy. Michelangelo, who could not tolerate in friendship any other relationship than that of complete self-surrender and equality, threw himself into the very dust before his love and debased himself almost to self-destruction.

His book of poems is filled with an unspeakable longing for the perfection of earthly beauty and for eternity; and his beloved mistress is the sole symbol of this metaphysical climax. Earthly beauty is but an imperfect semblance of the divine beauty, the embodiment of which is his love. We meet all the familiar motives; he is nothing before her; he is unworthy of existence; he is like the moon receiving her light from the sun; love has raised him from his base condition and is teaching him the futility of all he had hitherto valued.

> *Yea, well I see what folly 'twere to think*
> *That largess dropped from thee like dews from heaven*
> *Could ever be paid by work so frail as mine.*

> (*Transl. by* J.A. Symonds)

And of love he says:

> *From loftiest stars shoots down a radiance all their own,*
> *Drawing the soul above,*
> *And such, we say, is love.*

> (*Transl. by* Harford)

His poems, which would proclaim him a great poet if he were not an even greater sculptor, breathe an emotion unsurpassed in its intensity. They reveal to us in an almost unique manner the emotional process which culminated in the deification of the beloved. If we did not know that Vittoria Colonna was an historical individual, not much younger than Michelangelo himself, and (if we are to credit her portrait) a very plain woman with a large masculine nose, we might be tempted to believe her to be a mythical personage like Beatrice Portinari, or Margaret in *Faust*. But the conviction that all true perfection was centred only in her, now faced his art and threw its terrible shadow over it.

"Michelangelo conceived love in the Platonic sense," wrote his friend and biographer, Condivi; but this is only a part of the truth. In the heart of Michelangelo there took place the tremendous reconciliation between the Greek cult of beauty and the religion of the beyond; he blended the finest blossom of Hellenism with the profoundest spirit of Christianity; he sublimated Plato and Dante into a higher intuition; the *eroico furore* of his contemporary, Giordano, had found an embodiment. The two great rays which illuminated his life: the perfect earthly beauty to which destiny had called him, and the boundless religious longing, the last fundamental force of his soul, converged in the glorified woman. Vittoria appeared to him as the solution of the world-discord, a solution which he had no right to expect, a miracle. She was the greatest experience of his great life, an experience which almost broke him. More than once the thought of Vittoria filled him with sudden dread. In her he had seen God and the world in one. The powerful effect of this on so self-reliant a character, a man who had been unable to find much sympathy with patrons and friends, to whom women had meant nothing, may easily be imagined. All at once he had found a centre, and more than that—a solution of all the discords of life, of the eternal dualism of the earthly and the divine. His love was not the love of a youth stretching out feelers to the world beyond, but the final creed of a lonely life which had known nothing but beauty and divinity. With the passion characteristic of him, he threw himself into this new experience and made it his fate, flinging world and art aside. Before Vittoria he ceased to be a sculptor and became a worshipper.

We realise the great difference between this worship and the worship of Dante. The latter formed the consciousness of eternity, and became a poet, early in life. He never doubted the profoundest truth, the metaphysical importance of his love; but in the case of Michelangelo, the love of an old man was the last event in a life consumed by restlessness. The adoration of this mysogynist was almost an act of despair; not a sweet delivery from doubt, but a source of fresh shocks. It problematised his whole previous existence and nullified the work of his life. For before this new experience—perfection, met in the flesh—art broke down. The greatest of sculptors never made an attempt to imprison the beauty which had appeared to his soul in marble or in canvas, deeply convinced that such an achievement was beyond the power of earthly endeavour.

Before Vittoria Michelangelo became deeply conscious of his inmost self; she gave direction to his longing and was its symbol; she was the perfection for which he had always striven—and he despaired of his art.

> *Thy beauty it befell in yonder spheres:*
> *A symbol of salvation, bright'ning heaven*
> *Th' Eternal Artist sent it down to earth;*
> *If it diminish, years succeeding years,*
> *My love will lend it but a greater worth.*
> *Age cannot fade the beauty God has given.*

And the conviction that only the idea of eternal beauty has any value, and that all earthly things are as nothing before it, became stronger and more tormenting. One instance from many:

> *As heat from fire, from loveliness divine*
> *The mind that worships what recalls the sun,*
> *From whence she sprang, can be divided never.*

> (*Transl.* by J.A. SYMONDS)

In the same way he realised the futility of earthly love compared to metaphysical love:

> *The one love soars, the other downward tends,*
> *The soul lights this while that the senses stir.*

And:

> *The highest beauty only I desire.*

It is extraordinary, however, that even this ecstatic adorer vaguely suspected that he himself might be the creator of the beauty which he saw in his mistress. In a sonnet he asks Cupid whether her beauty really exists, or whether it is a delusion of his senses, and he receives the reply:

The beauty thou discernest all is hers;
But grows in radiance as it soars on high.

(J.A. Symonds)

It is indescribably tragic to watch Michelangelo slowly despairing of his own genius and art, and becoming more and more dominated by the thought of the futility of all earthly things and all earthly beauty. The religious conception of eternity and transcendent beauty, the *forma universale* became his last refuge. After Vittoria's death Michelangelo said to Condivi: "I have only one regret and that is that I never kissed Vittoria's brow or lips when she lay dying." More and more he brooded on sin and salvation, incarnation and crucifixion. The beloved mistress had become the sole herald of eternal truths. Melancholy and mourning took possession of his soul with an iron grip; he could conceive of only one happiness, death closely following on birth. But the thought of death again was seized and symbolised with the old artistic passion:

And cleansed by fire, I shall live for ever.

And as the flames are soaring to the sky,
I, changed and purified, shall soar to heaven.

Oh, blissful day! When in a single flash
Time slips away into eternity—
The sun no longer rides across the skies. . .

Michelangelo was conscious of his near kinship with Dante; he illustrated a copy of the *Divine Comedy* which, unfortunately, is lost, and wrote a poem on Dante in which the following lines occur:

Were I but he! Born for like lingering pains,
Against his exile, coupled with his good,
I'd gladly change the world's inheritance.

(*Transl. by* J.A. Symonds)

The paintings in the Sistine Chapel, with their materialised thoughts of destiny, retribution and eternity, originated in a feeling akin to the feeling underlying the *Divine Comedy*. Both here and there the creation of celestial and infernal spirits was the outcome of the infinite longing of the artistic imagination. Both men could spend the human and creative passions with which their souls were thrilled only on the supreme and universal. The eternal destiny of man, fate, sin, the futility of all earthly things, the relationship of the world to God, love surpassing all human limits and aspiring to the eternal—these are the common objects over which they brooded. But while it was given to Dante to create his picture of the world in harmony with his own soul, and account it a true representation of the world-system; while his world was a definite place with a beginning and an end, and his life-work remained in harmony with his own soul, and the universe, Michelangelo's lacerated soul could find peace only in the ultimate truth, which filled his heart, and to which he yearned to give plastic life, only to be unsatisfied after achieving it. George Simmel, in a profound work, draws our attention to the infinite melancholy which overshadows all Michelangelo's figures, because his genius aspired to express the inexpressible. Even the supremest plastic representation of the passion and longing for the transcendental which thrilled his soul did not satisfy him. This tragedy is the tragedy of the metaphysical erotic overflowing its own specific domain. Dante's faith in the absolute value of his work and in the truth of the consummation of his love in eternity—which was the sustaining power of his life—remained unshaken, but Michelangelo lost his faith in his work; art and love forsook him and withdrew into a transcendental world which he could divine, but could not grasp. His faith was no blissful certainty; he knew no more than the dark aspect of things; the imperfection of even the sublimest, of his art and his love.

Shakespeare's genius could breathe life into all things human, and he found satisfaction in doing so. Michelangelo's creative, plastic power seemed illimitable; he possessed all the gifts an artist could possibly have, but from year to year his conviction of the futility of all earthly things grew to a profounder certainty. He had knocked at the iron gate of humanity with his hammer and his chisel; they had broken into fragments and sorrow made him dumb. There is a stage in the life of every genius when he comes to this gate, when he has to show his credentials and reveal the inmost kernel of his being. Dante attempted to grasp the transcendental in one gigantic vision, Goethe timidly shrank back from it.

In examining the prophets and youths in the Sistine Chapel, or the chained men in the Louvre, who seem unable to bear existence, and are therefore "slaves" of the earth; or in contemplating the half-finished slaves in the Boboli Gardens, who seem almost to burst the stone in their wild longing for a higher life; or in reading his last sonnets, we can conceive a vague idea of the deep melancholy darkening the life of this man, a gloom which was not the melancholy of the individual, but of all humanity, unable and unwilling to deceive itself further. Can there be a greater tragedy than the tragedy of this incomparable artist, looking back at the work of his lifetime with despair?

> *For art and wit and passion fade and vanish,*
> *Countless achievements, ever new and great,*
> *Are naught but dross within the sight of heaven.*

To Vasari he sent a sonnet denouncing the artistic passion which abandons itself completely to art:

> *Now know I well that that fond phantasy*
> *Which made my soul the worshipper and thrall*
> *Of earthly art is vain.*

> *(Transl. by* J.A. SYMONDS)

Faith, is to him "the mercy of mercies," for he has never possessed its deepest conviction.

But the passion which burned in him remained unquelled to the last: his soul is torn between love and the thought of death.

> *Flames of love*
> *And chill of death are battling in my heart.*

He longed to break away from love and find peace, and he called on death for delivery, but in vain:

> *Burdened with years and full of sinfulness*
> *With evil customs grown inveterate,*
> *Both deaths I dread that both before me wait,*
> *Yet feed my heart on poisonous thoughts no less.*

> *(Transl. by* J.A. SYMONDS)

And later on he thanks love again for being his deliverer, and not death.

Michelangelo poured all his heart into these last sonnets. We see his solitary and heroic age overshadowed by the thought of death. His whole soul is wrapped in gloom; art is vanity, love is sorrow, the thought of the futility of all things frames the portrait of his love with a wreath of black laurel. He ponders on his life, and comes to the conclusion that

Among the many years not one was his.

This man, the supremest creative genius the world has known, accused himself of having wasted his life.

No song of praise ever rose to the Deity from Michelangelo's heart, as it did at least once or twice during his lifetime from the heart of Beethoven. He never had one hour of true inward peace. He represents the metaphysical world-feeling which (in addition to love) is the foundation of the deification of woman, but it has grown into immensity, and has been lifted to a higher plane; not only love, but all life is felt as fragmentary and pointing to a world beyond. If at an earlier stage it was the love of woman which could not find its consummation on earth, it is now the whole of our earthly life and all our aspirations which can only attain to their highest meaning and to final truth in a metaphysical existence. The tragedy of metaphysical love has deepened into the supreme tragedy of life.

III

Perversions of Metaphysical Eroticism

(a) The Brides of Christ

Hitherto I have confined myself to the analysis of the emotional life of man, but there are two other points which must be taken into account. The first is the question of woman's attitude towards the lofty position assigned to her by man; the second and more important one is the question as to whether the women of that period exhibit in their emotional life any traces of a feeling akin to the deification of their sex? The reply to the first question is simple enough. Naturally the adoration and worship of their lovers could not have been anything but pleasant to women. There is a poem by the talented Provençal Countess Beatrix de Die, which betrays genuine sorrow at the infidelity of her friend, and at the same time leaves no doubt that she—and probably a great many others—took the eulogies showered upon them by the enraptured poets, literally. Once again woman accepts the position thrust upon her by man, not this time the position of a drudge, but that of a perfect and godlike being. Countess Beatrix credits herself with all the qualities with which the imagination of her worshipper had endowed her, as if they were unquestionable facts.

> *Hence all my songs will be with sadness fraught.*
> *My lover fills my soul with bitter woe,*
> *And yet is all the happiness I know.*
> *My grace and favour all avail me naught.*
> *My sparkling wit, my loveliness supreme,*
> *They cannot hold his love and tender thought,*
> *Of all my lofty worth bereft I seem.*

But far more interesting than this psychological misunderstanding on the part of the much-lauded sex, is the question as to whether the emotional life of woman matured anything that can be called a worship of man? The answer to this is a decided "no." At no time in the history of woman do we find even the smallest indication of a parallel phenomenon; the profound and tragic dualism of the Middle Ages—one result of which was the spiritual love of woman—passed her by without touching her. In the feminine soul conflict apparently results not in tragedy and productivity, but in morbidness and hysteria.

It may be argued that the love of Jesus, which inspired both the nuns of the Middle Ages and those of a later period, represents a type of man-worship; but in examining all these more or less famous nuns and ascetics we find, instead of genuine spirituality, a concealed and often morbid condition, which in some cases degenerated into hysteria. The dualistic period, the age of metaphysical love, made no impression upon the female soul. There can be no doubt that the emotional life of woman, in strict contrast to the emotional life of man, has had no evolution, and can therefore have no history. It is unadulterated nature and, in its way, it is perfect.

In studying the female mystics, we find an imitation of metaphysical eroticism sufficiently transparent to be easily recognised, even by the layman, as belonging to the domain of pathology. These ecstatics were animated not by a pure, but by an impure spirit. Perverted sensualists, they believed their hearts to be filled with spiritual love. Contrary to the striving of the greater number of the men, who raised their love into heaven so as to keep it pure, and made it one with their religious aspirations, all the figures and symbols of religion were used by these women as an outlet and a foil to their sexuality. The loving soul repairing to the nuptial chamber is the transparent veil of desire half-concealed by religious conceptions. Women have described similar situations in metaphors which—for sensuous passion—leave nothing to be desired, even the famous love-potion of Tristan is not wanting.

The material is abundant, and I have repeatedly touched upon it in previous chapters. At the period of great mystical enthusiasm (the twelfth and thirteenth centuries) this morbid love of God was a sinister attendant phenomenon of true mysticism. Whole convents were seized by epidemics of hysteria, the women writhed in convulsions, flogged each other, sang hymns day and night and had hallucinations—for all of which the love of God, or the temptation of the devil, were made responsible.

Among the more notable of these pseudo-mystics are Christine Ebner (the author of a book entitled, *On the Fullness of Mercy*), and Mary of Oignies, a passionate worshipper of Christ who mutilated herself in her ecstasies and who, on her deathbed, still sang: "How beautiful art Thou, oh, my Lord God!"

A shining exception among the German nuns of that time was Mechthild of Magdeburg, a woman of rare gifts. She was a genuine mystic, but she, too, revelled in fervent, sensuous metaphors, and it would be an interesting task to separate the two elements in her case; but, having admitted her genuine mysticism in a previous chapter, I will here restrict myself to a few quotations which show her from her other side. Her *Dialogue between Love and the Soul* abounds in passages like the following: "Tell my beloved that his chamber is prepared, and that I am sick with love of him." "The closer the embrace, the sweeter the kisses." "Then He took the soul into His divine arms, and placing His fatherly hand on her bosom, He gazed into her face and kissed her right well." Mechthild, too, was ready to die with love.

Everyone of the most celebrated Brides of Christ belonged to the Latin race; they were hysterics, and as such have long been claimed by the psychopathist.

The love of Jesus professed by Catherine of Siena (1347–1388), a clever politician, who was in correspondence with the leading statesmen of her time, found vent in passages like the following:

"I desire, then, that you withdraw into the open side of the Son of God, who is a bottle so full of perfume that even the things which are sinful become fragrant. There the bride reclines on a bed of fire and blood. There the secret of the heart of the Son of God is revealed and made manifest. Oh! Thou overflowing cup, refreshing and intoxicating every loving and yearning heart." "I long to behold the body of my Lord!" And straightway the bridegroom appeared to her, opened his side and said to her: "Now drink as much of my blood as thou desirest."

But the saint who enjoyed the greatest fame—partly on account of her frequent portrayal by the plastic arts—was doubtless St. Teresa (Teresia de Jesus), a Spanish nun (1515–1582). During childhood and early youth she suffered from serious illnesses, and on one occasion was even believed to be dead. "Before I felt the presence of God," she says in her biography, "I experienced for some time a very delightful sensation, a sensation which I believe one is partly able to produce at will (!), a pleasure which is neither quite sensuous, nor quite spiritual, but which comes from God." She describes in her "Life" four stages of prayer, which gradually lead the soul to God: "There is no joy to be compared with the joy which the Lord giveth to the soul in its exile. So great is this delight that frequently it seems that the least thing would make it forsake the body for ever." "When the soul seeks God in this way," the saint feels with supreme delight her strength ebbing away and a trance stealing over her until, devoid of breath and all physical strength she can only move her hand with great pain. The delights experienced by her are described in great detail and very sensuous language; hysterical conditions, such as painful convulsions, and hallucinations, are represented as religious phenomena. "It is dreadful what one has to suffer from confessors who do not understand these things," she says in one of her writings with deep regret.

St. Teresa relates her life with the well-known long-winded self-complacency of the hysterical subject. She frequently had visions of Jesus, and again and again she emphasised the beauty of his hands. "Standing by my side, he said to me: 'I have come to thee, my daughter, I am here; it is I; show me thy hands.' And it seemed to me that he took my hands in his, and laid them in his side. 'Behold my wound,' he said, 'thou art not separated from me; bear this brief exile on earth. . .'" etc.

On one occasion she had a vision of an angel whom she describes as follows: "He was not tall but small, very beautiful, his face so radiant that he seemed to be one of the highest angels, who are, I believe, all fire. . . in his hand he held a golden spear, at the point of which was a little flame; he appeared to thrust this spear into my heart again and again; it penetrated my entrails, and as he drew it out he seemed to draw them out also, and leave me on fire with a great love of God. The pain was so intense that I could not but sigh deeply; yet so surpassing was the sweetness of this pain that it made me wish never to be without it. It is not physical, but spiritual pain, although the body often suffers greatly from it. The caressing love between God and the soul is so sweet that I implore Him of His mercy to let all those experience it who believe that I am lying."

The treatise *Thoughts of the Love of God on some Words of the Song of Songs* is crowded with purely sensuous passages. In accordance with the general custom, she interprets this naïvely sensual Semitic poem allegorically, becomes tremendously excited in meditating on the kiss of the beloved and discusses the question of what the soul should do to "satisfy so sweet a bridegroom."

In the pamphlet *The Fortress of the Soul and its Seven Dwellings*, St. Teresa describes similar states of mind: "The bridegroom commands the doors of the dwellings to be closed and also the gates of the fortress and its surrounding walls. In freeing the soul from the body, he stops the body's breathing so that, even if the other senses are not quite deadened, speech is impossible. At other times all sensuous perceptions disappear simultaneously; body and hands grow rigid and it seems as if the soul had left the body, which is scarcely breathing. This condition is of short duration. The rigidity passes away to some extent, the body slowly regains life, the breath comes and goes, only to die away again and thus endow the soul with greater freedom. But this deep trance does not endure long." She continues to describe her ecstasies and is careful to point out the complete fusion of supreme delight and bodily pain. Perhaps no hysterical subject has ever described her states of mind so well. Her avowal (made in a letter to Father Rodrigue Alvarez) of her complete unconsciousness of her body is quite in harmony with those states of rapture. She wrote a number of spiritual love-songs which are said to be conspicuous for their ardour and beauty; probably they have never been translated from the original Spanish.

Finally there is the famous Madame Guyon (1648–1717), who—in addition to many other works—wrote a very detailed autobiography. She lived with her husband, whom she treated with coldness, finding her sole joy in her spiritual intercourse with God. "I desire only the divine love which thrills the soul with inexpressible bliss, the love which seems to melt my whole being." God burns her with His fire and still trembling with delight, she says to Him: "Oh, Lord! The greatest libertine, if Thou didst make him experience Thy love as Thou didst make me experience it, would forswear carnal pleasure and strive only after Thy divine love." "I was like a person intoxicated with wine or love, unable to think of anything but my passion," etc. The fact that she sought in this love the pleasure of the senses is very apparent.

We are not concerned here with the problem of how far these women may be regarded as pathological cases; all of them were filled with a vague feminine desire for self-surrender, which they projected on a celestial being, either because they did not come into contact with a suitable terrestrial object, or because the impulse was abnormal from the beginning. But their spiritual love never rose above empty sentimentality and hysterical rapture. All of them, and some of them were highly gifted, were thrilled with the love of Jesus, they had visions of the "sweet wounds of the Saviour," and so on; but their emotion did not kindle the smallest spark of creative power. The Queen of Heaven, on the other hand, was a free creation of spiritually loving poets and monks.

The women imitated metaphysical love and distorted it; sexual impulse, arrogantly attempting to reach beyond the earth, reigned in the place of spiritual, deifying love.

I have included these phenomena not for their own sakes, but to indicate my boundary-line, for very frequently these women are cited as genuine mystics. Even Schopenhauer mentions these "saints" in one breath with German mystics and Indian philosophers; he calls Madame Guyon "a great and beautiful soul whose memory I venerate." And yet there can be no doubt that it is not the fictitious object of love which is conclusive, but the emotion of the lover: the sensualist can approach God and the Virgin with inflamed senses, but to the lover every woman is divine.

The result of this chapter is as far as our investigation is concerned, negative. The deifying love of man has no parallel phenomenon in the emotional life of woman.

(*b*) Sexual Mystics

Sexual mysticism is a contradiction in itself, because true mysticism has nothing whatever to do with sexuality. But frequently suppressed sexuality, secretly luxuriating, takes possession of the whole soul, and a religious construction is put on the results. The sexually excited subject attributes religious motives to his ecstasy. I have no hesitation in asserting that the majority of these ecstasies—especially in the case of women—are rooted in sexuality, and that this so-called mysticism is nothing but a deviation or wrong interpretation of the sexual impulse. The same thing applies to the flagellants of the declining Middle Ages, and some Protestant sects of modernity. The raptures of St. Teresa and Madame Guyon, also, belong to this category, however much the fact may be concealed by pseudo-religious conceptions. I have no doubt that Eastern mysticism, too, grew up on a sexual foundation, but (as I have done all along) I will limit my subject to the civilisation of Europe.

This counterfeit mysticism, fed from dubious sources and calling itself love of God, taints the pure intuitions of some of the genuine mystics and metaphysical erotics; they were not always able to steer clear of spurious outgrowths. (Here, too, the psychological naïveté of mediaeval times must to some extent be held responsible.) Conspicuous amongst these is St. Bernard of Clairvaux, who in his *Sermones in Canticum* took the "Song of Songs" as a base for mystically-sexual imaginings.

There is nothing really new in this direction. But I will cite a few stanzas written by St. Bernard which might equally well have come from one of the amorous nuns:

To The Side-Wound Of Christ

Lord, with my mouth I touch and worship Thee,
With all the strength I have I cling to Thee,
With all my love I plunge my heart in Thee,
My very life blood would I draw from Thee,
Oh, Jesus! Jesus! Draw me unto Thee!

How sweet Thy savour is! Who tastes of Thee,
Oh, Jesus Christ, can relish naught but Thee!
Who tastes Thy living sweetness lives by Thee;
All else is void; the soul must die for Thee,
So faints my heart—so would I die for Thee!

(*Transl. by* EMILY MARY SHAPCOTE)

The greatest religious poet of all times after St. Bernard was Jacopone da Todi, who also, though rarely, revelled in fervid utterances. The Latin hymn, *Stabat Mater Speciosa*, ascribed to him, is spurious. I quote a translation taken from the Rosary of the B.V.M.

Other Virgins far transcending,
Virgin, be not thou unbending,
To thy humble suppliant's suit.

Grant me then, to thee united,
By the love of Christ excited,
Here to sing my jubilee.

But he is undoubtedly the author of the following stanzas:

Soaring upwards love-enkindled,
Does the soul rejoice, afire
In her glad triumphant flight.
Earthly cares to naught have dwindled,
Love's sweet footfall's drawing nigh her
To espouse his heart's delight.
All transformed and naked quite,
Laughing low, with joy imbued,

> *Pure, and like a snake renewed,*
> *Love divine will ever tend her.*

But poems like the following undoubtedly originated in a truly religious and pure sentiment:

> *Enwrapt in love thine arms Him fast enfolding,*
> *So closely clasp Him that they loose Him never;*
> *And in thy heart His sacred image holding,*
> *Far from the path of sin thou'lt journey ever.*
> *His death in twain shall blast thy callous heart*
> *As once the solid rock He rent apart.*

The most distinguished among the fervid lovers of God of later times were the saints Jean de la Croix, Alfonso da Liguori, and François de Sales. The *Tract of the Love of God*, written by François de Sales, surpasses everything ever achieved in this direction.

I will not dilate further on this barren aspect of emotionalism so easily traceable through the later centuries in many a Catholic and Protestant sentimentalist, but will conclude this chapter with a brief discussion of Novalis. If I mention this poet in this connexion it is not because I desire to depreciate his genius, but because, possessing as he did, in a rare degree, depth of feeling and power of expression, he is an important witness of an unusual type. True, here and there his poems are reminiscent of Jacopone, but he is not sufficiently ingenuous, and is altogether too morbid to be classed with that ardent fanatic. He shares with Jacopone and other poets the yearning to grasp transcendental things with the senses, to approach the Deity with a love which cannot be called anything but sensuous. Novalis' *Hymns to the Night* are the most magnificent example of this perfect interpenetration of sensuous and transcendental love, and at the same time represent a complete fusion of the love he bore to his fiancée, who died young, and the worship of Mary. Night has opened *infinite eyes* in us, and we behold the secret of love unfolding itself in the heart of this poet, at once unique and pathetic, lofty and morbid. The whole universe he conceives as a female being for whose embrace he is longing. It is a new emotion: neither the chaste worship of the Madonna, nor the sexually-mystic striving to embrace with the soul. The night gives birth to a foreboding which excites and soothes all vague desires. The lover thus soliloquises of the night:

In infinite space.
Thou'dst dissolve,
If it held thee not,
If it bound thee not,
And thrilled thee,
That afire
Thou begettest the world.
Verily before thou art I was,
With my sex
The mother sent me
To live in thy world,
And to hallow it
With love.

Here the ancient, mystical longing to become one with God is conceived under the symbol of the night. (A symbol which we shall meet again, magnified, in Wagner's *Tristan*.)

Lo! Love has burst its prison.
No parting now shall be,
And life's full tide has risen
Like to a boundless sea.
One night of love supernal,
Only one golden song,
And the face of the Eternal
To light our path along.

In addition, Novalis was a perfect woman-worshipper. He loved the Middle Ages and Catholicism. "The reformation killed Christianity; henceforth Christianity has ceased to exist." "Catholicism preached nothing but love for the holy, beautiful Lady of Christianity, who, endowed with divine virtue, was able to deliver all loyal hearts from the most terrible dangers." He wrote hymns to Mary in the style of the pietists, emphasising more especially the principle of motherliness:

Oh, Mary! At thy altar
A thousand hearts lie prone,
In this drear life of shadows

They yearn for thee alone.
All hoping to recover
From life's distress and smart,
If thou, oh holy Mother,
Wilt take them to thy heart.

He idolised his fiancée, who died young. "Her memory shall be my better self, a sacred image in my heart before which a sanctuary lamp is ever burning, and which will save me from the temptations of the Evil One." And through the mouth of Heinrich of Ofterdingen he proclaims: "My beloved is the abbreviation of the universe; the universe is the elongation of my beloved." "Heaven has given you to me to worship. I adore you, you are a saint, you are divine glory, you are eternal life!"

This sentimental worship of woman, combined with an all-transcending insatiable sensuousness, produced the peculiar sexually-mystic world-feeling which is so characteristic of him. Night deeply moves his soul, longing, the memory of the beloved woman, adoration for the Virgin, his fantastic conception of an incarnated universe are fused into one great emotion:

Praise to the Queen of the World!
The lofty herald
Of the sacred world.
The patroness
Of rapturous love!
Thou art coming, beloved—
Night has descended—
My soul is ravished—
Over is this earthly journey
And thou art mine again.
I gaze into thy dark, deep eyes,
And see naught but love and happiness.
We sink down on the altar of the night,
The soft couch—
The veil falls,
And kindled by the rapturous embrace,
Glows the pure fire
Of the sweet sacrifice.

The climax and unique example of sensuousness, unsurpassed for its symbols of the physical embrace, is the hymn: "Few know the Secret of Love." It is too long to give in full. The following are a few stanzas:

Would that the ocean
Blushed!
And in fragrant flesh
Melted the rock!
Infinite is the sweet repast,
Never satisfied is love;
Nor close, nor fast enough
Can it hold the beloved.
By ever more tender lips
Transformed, the past ecstasy
Grows closer, more intimate.
Rapturous love
Thrills the soul;
Hungrier and thirstier
Grows the heart.
And thus the transports of love
Endure for ever.

Here the remotest limit has been reached—sensuousness seems to flow into eternity, voluptuousness would shatter the world to pieces and create a new relationship of things. Before this poem all ecstasies of sensuousness masquerading as cosmic emotion are dull and timid. The transcendent symbols of Catholicism are used to guide the insatiable sensuous imagination to metaphysics. "Who can say that he understands the nature of blood?" Novalis may ask this question. It is truly blood, human blood, longing to gush forth and pulsate through the body of the universe.

In time to come all will be body
One body;
In celestial blood,
Float the enraptured twain.

The human blood has become *celestial blood*; the voluptuousness of man, the voluptuousness of the world, and because the whole world is one body, it needs no duality; sexuality which has become a cosmic law rules over humanity, God, Christ and the universe. This hymn is the immortalisation of voluptuousness. If the love-death is the immortalisation of love unable to find satisfaction on earth, so its counterpart, cosmic sensuousness is, in the last sense, orientalism. Only a genius could invent a new, symbolic language to express feelings so alien to the European. Earthly sensuality did not satisfy Novalis, voluptuousness detached from man, voluptuousness in itself, was his dream and his religion—the supremest creation ever achieved by sexuality intensified into a cosmic emotion.

I think that I have now made clear the fact that the emotional life of man is rooted in two elements, completely distinct from the beginning: the sexual impulse and personal love. It is in studying the love of the transcendental, that culminating point of so many feelings springing from various sources, that the inherent contrast between the two fundamental principles becomes most apparent; and that we realise why they have always been intermingled both in theory and in reality.

We have last examined the attempt of sexuality to possess itself of the whole universe; we will now turn our attention to the true union of both erotic elements. This union occurred at the time when Goethe and Novalis were bringing spiritual love and cosmic sensuousness to their highest summit.

THE THIRD STAGE
(THE UNITY OF SEXUAL IMPULSE AND LOVE)

I

The Longing for the Synthesis

Humanity inherited the pairing-instinct from the animal-world; but as differentiation progressed, this instinct tended to restrict itself to a few individuals—sometimes even to a single representative only—of the other sex. In the beginning of the twelfth century a new and unprecedented emotion—spiritual love of man for woman based on personality—made its appearance, and until modern times the two fundamental erotic principles existed side by side without inner relationship. Sexuality with its various manifestations has existed from the beginning; the ultimate object of sexual intercourse is pleasure; but here and there, and parallel with sexual pleasure, there have been, in varying degrees of intensity, instances of spiritual love. In the second half of the eighteenth century there appeared—timidly at first, but gradually gaining in strength and determination—a tendency to find the sole course of every erotic emotion in the personality of the beloved, a longing no longer to dissociate sexual impulse and spiritual love, but to blend them in a harmonious whole. Personality should knit body and soul together in a higher synthesis. The first signs of this longing became apparent in the period of the French revolution; (we find traces of it in the works of Rousseau and in Goethe's *Werther*); it was developed by the romanticists and represents the typical form of modern love with all its incompleteness and inexhausted possibilities. The achievement of this eagerly desired unity, which would be synonymous with the victory of personality over the limitations of body and soul, is the great problem of modern time in the domain of eroticism. The characteristic of this third stage of eroticism is the complete triumph of love over pleasure, the neutralisation of the sexual and the generative by the spiritual and the personal. The physical and spiritual unity of the lovers has become so much supreme erotic reality, that the line of demarcation between soul and senses is completely obliterated. In extreme cases—which are not at all rare—the bodily union is not realised as anything distinct, specifically pleasurable; it does not occupy a prominent position in the complex of love; sensuous pleasure, the universal inheritance from the animal world, has been vanquished by personality, the supreme treasure of man. The characteristic of the first stage was the unquestioned sway of one of the elements of erotic life, sensual gratification (this stage has, of course, never ceased to exist), as well as the aesthetic pleasure in the beauty of the human form. The second stage gave prominence to all those spiritual qualities which were most appreciated, virtue, purity, kindness, wisdom, etc., because love rouses and embraces everything in the human soul which is perfect. In the third stage, sensuous pleasure and spiritual love no longer exist as separate elements; the personality of the beloved in its individuality is the only essential, regardless as to whether she be the bringer of weal or woe, whether she be good or evil, beautiful or plain, wise or foolish. Personality has—in principle— become the sole, supreme source of eroticism. In this stage there is no tyranny of man over woman—as in the sexual stage—no submission of man to woman—as in the stage of woman-worship; it is the stage of the complete equality of the sexes, a mutual giving and taking. If sexuality is infinite as matter, spiritual love eternal as the metaphysical ideal, the synthesis is human and personal.

Before the eighteenth century, this new erotic union did not exist as a phenomenon of civilisation, but occasionally we find it anticipated or vaguely alluded to. Some of the early German minnesingers (such as Dietmar von Aist and Kürnberg) sometimes betray, especially when speaking through the medium of a woman, sentiments prophetic of our modern sentimental ballads. The following verses by Albrecht of Johansdorf, express the reciprocity characteristic of modern love:

When two hearts are so united
That their love can never wane,
Then I ween no man should blight it,
Death alone should part the twain.

Even more modern in sentiment are the following stanzas:

This is love's measure:
Two hearts and one pleasure,
Two loves one love, nor more nor less,
And both right full of happiness.
In woe one woe,
And neither from the other go.

Though Walter von der Vogelweide adopted the contemporaneous conception of love as the source of everything good and noble ("Tell me what is Love?") he never quite accepted it:

> *Love is the ecstasy of two fond hearts,*
> *If both share equally, then love is there.*

More ancient evidence even is the definition of marriage by the scholastic Hugo of St. Victor, who had leanings towards mysticism: "Marriage is the friendship between man and woman," he says.

My knowledge of the subject cannot, of course, be unexceptional, but I do not believe that personal love of the third stage, that is, the blending of both erotic elements, was quite definitely expressed before the second half of the eighteenth century. We may be justified in maintaining that the tension between sexuality and spiritual love had been slackening in the course of the centuries, that sexuality was conceived as less diabolical, and love as less celestial than heretofore; but the principle had remained unchanged. Only the female portraits of Leonardo da Vinci are deserving of special mention; the great artist was possibly the first who artistically divined, if he did not achieve, the synthesis. The exceptional position always granted to his women—particularly to his Mona Lisa—must doubtless be ascribed to this premonition. We may be certain that Leonardo not only as artist, but as lover also, was ahead of his time; but he must be regarded as an isolated instance. The three stages apply to the eroticism of man only. His emotion soared from brutality to divinity, and then gradually became human; his feeling alone has a history. The force which seized, moulded and transformed him, had no influence over woman. Compared to man, she is to-day what she was at the beginning, pure nature. Her lover has always been everything to her; never merely a means for the gratification of the senses, nor, on the other hand, a higher being to whom she looked up and whom she worshipped with a purely spiritual love; but at all times he possessed her undivided love, unable in its naïve simplicity to differentiate between body and soul. The higher intuition, the object of the supreme erotic yearning of man, for the possession of which he has struggled for centuries, and even to-day does not fully possess, has always been a matter of course to her. She whose truest vocation is love, received from nature that which the greatest of men have striven hard to win and only half succeeded in winning. Man's profound dualism is alien to her; her greatness—

but also her limitation—lies in the simplicity and infallibility of her instinct, which has had no evolution and is consequently not liable to produce atavisms and aberrations. She is hardly conscious of the chasm between sexual instinct and personal love. Wherever this is not so, we *may* find intellectual greatness (as for instance in the case of the Empress Catherine of Russia), but as a rule we find only morbidness, despondency and callousness. To the normal woman the phenomena of dualistic eroticism appear unintelligible, even unwholesome. The unity of love is a matter of course to her, so that the third stage is practically male acquiescence to female intuition.

Even in our time, when so much is said and written about modern woman and her claims, her feeling is still perfect in itself; compared to the discord and heterogeneity of man, she represents simplicity and harmony. Both purely spiritual worship and undifferentiated sexual desire are exceptions as far as she is concerned and must still be regarded as abnormal.

This unbroken, determinative female eroticism may possibly be explained (as Weininger explains it) by woman's sexuality, which is absolute, and does not rise above the horizon of distinct consciousness, but Weininger's dualism is in this direction attempting to value and standardise something which in its essence is alien to his standard.

Psycho-physical unity, then, is the basic characteristic of female eroticism, but the state of affairs in the case of male eroticism is a very different one. A study of the gradual origin of the erotic elements will facilitate a better understanding of the relevant phenomena.

In the case of woman, the primary sexual instinct pervades the whole being; it has been refined and purified without any great fluctuations or changes; in the case of man it has always been restricted to certain regions of his physical and psychical life, and an entirely novel experience was required before it could win to the final form of personal love. This prize, in his case, is therefore enhanced by the fact of being the outcome of a long conflict; the reward of a task still showing the traces of the struggle and pain of centuries. The truth of the words "Pleasure is degrading" had been established by experience.

A few historical instances, illustrating female eroticism, will uphold my contention. In the remote days of Greek antiquity, we find an example of undivided wifely love in Alcestis, whose devotion to her husband sent her to voluntary death in order to lengthen his life. Wifely devotion accomplished what parental love could not achieve. The

Alcestis of Euripides represents a feeling very familiar to us. Penelope, the faithful martyr, is a similar instance.

At the time when spiritual love, accompanied by eccentricities and Latin treatises, gradually, and amidst heavy conflict, struggled into existence, the soul of woman was already glowing with the emotion which we, to-day, realise as love. I have three witnesses to prove this statement. The *Lais* of the French poetess Marie de France, based on Breton and Celtic motifs, are permeated by a sweet sentimentality, very nearly related to the sentiment of our popular ballads. They tell of simple feelings, of love and longing and the grief of love. One of her *lais* treats the touching story of Lanval and Guinevere, and another an episode of Tristan and Isolde.

> *De Tristan et de la reine,*
> *De leur amour qui tant fut fine,*
> *Dont ils eurent mainte doulour*
> *Puis en moururent en un jour.*

The naïve sentiment of these poems forms a delicious contrast to the contemporaneous mature and subtile art of Provence, and the entire erudite armoury of love.

A great baron declared that only the man who could carry his daughter in his arms to the summit of a certain mountain—an impossible feat—should win her hand in marriage. No man possessed strength to carry her farther than half way. But the knight whom she loved secretly went out into the world, and after years of searching, discovered a magic potion able to endow him who quaffed it with enormous strength. Full of joy he returned home and, his beloved in his arms, began the laborious ascent. Strong and jubilant, he laughed at the potion. But after a while, feeling his strength ebbing away, the maiden implored him: "Drink, I beseech thee, beloved!" "My heart is strong, to drink were waste of time." And again she pleaded: "Drink now, beloved, thy strength is diminishing fast." But he, eager to win her only by his own effort, staggered on and reached the summit, only to sink to the ground and expire. The maiden, throwing herself on his lifeless body, kissed his eyes and lips and died with him.

We recognise in this simple tale the new form of love, mutual devotion, and the thought of the consummation of this love, the *Love-death*, which was not definitely realised until six hundred years later. It originated in the Celtic soul, as the worship of woman originated in the Romanesque (the Teutonic soul shared in the development of both). It was a dream of the suppressed Celtic race, spending its whole soul in dreams and producing visions of such depth and beauty that even we of to-day cannot read them without being profoundly moved.

Next there are three love-letters written in Latin by a German woman of the twelfth century. In very touching words she tells her lover that the love of him can never be torn out of her heart. "I turn to you whom I hold for ever enclosed in my inmost heart." She promises and claims faithfulness until death: "Among thousands my heart has chosen you, you alone can satisfy my longing, and you will never find my love wanting. I trust myself to you, all my hope is centred in you. I could say a great deal more," she concludes, "but there is no need of it." And then follow the charming German stanzas:

Thou to me and I to thee,
Knit for all eternity.
In my heart art thou imprisoned,
And I threw away the key.
Nevermore canst thou be free.

In the third letter she drops the formal Latin and addresses him in intimate, simple German. But the man's replies are clumsy and strange, and plainly evidence his uncertainty of himself: "You have put a human head on a horse's neck, and the beautiful female form ends in an ugly fish's tail." It looks as if a parting were inevitable.

But the most touching testimony from the Middle Ages is the famous love story of Abélard and Héloïse. We probably possess no older document of the passionate devotion of a woman, differing in nothing from the sentiment of the present age, than the letters of Héloïse. Abélard persuaded her to take the veil and repent in a convent the sin of voluptuousness—but she knows nothing of God—her whole soul is wrapped up in her lover: "I expect no reward from God, for what I did was not done for love of Him. . . I wanted nothing from you but yourself; I desired only you, not that which belonged to you; I did not expect marriage or gifts; I did not seek to gratify my desires and do my will, but yours, and well you know that I am speaking the truth! The name of wife may seem sacred and honourable to you, but I prefer to be called your mistress or even your harlot. The more

I degraded myself for your sake, the more I hoped to find grace in your eyes. . . I renounced all the pleasures of the world to live only for you; I kept nothing for myself but the desire to belong entirely to you." Abélard's replies are pious sermons and theological treatises; he thinks of the love of the past only as *the cursed desires of the flesh*, the snare in which the devil had caught them, and urges Héloïse to thank God that henceforth they are safe. "My love which entangled both of us in sin," he says in one of his letters, "deserves not the name of love, for it was naught but carnal lust. I sought in you the gratification of my sinful desires," etc. He blessed the savage crime committed on him because it saved him for ever from the sin of voluptuousness. What Héloïse loved and treasured as her sweetest memory, was to him hell and devil's work. He wrote to her almost as if in mockery: "What splendid interest does the talent of your wisdom bear to the Lord day after day! How many spiritual daughters you have borne to Him! What a terrible loss it would have been if you had abandoned yourself to the lust of the flesh, had borne, with travail, a few earthly children, while now, with joy, you bear a great number of daughters for the kingdom of Heaven. You would have remained a woman like all the rest, but now you are far exalted even above men." This correspondence plainly reveals the tragedy of the lacerated man of the Middle Ages, as compared to the never-varying woman, emerging perfect from the hands of nature. A long and toilsome road still stretches out before him; she had reached the goal, without a struggle, at the outset. How strange is this cry of a mediaeval nun: "It seems as if the world had grown old, as if all men and all living creatures had lost their freshness, as if love had grown cold not in many, but in all hearts."

What was really the final cause of the hostility to sensuousness displayed by dualistic mediaeval Christianity? Was it not contained in eroticism itself?

This hostility was based on the fact that the world knew as yet only spiritual love and its antithesis, the sexuality which man shares with the animals; the only salvation, not merely in the Christian sense, but from the point of view of every lofty conception of civilisation, lay in the victory over animalism. The contempt of and the struggle against the lower form of eroticism animating the dualistic period was absolutely consistent; asceticism represents the highest form of culture attainable by that period. (The rejection of spiritual love was an inconsistency on the part of the clergy.) The principle of personality was the fundamental principle of Christianity; this is clearly expressed by the fact that Christianity regarded the soul as the supreme value. And what is the soul but the consciousness of human personality conceived naïvely as substance? In the light of this higher intuition sensuousness was bound to appear base and degrading.

It is therefore historically correct, though essentially an error, to regard Christianity as the religion of asceticism, for the asceticism of the Middle Ages was nothing but the immature stage of the principle of personality. Directly spiritual love was no longer in opposition to sexuality, directly a synthesis had been effected, Christianity should have drawn the obvious conclusion from its fundamental principle and acknowledged love, which united the hostile elements. Protestantism did so, half-heartedly. Luther's vacillating attitude towards sexuality is typical of this indecision. At heart he could not justify sexuality; he regarded it, in the same way as did the Fathers of the Church, as an evil with which one had to make terms. His sanction of marriage was nothing but a crooked and ill-founded compromise; and as he remained at the old dualistic standpoint, it could not have been otherwise. But the moment the new sensuous-supersensuous form of love had come into existence, it behoved Christianity, as the religion of personality, to acknowledge it.

After this digression I return to the period of the inception of the third stage of love. If I were writing a history of eroticism, I should now have to describe the rococo period, a period essentially rationalistic and devoted to pleasure, a period which believed in nothing but the obvious and understood love only in the sense of sensual pleasure. If sensuality had hitherto been evil—at least theoretically—it now became obscene. Stripped of every grand and cosmic feature, it degenerated into the principal form of amusement. The eighteenth century, though instructive and interesting to the student of eroticism, produced nothing new. Under the undisputed sway of France, a period of sensuality set in, unparalleled by any other epoch in the history of the race, except, perhaps, the early oriental epoch; even the gynecocratic family of remote antiquity was openly revived by the ladies of Paris. Casanova was the sexual hero of the age (as he is to some extent the hero of our present impotent epoch). Indefatigable in the pursuit of woman and successful until old age, he was a well-bred sexualist without subtlety or depth. The Vicomte de Valmont, the hero of Choderlos de Laclos' famous and realistic novel *Les Liaisons Dangereuses*, an absolutely cold and cunning seducer, was its god. They were seconded by the pleasure-loving Ninon de l'Enclos, who was still desired at the age of eighty.

This ultra-refinement was followed by the loathing of civilisation and love of nature expressed by Rousseau, Werther and Hölderlin; closely allied to these passions was sentimental love, the direct precursor of our modern conception of love. Its peculiarity lay in the fact that although spiritual in its source, it yearned for psycho-physical unity, and was therefore always slightly discordant. Rousseau was the first exponent of this romantic nature cult and sentimental love of woman. He represents the sharp recoil from the frivolity of the *ancien régime*, and the beginning of the third stage of love. His *Nouvelle Héloïse* (1759) was probably the first work in which sentimental love found expression. In Goethe's *Werther* (1774), which is a faithful portrayal of the poet's personal feelings, it was represented more powerfully. Werther's love was purely spiritual at its inception. "Lotte is sacred to me. All desire is silent in her presence." But in the end he desires her with unconquerable passion; a dream undeceives him about the nature of his feelings, and as he clasps her in a passionate embrace he is conscious of having reached the summit of his longing. This would seem the goal of modern love, embodying all its previous stages. It is interesting to find embodiments of the extreme poles in two incidental characters; one has been driven mad by his adoring love for a woman and wanders about the fields in November to gather flowers for his queen; the other is a young peasant who kills his rival in jealous rage. But Werther himself, steering a middle-course between these two extremes, walks straight into modern love, which means death to him.

Both the *New Héloïse* and *Werther* are, sentimentally, efforts to reach the synthesis *via* the soul. Friedrich Schlegel, in his famous *Lucinda* (1799), tried the opposite way. He has been savagely attacked for it by one side and lauded to the skies by the other, and when "the emancipation of the flesh" became the motto of the day, he was glorified as a martyr. The philosopher and theologian Schleiermacher saw in *Lucinda* a delivery from the tyranny of centuries. "Love has become whole again and of one piece," he exclaims, joyfully calling the poem "a vision of a future world God knows how distant." "Love shall come again; a new life shall unite and animate its broken limbs; it shall rule the hearts and works of men in freedom and gladness, and supersede the lifeless phantoms of fictitious virtues." Schleiermacher also voiced the idea of the synthesis: "And why should we be arrested in this struggle (*i.e.*, between love as the flower of sensuousness and the intellectual mystical component of love), when in all domains we are striving to bring the ideas, born by the new development of humanity, into harmony with the result of the work of past ages?" His *Confidential Letters on Schlegel's Lucinda* have made the Protestant pastor Schleiermacher the philosopher of the third stage of eroticism, as the chaplain Andreas was the theorist of the second. The third stage gained its first footing amongst the German romanticists. Women were largely instrumental in achieving its victory. I will not go into detail but will confine myself to mentioning in passing the names of Jean Paul, Henrietta Herz, Brentano, Sophy Mereau, Dorothy Vest, Schelling, Friedrich Gentz. W. von Humboldt records a conversation which he had in the year of the Revolution with Schiller. The latter unhesitatingly professed his faith in the unity of love. "It (the blending of love and sensuality) is always possible and always there." But Humboldt was diffident, unable fully to grasp the new conception. "I said that it would sever the most beautiful, most delicate relationships, that it was too heterogeneous to admit of coherence; but my principal argument was that in the majority of cases it was out of the question. . ."

There is a document from the year 1779 which contains in its entirety the modern conception of harmonious love, together with its ecstatic apotheosis, the love-death, a document which puts the later theorising romanticists and *Lucinda* completely in the shade. I am referring to the only one of Gottfried August Bürger's letters to Molly, which has been preserved. It contains the following passages: "I cannot describe to you in words how ardently I embrace you in the spirit. There is in me such a tumult of life that frequently after an outburst my spirit and soul are left in such weariness that I seem to be on the point of death. Every brief calm begets more violent storms. Often in the black darkness of a stormy, rainy midnight, I long to hasten to you, throw myself into your arms, sink with you into the infinite ocean of delight and—die. Oh Love! oh Love! what a strange and wonderful power art thou to hold body and soul in such unbreakable bonds! . . . I let my imagination roam through the whole world, yea, through all the heavens and the Heaven of heavens, and examine every delight and compare it to you, but by the Eternal God! there is nothing I desire so ardently as to hold you, sweetest and heavenliest of all women, in my arms. If I could win you by walking round the earth, naked and barefoot, through thorns and thistles, over rocks and snow and ice, and, on the point of death, with the last spark of life, sink into your arms and draw new life and happiness from your loving bosom, I should consider that I bought you for a trifle."

To adduce more historical evidence of modern love would serve no purpose; in the next chapter I shall discuss its metaphysical consummation, the love-death. But I will briefly point out the not quite obvious difference between synthetic love and sexuality projected on a specific individual. In several of the higher animals the sexual instinct is to some extent individualised, but nevertheless it is no more than instinct, seeking a suitable mate for its gratification. All the well-known theories of "sexual attraction," from Schopenhauer to Weininger, accounting love as nothing but a mutual supplementing of two individuals for the purpose of the best possible reproduction of the species, do not apply to love in the modern sense, but to the sexual impulse; they completely disregard the individual, and are only aware of the species; they apprehend individualisation as an instrument in the service of the race. But genuine personal love is not kindled by instinct; it is not differentiated sexual impulse; it embraces the psycho-physical unity of the beloved without being conscious of sexual desire. It shares with the purely spiritual love the eagerness of man to raise and glorify the beloved woman, without ulterior motive or desire. This distinction may be called hair-splitting, and I admit that it is frequently impossible to make it in practice, but it is important in principle because it goes back to origins and finds in the metaphysical climax of the third stage, the love-death, its practical anti-generic proof. But with all this it is of common occurrence that spiritual and sensual love are at different times projected on one and the same woman.

Schopenhauer's instinct of philoprogenitiveness has to-day become an article of faith with the learned and unlearned. Schopenhauer was the first, probably, to conceive the idea that love was the consciousness of the unconscious instincts in the service of the species, and had no other content or purpose than the will of the species to produce the best possible offspring. In a chapter of his principal work, entitled *The Metaphysics of Love*, he essayed to promulgate and prove his theory in detail. "All love, however ethereal it may pretend to be, is rooted solely in the sexual instinct; it is nothing more nor less than specialised, strictly speaking individualised, sexual desire." Schopenhauer's conception of love does not rise above this specialised impulse. He calmly ignores all phenomena such as those I have described because they do not fit his theory. With the exception of his cheap observation that contrasts attract each other (which is the pith of all his "truths") he does not adduce the smallest evidence for the truth of his myth of "the genius of the species spreading his wings over the coming generation." However much the results of breeders may be applicable to the human species, they have nothing to do with love, and the believers in the theory of the instinct of philoprogenitiveness are silent on the subject of the best and most suitable subject for the purpose; is it the law-abiding citizen? the restless reformer? or the artist and thinker? Strange to say, the legend of the instinct of philoprogenitiveness, intuitively conscious of the right way, is to-day accepted even by scientists who are in sympathy neither with Schopenhauer's nor with any other metaphysic. It is taken for granted that love can only serve the purpose of the species; the fact that this theory is both metaphysically and scientifically unsound is ignored. For even leaving the genius of the species out of the question, his intelligent comprehension of the "composition of the next generation" is nevertheless devoutly believed in. Even Nietzsche, that arch-individualist, was completely under the spell of this dogma, as is proved by many of his utterances, for instance, by the well-known socialistic definition of marriage as "the will of twain to create that which is higher than its creators," and also by his theory that man is not an end in himself but a bridge to something else. Nietzsche's pronouncement that he has not yet found the woman whom he would like to be the mother of his children, echoes the philosophy of Schopenhauer, the superstition of the genius of philoprogenitiveness. The intrinsic worth of love without any ulterior motive, without a view to pleasure or to offspring, seems to have been unknown to Nietzsche. Schopenhauer's hero puts the purport of love not in the actual individual, but in a conception, and annihilates the value of the individual and the unique. Every great emotion is an end in itself, and whatever we may read into it of "purposes" and "expediencies," is an invention, and independent of the emotion itself. The aim of the purely spiritual love of the second stage was not propagation, and yet it was an emotion whose loftiness cannot easily be surpassed. With the deification of woman love reached far beyond the beloved into infinitude, and the phenomenon of the love-death renders all the supposed generic purpose of love impossible. But even if we ignored love altogether and admitted the existence of the sexual instinct only, its mysterious endeavour in the interest of the species would still remain pure imagination, and a conception far inferior to that of the winged god of love. The instinct does not possess a trace of "discretion," takes no interest in the weal and woe of humanity, but is utterly selfish, seeking its own gratification and nothing else.

The theory which fits so well into Schopenhauer's metaphysics has, without it, neither sense nor support. There is no instinct of philoprogenitiveness, but rather a pairing-instinct, and in addition to this a conscious desire for offspring. The difference between these two instincts is great, for as a rule, the pairing-instinct is not accompanied by a wish for children (that it should be so unconsciously is a theory not worth considering seriously), and the longing for children very frequently exists without any sexual desire; to manufacture an instinct out of those two inherently dissimilar impulses is fantastic metaphysics and not spiritual reality. The history of antiquity furnishes ample proof of my contention, for in the days of the remote past the sexual impulse had its special domain, as well as the wish for progeny, which was often regarded in the light of a duty.

The legend of the instinct of philoprogenitiveness which is to-day so universally believed, is undoubtedly the result of the general feeling that sexual intercourse as such is base and degrading. But because of the more or less clear consciousness that sexual intercourse is really what is most desired in love, and because of the lack of courage openly to admit it, attempts are made to justify it from a social standpoint.

The task of establishing the equilibrium between love and sensuousness has not yet been accomplished. What is so often realised as *the sexual trouble* has its origin in the fact that the higher stage has not yet been finally reached. There is an infinite number of unions, all of which have a flaw. Witness modern literature with its indefatigable treatment of eroticism. If a complete unity is ever to be established, then doubtless it will be the privilege of the Germanic race to achieve it, for the Neo-Latin nations mean by love either the individualised instinct, or the rare, purely spiritual love. But it is not likely that the third stage will become a universal condition; in all probability it will, for a long time to come, be limited to special individuals, and even then only to specific phases of their lives. The feeling of the great majority of men has not changed; it is primitively sexual; in the state of mind which is called *to be in love* it is centred on an individual woman, to be, after a time, gradually stifled by other interests. The emotional life of the majority of women, on the other hand, is still what it was in remotest antiquity. Love impels woman into the arms of a man to whom she remains faithful, until slowly her instincts are transformed into love for her children. But in the case even of the average woman, body and soul are equally affected; there is no more terrible moment in a woman's life than the one in which she discovers that the man to whom she has given herself has merely used her as a means for gratification. Harmoniously organised woman has given herself to a merely sexual man who sought in her only the satisfaction of his senses. This also is the cause of the horror with which the normal woman regards the prostitute, for the latter has made of herself a means for the gratification of male sexuality, losing thereby her inherent harmony and individuality. And it is also the reason why, in spite of ethical convictions and logical conclusions, we should have different standards for the loyalty of the husband and the loyalty of the wife; in man sexuality is a distinct element, an element, it is true, which we do not value, but which nevertheless exists and has, as we have seen, a historical root. When a man gives way to his instincts, his individuality is not only not destroyed, but it is hardly affected. It is very different in the case of the woman; with her, emancipated sexuality is synonymous with inward annihilation, for it has not the support of the past and cannot exist independently. A man's spiritual annihilation from the emotional sphere is unthinkable because his organisation is naturally heterogeneous. The mere sexualist represents a past stage of male eroticism which has been largely overcome, but he is rarely so completely under the spell of sexuality that he cannot highly develop other parts of his entity. The *double morality* has, therefore, an objective reason (though perhaps not a higher justification), and would only be unjustifiable if man had achieved a complete erotic unity.

The more complicated life becomes, the more numerous and complex are the relations between individuals and groups. A man is a member of a trades union; he has political, artistic, sporting and social relations; he may be a collector or interested in certain social phenomena, etc. In modern civilisation every component part of the human personality is separated from the entire personality and brought into a systematic connection with similar component parts of other entities. Our social principle is division of labour, not only in the community but also in the individual. With one man one can talk only philosophy, with another music, with a third personal matters, and so on. But because in this way only one part of man, and never the whole being, can be satisfied at a time, the desire to expend one's whole personality in one great achievement, or in connection with another individual, is increasing exactly in proportion as specialisation is increasing in the community and in the individual. The more richly endowed and synthetic a man, the more inappeasable will be his yearning to find the talents scattered broadcast over humanity combined in one personality, and to give himself wholly and entirely to that personality. The splitting up of man caused by our social conditions is one of the principal causes of the longing for the great and strong love which we hear so much discussed. The yearning for the absolute, for perfection, no longer separating and selecting but embracing man as a whole, annihilating body and soul in a higher intuition, the longing for mutual self-surrender, for giving and receiving an undivided self, is growing stronger and stronger. The idea of modern love, a love embracing the whole breadth of human development, is unequalled in human history. A single person shall stand for all mankind. The lover has always been all the world to woman, but man has possessed many things in addition to the beloved. Our age claims (wherever it understands its own eroticism) that woman, on her part, shall give to man all things in existence in a higher and purer form; not only complete satisfaction of the senses, not only the lofty emotion of spiritual love, but also friendship as a fellow-man; she shall be to him the friend who meant so much to the Greek and the ancient Teuton. It is self-evident that the true erotic of our time has very little to spare for friendship, while on the other hand the man who is not erotic in the true sense of the word, but merely sexual, has generally a poor idea of woman and a great appreciation of male friendship. But modern love does not only seek to combine all human relationships; it would fain include work, recreation, art. The instinctive jealousy of every occupation which she does not share with her lover, is nothing more than a loving woman's fear that the things which belong to him exclusively may become a danger to the unity of love. Whether such an all-absorbing love is possible in richly-endowed natures, and whether it will not be the cause of new conflict, are questions which cannot here be entered upon. But one thing is certain: the great love cannot find its consummation on earth.

II

The Love-Death
(The Second Form of
Metaphysical Eroticism)

The craving for infinitude is latent in love; its essence is the longing to reach beyond the attainable, to find the meaning of the world in ecstasy. The great erotic is a man whose inward being rests on emotion, who must bring this emotion to its climax—and who is wrecked on the incompleteness of human feeling. We recognise in him one of the tragic figures at the confines of humanity. For it is the final tragedy of a soul impelled by the inexorable will to self-realisation, to be broken on the wheel of human limitations.

The tragedy of the great man of action is less conditioned by principle than the tragedy of other types of greatness, because he is not limited by the universal restrictions of humanity, but by individual and accidental ones. He recognises, partly because of his unmetaphysical constitution, no limits to human activity, and in gaining his individual object, he reaches a relative end. It is otherwise with the thinker, the artist, the religious enthusiast and the lover. The thinker possesses the highest intellectual endowments; he represents cognisant humanity, and his portion is the anguish of realising that the essence of being cannot be grasped by the intellect. The great artist creates a masterpiece; his heart is aglow with the ideal of perfect beauty beheld by none but him, but his ideal eternally eludes him; the saint has achieved perfection as far as perfection is possible to humanity, and stands aghast at the burden of insufficiency which weighs down mankind; the great erotic is the hero in the world of feeling, his soul yearns for the consummation of his love—and already he has reached the confines of life.

There are various paths by which the erotic may travel towards perfection; they correspond to the principal erotic types. I have devoted a special chapter to the seeker of love, or the Don Juan; the woman-worshipper who cannot find satisfaction on earth has been dealt with already. The great and rare lover, however, the exponent of the final form of love, who loves a woman of flesh and blood with every fibre of his being, differs very essentially from either of these types. The profounder the emotional depth of the soul, the greater is the difficulty of finding a complementary being. The erotically undifferentiated nature (whose intellectual level may, however, be a high one) finds, and in case of loss replaces, the complementary being comparatively easily. The difficulty both of finding and of substitution increases in proportion to the differentiation and the intensity of feeling. The true erotic, once he has found his complementary being, is overwhelmed by the will to the perfect realisation of his passion. It appears with the unanswerable logic of the unique and final, carrying in its train supreme happiness and infinite sorrow. A love able to deliver a soul from its solitude is rare; once there, the whole world is as nothing to it. All life is embraced and brought under its spell. (In this connection I need only mention Michelangelo.) A lover of this type surrenders himself to love unconditionally—love shall completely annihilate, completely renew him.

But it is just in this overwhelming love that the impassable barrier becomes apparent. The lovers are two beings and not one indivisible entity. The fundamental fact of individuality stands between them as the last obstacle to their complete union. The more intense the emotion, the more desperately it tilts against this barrier, against the impossibility of complete mutual absorption, and the more passionately it demands another common form of existence. Individuality and the eternal duality of being is felt as a curse. The lovers cannot endure the thought of continuing life as distinct personalities.

The great erotic who, against all expectation, finds the being to whom he can surrender himself unreservedly and with a sense of immortality, discovers within himself the supreme and only happiness, and by that very fact has himself become the source of his unhappiness. Personality, the greatest gift bestowed upon the children of man, has flashed its light upon the tragedy of life: solitude, eternal duality. The soul recognises with unspeakable dismay in its own fundamental principle the cause of its isolation and the impossibility of final union with the beloved. The supreme value of European civilisation, the value of complete personality, into whose gradual development and perfecting all human forces had been built, and in whose interest countless sacrifices had been made, knows itself as the cause of supreme suffering, as an element which ought on no account to exist. Not its completion, but its annihilation is what should really be desired. We have here arrived at the very confines of humanity. If the great thinker has found the boundaries of all knowledge in the limitations of the intellect, and is thus the representative of the human mind with its unattainable goal: knowledge of the secret of being, the erotic has gone a step further. He has found the boundary in the very perfection of his personality and, to him, the barrier is unendurable. In the rare love of the rare personality is discovered the eternal separateness of the ego; only the destruction of its origin, the annihilation of itself, might, perhaps, throw down the barrier which separates the lovers. Inevitably there arises in the soul the desire and the will to escape, together with the beloved, the insufferable solitude of existence; to achieve in death what life denies; to realise another, a higher condition, divined in dreams and seen in visions; to become one with the beloved, to transform all human existence into a new, divine universal existence: "Then I myself am the world!" Everything individual, all life, is blotted out; the death of the lovers from love and through love is the mystic portal of a higher state of being. It is the last ecstasy of unity—the love-death—an ecstasy which life cannot give because it must always be wrecked on duality. It is the despairing attempt to escape from separateness, to effect a delivery which to human understanding seems final, and it is characteristic that Wagner, who made the problem of redemption peculiarly his own, should have expressed this attempt uniquely and with unparalleled grandeur.

It would be a mistake to read into the idea of the love-death a rejection of the European view of life, a denial of the world-feeling of personality, and a victory of the impotent philosophy of the East which exalts non-existence above existence (that is to say, individual existence). For the essence of the love-death is contained in the determination of personality to realise itself in a new and positive form of existence. It is felt as the final synthesis, exactly as (in other spheres) the union of the ideal with the personal is seen as the perfection of human life. How would it be possible at once to annihilate and to transcend the individual soul, the source of personal love, if this soul were not first presupposed as the essential and supreme value? Where personal love does not exist, as in the Orient and Japan, the thought of the love-death would be an absurdity. The burning of Indian widows is a phenomenon widely differing from the love-death. The Indian widow slavishly abandons a life which has become aimless through her master's death; she does not make a sacrifice in the true sense of the word, and is not actuated by love.

The complete unity of the lovers is possible on earth for a brief hour and it will, in most cases, satisfy erotic yearning. It can be realised in two ways: by the blissful rest of the lovers in each other, which silences all desires and apparently robs time of its tyranny.

> *The heart is still, and nothing can disturb*
> *The deepest thought, the thought to be her own.*

says Goethe; and a newer poet:

> *Close around me, wondrous being,*
> *Wind thy magic veil oblivion,*
> *All my heart from unrest freeing,*
> *Let there be untroubled calm.*

> *Give me peace; the helter skelter*
> *Of the wide world has gone by;*
> *And this narrow, silent shelter*
> *Holds the potent healing balm.*

By the side of this idyllic consummation of the longing for love, there is the other, the ecstatic consummation of mutual rapture. It almost blots out individual consciousness in the singly (no longer doubly) felt, body and soul entrancing ecstasy; it is such sheer delight that pleasure is no longer perceived as a distinct element, but rather is there the consciousness of a complete transformation of life. Pleasure, which, a great psychologist maintains, "craves eternity" is annihilated in its perfection, knows no more of itself, and is a part of the lovers' sense of complete unity. It does not "crave eternity"; such a craving is its last stage but one, the outer court (further than which Nietzsche as far as eroticism is concerned never penetrated); in the innermost sanctuary pleasure disappears; it has no longer any meaning, it becomes void before the new consciousness. The supreme ecstasy of great love proves that the summit of human emotion is beyond pleasure and pain, and does not acknowledge the limitations of bodily existence. Thus, of necessity, the rapture of love must engender the idea of its own eternity, the destruction of individual consciousness. I will quote in this connection a few verses by Erika Rheinsch:

To open now my lips were vain indeed,
Nor word nor even kiss could e'er confess
What sighs and joy and grief and happiness
Would flash from me to you with lightning speed.

Nor hope nor pray'r can still the soul's desire,
For God Himself can never join us twain;
My bitter tears fall on my heart like rain
And cannot quench its all-consuming fire.

Oh! Now to break the spell—the storm to breast
With broken heart and life-blood ebbing fast,
Bearing the pangs of death for you, at last,
Dark troubled love—at last thou wert at rest!

We perceive that love can no longer content itself with the penultimate—it must dare the last heroic step which creates beyond body and soul something new and final, for "God Himself can never join us twain." The love-death is the last and inevitable conclusion of reciprocal love which knows of no value but itself, and is resolved to face eternity, so that no alien influence shall reach it. The two powers, love and death, tower above human life fatefully and mysteriously; an isolated experience cannot appease them, they involve the whole existence. To the individual who loves with an all-absorbing love, and to the individual on the point of death, everything dwindles into insignificance. Before the majesty of the love-death life breaks down, to be laid hold of and transcended in a new (divined) sphere.

The thought of the love-death, the will that the world should be governed by love, is the most unconditional postulate of feeling ever laid down. For the love-death is the definite and irrevocable victory of emotion; it is ecstasy as a solution of the world-problem and the world-process. It is human to regard love and death as antitheses; to consider them far removed from each other; marriage and funeral are the poles of social life. The ecstasy of the love-death, however, owing to its all-transcending claim, unites the two poles. The climax of life shall also be its end.

It is here, in the voluntary surrender of life in order to attain a divined unity, and not in the union of begetting and destroying, that the frequently assumed connection between love and death is to be found.

Voluptuousness and death are not interlinked, as is so frequently asserted since Novalis (not on the higher plane of eroticism), but voluptuousness has immolated itself, has been annihilated in the love-death. The view that begetting and destroying are related functions, is based on the supposition that love is bound up with propagation. This is the fateful error of the modern theory of love, a rationalistic, metaphysical abstraction, which touches no corresponding chord in the human soul. To base the relationship of love and death on an association of becoming and declining is a beautiful idea, but nothing more. Modern synthetic love produces this relationship in its metaphysical perfection out of itself; it is foreign alike to pure sexuality and to spiritual love. (Wherever the desire to destroy is found hand in hand with sensuality, morbid instincts are at play.)

It frequently occurs that lovers commit suicide together because external circumstances prevent their union. This is a step corresponding to suicide from offended vanity or incurable disease; life has become unbearable to the individual haunted by a fixed idea, and he throws it away. But this has nothing whatever to do with the love-death; it is a purely negative act of despair, whereas the love-death is an altogether positive act, namely, the will to win to a higher (and to the intellect inconceivable and paradoxical) metaphysical unity. The love-death aspires to perform a miracle. It has, possibly, never been realised in its full greatness; the evidence of the common death of Heinrich von Kleist and Henrietta Vogel must be rejected. During the last days of his life Kleist was wrapped up in the idea of their common death, and in a letter to his cousin, Marie von Kleist, he says: "If you could only realise how death and love strive to beautify these last moments of my life with heavenly and earthly roses, you would be content to let me die. I swear to you I am supremely happy." In the same letter he speaks of "the most voluptuous of deaths." And yet it was no real love-death, that is to say, death following as a necessary corollary in order that love may be consummated. Kleist as well as Henrietta had separately resolved to commit suicide, and when they—almost accidentally—heard of this mutual intention, they conceived the idea of the new voluptuousness of a common death. Love did not play a very great part in this. Kleist further says in the same letter: "Her resolution to die with me drew me, I cannot tell you with what unspeakable and irresistible power, into her arms. Do you remember that I asked you more than once to die with me. But you always said 'No.'" From this and other passages it is clear that Kleist would have taken his life in any case, and that he only seized this specific opportunity to plunge into the ecstasy of a common death.

The thought of the love-death is often present in the hearts of individuals who are genuinely in love. We read in Schlegel's *Lucinda*: "There (in a transcendental life) our longings may perhaps be satisfied." And in Lenau's letters to Sophy the same thought is more than once apparent.

The idea reached perfection and immortality in Wagner's "Tristan and Isolde." It is Wagner's world-famous deed to have lived through and embodied this complex of emotion for the first, and so far for the last time; his lovers are in a superlative degree representative of human love; they typify the climaxes of human emotion. Wagner has immortalised the metaphysical form of synthetic love; his importance to synthetic love surpasses Dante's importance to deification.

Already in the first act the exchange of love-potion and death-draught is profoundly significant: both Tristan and Isolde seek death because they are alarmed by the external obstacles to their love. But the thought of death and love, the foreboding that their love can find rest only in the ultimate, in finality, has been in their hearts from the outset. Together they receive new life from love, and together love leads them, step by step, to death. In the profoundest sense no exchange of potions has taken place, but the power of the love-potion has made them conscious of what was latent in their souls, waiting to burst into life. At the very moment when Isolde proffers Tristan the death-draught, the conviction flashes into his soul that she is giving him death through love: "When thy dear hand the goblet raised, I recognised that death thou gav'st." And in the same way Isolde: "From golden day I sought to flee, in darkest night draw thee with me, where my heart divined the end of deceit, where illusion's haunting dream should fade, to drink eternal love to thee, joined everlastingly, to death I doom'd thee."

The second act leads them further and further into the coils of their love; they are more and more convinced that death alone is left to them, step by step they discover the secret of the mystical union—and yet they are still completely imprisoned within the limits of their personalities and cannot quite understand the miracle: "How to grasp it, how to grasp it, this great gladness, far from daylight, far from sadness, far from parting?" For it is the profoundest secret of the world which here must be guessed by love—the final unity of two souls and through it unity with all life. Clearer and clearer and more and more compelling looms the thought of a common death, until it is grasped and comprehended; the lovers realise that to be completely one they must surrender their lives, and that by losing life they can lose nothing essential. "All death can destroy is that which divides us." Ultimately Tristan pronounces the final decision, and Isolde repeats it word by word, follows it step by step like a sleep-walker, so as to make it quite her own. "Thus should we die no more to part, in endless joy, one soul, one heart, never waking, never haunted by pale fear, in love undaunted, each to each united aye, dream of love's eternity." The grand, artistic symbol for this state of consciousness touches metaphysic. Wagner introduces night as the visible emblem of an existence in a world—inconceivable by our senses—beyond the grave, in contrast to the earthly day, to "the day's deceptive glamour." (Nietzsche later on adopted this symbol "midnight" as the emblem of everything lofty.) The lovers who in their day-consciousness believed that they hated each other, now that they are walking towards eternal night divine that which is beyond the reach of their separated selves, beyond all illusion and duality. The duality is outwardly expressed by their different names, separated and united "by the little word *and*." All at once the knowledge dawns upon them that great love cannot be consummated in the day of the world, but that it points to a life beyond. They have discovered the final meaning of life and the world—the annihilation of individual life and death through love—analogous to the last wisdom of the mystic: "To become God." "I myself am the world." Death is the inevitable corollary of supreme love. But as they tremblingly yearn for and await the inconceivable, earth once more stretches out her arms to them, the dream of metaphysical existence melts slowly away. In the orchestration *phantoms of the day, dreams of morning*, suppress the new, the divined conception.

At the opening of the third act the motif for horns and violas gradually ascending and dying away, expresses the unspeakable dreariness and senselessness of material life, after its profound meaning, the re-creation of the world by love, has been lost. This feeling of absolute senselessness dominates the awakening sleeper; Tristan, interpreting it in the sense of Schopenhauer as the universal aimlessness of the world and of life, is merely expressing the doom of his own longing for the supreme: he has divined and has lost the loftiest value. Wagner intuitively perceives that sin is a component part of the supreme sublimation of love and personality; Tristan must curse himself and the beloved woman because love, as the last consequence of sin, demands the love-death, which can never find completion; "The terrible draught myself I have brewed it! A curse on thee, terrible draught! A curse on him who brewed it!"

In the music at the end of the third act, which is known by the (not quite relevant) title of "Isolde's Love-death," Wagner, after previously expressing by Tristan's last words, "Do I near light?" the inadequacy of the physical senses—attempts to describe the metaphysical condition of the unity of love, which to our consciousness can only have the negative characteristics of the unthinkable and intangible—the unconscious. This he tried to accomplish artistically by making use of the senses, by trying to convey in terms of sound, light, scent, what he understood by this complete immersion in the swirling totality of cosmic life—"*in des Weltatem's wehendem All.*" The essence of this condition is that the duality of the souls, and finally the multiplicity of the world, is resolved in a higher unity. But as we are concerned with the emotional life of the lovers and not with vague metaphysical propositions, we may say that such a death is not a being dead, destroyed, annihilated, dispersed, but a being transformed, perfected in love. The amazing phenomenon of this complex of feeling is the fact that real life has become unbearable, and that another life is created without the least regard to possibility or truth; it is as if the emotion of the lovers were endowed with divine, creative power.

Those who realise the love-death as a necessity of their inmost being, resemble the great ecstatic whom earthly life can no longer satisfy, because he is conscious of a force compelling him to enter into a higher cosmic existence. His inmost experience is the annihilation of the individual soul in God; he aspires to a direct pouring of the soul into the divine love. Those who die in love are directly seeking complete unity with each other, and only indirectly, through this unity, the divined annihilation in metaphysical being. The love-death is the erotic, bi-human form of mystic ecstasy, and could not be evolved until the highest form of love had been developed.

Metaphysical eroticism is a product of the spirit of Europe, for it is linked to personality whose will is the immortalisation of love. Orientalism neither comprehends nor appreciates this emotion, for it lacks the foundation of the culture of personality. The Semite, the Indian and the Japanese experience only the rapture of the senses; and gratification, restlessly revolving round itself between enjoyment and exhaustion, is condemned to eternal sterility. All religio-sexual orgies of which history tells us are so many attempts of sensuality to possess itself of a higher intuition—vain attempts, because casual intercourse and the annihilation of the individual can never produce new values. According to Hegel the immanent sense of everything that happens in the world is the destiny of the individual to grow from slavery into freedom; but is it not rather the meaning of increased culture that man should realise himself as an individual (which is by no means a contradiction to the first proposition)? Metaphysical eroticism is the completion of personality in love. Simultaneously with the birth of personality originated the deification of woman; the destruction of the most highly evolved personality, the last painful consequence of its blessed-unblessed nature, gives birth to the conception of the love-death. Like antique torch-bearing genii the two metaphysical forms of love stand at the head and the feet of self-conscious man. Here and there erotic emotion, transcending all limitations, becomes the pathway leading to the ultimate secrets of life: deification creates a supernatural female being as the erotic representative of everything divine. This is a productive act, erotic, artistic and religious at the same time. It produces out of its own fulness new forces for the service of higher ideals; it creates a new world of emotion with new contents.

Simultaneously with the projection of the love of woman into eternity were sown the seeds of those great things on which the higher spiritual life of to-day is based. Deification demands shape and individuality beyond the earthly sphere, in eternity. But from one side it is love, love without response (unless the lover finds response in and through artistic expression), the eroticism of the solitary man, and it occurs as such to this day in rare minds. Woman-worship is the natural and the highest form of love for the man who does not seek his own perfection in duality—a reciprocal relationship with another being— but solitarily, and yet not, as the mystic, shapelessly, but rather in a love definitely projected on another being. The dream of the perfect woman is the only erotic dream which reality can never disappoint, for it makes no claim on reality. Doubtless it is to some extent paradoxical that the inherently social feeling, anchored in duality, should be experienced and perfected solitarily, that it should waive all claim to response and reciprocity, to all appearances the most important elements of love.

The love-death corresponds more completely to the erotic ideal inasmuch as it is founded on absolute equality in reciprocity. It finds its climax not in solitude but in the company of the beloved. The idea of complete abandonment is revolting to the solitarily loving individual; the lover whose whole soul turns to the beloved cannot understand the love of the solitary soul; it appears to him unnatural and cold, perhaps meaningless and crazy. Woman does not know true solitude, the thought of deification is foreign to her nature; she attains to the supreme only with and through man; it is easier to her to give herself to her lover entirely, and even to follow him into death. But in this connection I am unable to suppress a doubt as to whether the fundamental emotion of the mystical world-union is altogether present in woman, whether she really divines behind her lover—eternity.

While deification is universally creative, while it is fresh as the spring and full of faith, the love-death with its gloomy pathos demands the entire individual and destroys everything but itself. It has no creative power, for there is nothing beyond it. One may justly maintain that the love-death realises the mystico-ecstatic religious emotion, while in the deification of woman the religious need to worship finds satisfaction. Both are combinations of love and religion, both are metaphysical eroticism, paradoxical and yet logical conclusions of human emotion.

The overwhelming longing which is connected at least with the first stages of a great love, may be interpreted in another, in a social sense. Love is the intensest and most direct relationship which can exist between two beings, and the impossibility of realising its final longing represents the most genuine tragedy of life among men and women of the social world. The need which impels two beings to each other lacks, in this union too, the possibility of complete consummation. And if the most powerful of all social emotions (and as many believe the root of all others) suffers from an inner duality, to how much greater an extent must the less intense feelings which unite individuals share the same lot! Humanity, wherever it is comprehended profoundly and spiritually, not economically, carries within itself the germ of its tragical imperfection. Whatever social relationship we may enter, we find that it has a flaw, and the more genuine and profound the relationship, the less dictated by utilitarian considerations (which in this connection correspond to the element of sensuality in eroticism), the more painfully does this flaw make itself felt,—whether it be in friendship, in the relationship of master and man, or in free companionship. Every relationship between individuals is stricken with the curse of incompleteness— even love cannot escape this fate. Love enforces in the deification of woman a transcending of earthly life—and it throws itself into the last embrace of a common death—that is to say, it shudderingly admits the impossibility of its consummation.

III

THE CONFLICT BETWEEN SEXUALITY AND LOVE

The Seeker of Love and The Slave of Love

It is obvious that even an equilibrium between sexuality and love cannot always be established, while a genuine and complete unification is very unusual and may, perhaps, be called utopian. In the previous chapters I have dealt with the blending of both elements in the highest form of eroticism; in the following I will attempt to throw light on some of the principal phenomena resulting from a defective union of sexuality and love, phenomena which I am convinced have never been correctly interpreted. I allude to perversions which are not inherently pathological, although they are as a rule only observed and described in their pathological form.

The fundamental form of so-called sadism may be discovered in an erotic type which I will call the seeker of love. A lover of this type is characterised by an unappeasable longing for pure, spiritual love; he passes from woman to woman in the hope of realising this desire, but owing to his own material disposition he is unable to do so. Time after time he succumbs to sexual promptings. Thus groping, frequently quite unconsciously—for a fictitious being, he hates every woman whose fate it is to rouse his desire, for each one cheats him out of that which he seeks. A genuine illusionist, he knows nothing of the woman of flesh and blood, and continues seeking his ideal, only to be again and again disappointed. He blames every woman he conquers for what is really his own insufficiency; he despises her or revenges himself on her, punishes and ill-treats her; we recognise the true Don Juan and his morbid caricature, the sadist. But even the most brutal representative of this type may still be psychologically described as "a man who seeks spiritual love in woman after woman and, finding only sexuality, revenges himself on her." Quite a number of men harbour sadistic feelings for only one woman, and that the one to whom they owe their great disillusionment. Doubtless many men have almost lost the psychical roots of their perversions and are completely involved in physical acts. There is nothing remarkable in this fact; it occurs in every sphere of human life. The vague instinct of revenge on woman animates also, though perhaps unconsciously, the pathological sadist.

There is one thing which the seeker of love and the woman-worshipper have in common: both seek a higher ideal far beyond the woman of every-day life; but while the worshipper safeguards the purity of his feeling by putting the greatest possible distance between him and the object of his worship (and is therefore never disappointed), the seeker of love, blinded by the illusion that he has at last found the object of his quest, draws every woman towards him and again and again discovers that he is nothing but a sensualist. Every fresh conquest destroys his dream afresh, and he revenges himself, if he is a Don Juan, by despising and disgracing the unfortunate victim, and if he is a sadist, by maltreating her. And yet he never entirely loses his illusion; he craves for complete satisfaction, and as he is incapable of self-knowledge, he never abandons the hope of meeting the woman he seeks. He differs very little from the type represented by Sordello, who loved one woman spiritually, but regarded all the others from the standpoint of sex. It is the tragedy of Don Juan to revolt from the low erotic sphere which is his portion, and where he rules supreme, and for ever to aspire to a realm from which he is shut out. He is convinced that with the help of a woman he may redeem himself—and sinks deeper and deeper into the slough of his own sensuality. He becomes malevolent, cruel and callous; the pleasure whose slave he is repels him:

> *From craving to enjoyment thus I reel,*
> *And in enjoyment languish for desire.*

He is insatiable, but not as the primitive hedonist, whose natural element is pleasure, but because he again and again mistakes pleasure for love. He knows only "women," and thus he sins against personality and the love which is the outcome of personality.

The opinion that Don Juan is no more than a votary of pleasure is not worthy of criticism; the famous Casanova, for instance, has nothing in common with him. Casanova was a sensualist without psychical complexity and without tragedy. His sole endeavour was to wring the utmost measure of enjoyment out of life. He knew the woman of reality and did not waste his time in running after phantoms. In his old age he revelled in the after-taste and settled down to write his memoirs. Don Juan, on the contrary, has such a loathing for all the women he betrays, that he hardly remembers them, and certainly has the strongest disinclination to evoke their memory. Casanova was an entirely unmetaphysical and unproblematical nature. His philosophy is clearly expressed in the preface to his Memoirs: "I always regarded the enjoyment of sensual pleasures as my principal object; I never knew a more important one." Casanova, who, strange to say, enjoys such high erotic honours, was merely an ordinary, very successful man of the world, and is of no importance to the subject in hand. But even the greater and wilder Vicomte de Valmont (the hero of the famous novel of Choderlos de Laclos) is in spite of all his art and *esprit* and perverse principles no seeker of love and no Don Juan, but a fop and a braggart, seducing women in order to boast of his success. He is moreover only a representative of the bored Upper Ten of the *ancien régime*, and not by any means unique.

Thoughtful critics contend that Don Juan was an autocrat, a destroyer, a criminal nature with satanic tendencies, bent on the enslavement of women, on their social and moral death; that conquest only, not enjoyment, was his passion. I do not altogether reject this interpretation, but it fastens too exclusively on the external and the obvious, and overlooks the essential. What is the reason of his preposterous procedure? Is he really actuated by the evil desire to injure the women he woos? Such a motive may occur occasionally (the Vicomte de Valmont was so constituted), but it cannot be regarded as the guiding principle of a life—and above everything its pettiness is the exact reverse of so great and demoniacal a character as Don Juan. Were he conqueror in the highest sense, then—ascetic and proud—he would be content with the mere consciousness of victory. But his whole attitude belies the idea of a conqueror; he is not in the least interested in the women to whom he makes love. They are as necessary to him as "the air he breathes," but they are unable to give him what he seeks. At the moment of disappointment he abandons them in disgust, innocent of any despotic desires (which would pre-suppose interest). As far as he is concerned, women exist only for the purpose of quickening something in his soul. But his soul remains dead; divine love has no part in him, he cannot be saved and is doomed to eternal damnation.

But what is the reason why women cannot resist him? Let us first settle the point as to why women are attracted to men. I will answer this question briefly, and though my answer may appear dogmatical, it need not therefore be wrong. Women know very little of man, but there is one thing they feel with unfailing certainty, and that is whether their sex is of great or of small significance to him. (I am only alluding to the general effect of men on women, not to genuine personal love which is always incommensurable.) The greater the importance a man attaches to women, the more readily do they respond to his influence. They are attracted by his erotic will, not by one or the other of his spiritual or physical qualities. Women cannot resist a man to whom they mean much, everything. It is as if they were compelled to throw themselves into the chasm of his vacuity—every fresh victim with the fond hope of filling it—but all of them perish. And yet, at the moment of their defeat they are supremely happy, for they experience the full intensity of his passion and the boundlessness of his longing. The erotic craving of a man simply means that women are to him the most important thing in life. Women instinctively yield to that man who most eagerly desires them. The coarse sensualist, to whom all women are alike, attracts sensual women, not exactly because they find in him the satisfaction of their craving, but because they themselves act on him indiscriminately. But a woman will adapt herself with the greatest ease to the needs of the differentiated erotic (for instance, she will become really sentimental to please the man who prefers sentimental women), for she loves to give herself to the man who most desires her and as he desires her.

Don Juan, animated by illimitable erotic yearning, is therefore the undisputed master of the other sex. He has the power of bestowing absolute happiness, even if only for a brief hour, because in his boundless love (which is projected on anything but her) a woman receives the supreme value. Maybe he would be saved if a woman denied herself to him—maybe he would cease to be a seeker of love and become a worshipper, for he could not refuse to believe in the woman who rejected him; but it is his fate that no woman he woos can resist him, that all throw themselves into his arms without an exception and without a struggle.

Thus the seeker of love, too, though in a restricted sense, may be regarded as a metaphysical erotic, for he loathes sexuality—his portion—and yearns for a higher form of love. He shares this attitude with the slave of love, who is also a sensualist and a would-be lover. The slave of love imitates the attitude of the worshipper, but he infallibly sinks into the sexual sphere. What the psychopathist since Kraft-Ebbing designates as masochism, is the pathological degeneration of this particular emotion, which is very common and appears in various forms, but does not seem to me to be at all morbid. Certainly it is morbid when a man allows himself to be insulted, bound and flogged, but it is fairly normal when his passionate admiration is roused by an imperious woman, who passes him by like a queen without even noticing his abject adoration; when he longs to kneel down before her and kiss her feet, which in reward would spurn him. Quite normal, too, is the boyish happiness in serving an admired and adored woman (Kraft-Ebbing calls this pageism) described so beautifully in Dostoievsky's novel, *A Young Hero*, and fairly common among troubadours and minnesingers. (I need only mention Ulrich von Lichtenstein.) There are numerous degrees of this feeling—we frequently come across it in the novels of Dostoievsky, Jacobsen, Strindberg, D'Annunzio, and others—but the essence of it is always contained in the fact that the man, although yearning to worship the beloved woman, cannot maintain himself in the sphere of spiritual love, and aspires to direct physical contact. His attitude, which closely imitates purely spiritual love, cannot be other than sexual. The blending of love and sexuality together with the incapacity of effecting a real synthesis, the confusion of value and pleasure is most clearly shown in the masochist—far more clearly than in the case of the (rare) seeker of love. The outward modes preferred by the individual are a matter of indifference; for the most part they are symbolical acts, indicating the lover's inferiority and the loftiness and power of his mistress. What is really of importance is the spiritual attitude which induces him to commit these strange acts, and in these we find the characteristic attitude of the woman-worshipper: that of the slave before his queen. The slave of love is a sensualist incapable of approaching woman in a normally manly, instinctive and natural way, but requiring the pose of the spiritual worshipper. One might be tempted to believe that he harboured the secret wish to atone for his incapacity of feeling a pure love by being degraded and ill-treated. Thus from a human point of view the slave of love is a higher type than the seeker of love; all his transgressions, the fault of his morbid disposition, come home to him; he takes the blame of his sin upon his own shoulders, while the seeker of love revenges himself on his victims for his own shortcomings. The seeker of love is by nature polygamous, while the slave of love is, as a rule, monogamous (and consequently has little success with the opposite sex). Both aspire to a union of sensual and spiritual eroticism, but in both cases the union is a failure. All the repulsive and terrible manifestations of these perversions which have been recorded, can easily be shown to fit my theory. In psychological research it is merely a question of selecting the great types from the mass of phenomena and determining them correctly.

The so-called *fetichist*, too, whose passion is roused by indifferent objects which belonged, or might belong, to the beloved, or in fact to any woman, is a variant of the slave of love. The classical representative of fetichism is the mediaeval knight who carried a handkerchief, a glove, or any other article of clothing belonging to his lady, next to his heart, thus believing himself proof against evil influences. There we see already spiritual love groping for material objects in order to gain earthly support; not every man is a Dante, not every man is capable of keeping his soul free from the taint of this earthly sphere. But even the "plait-cutter," so well known to the reader of newspapers, the collector of garters, and similar desperadoes, require a relic, a fetich which they apparently worship. To the same category belongs the idolatrous cult which some men, especially artists—but also madmen—practise with female pictures and statues (more especially with heads). In this case the fundamental feeling of the love of beauty, which we know as an essential factor of purely spiritual eroticism, is made to serve sensual purposes. The desired illusion of spiritual worship is facilitated, and is protected from self-revelation, owing to the fact that a painted head rouses in the normal individual no passion, but inspires him with purely spiritual sentiments.

I have briefly touched on this subject because my theory of the two roots of eroticism permits of a new, and in my opinion plausible, explanation of erotic perversions; one might even go as far as to say that the existence of perversions follows as a necessary consequence; that they must exist because it obviously cannot *always* be possible to maintain a harmonious balance of sensuality and love. This chapter is therefore a necessary supplement to the previous ones in which the perfection of modern love is dealt with. The seeker of love and the slave of love are phenomena of dualistic eroticism incapable of attaining to unity. For this reason they neither existed in antiquity, nor do we find genuine examples of them in the female sex. All female perversions closely examined are hysteria—that is to say, want of inner balance—in various forms; a woman's subjection to the will of a man is in very many instances a natural symptom, and cannot be regarded as perverse. And thus we again perceive that the eroticism of woman is more harmonious and natural than that of the eternally groping and eternally erring man.

IV

THE REVENGE OF SEXUALITY

The Demoniacal and the Obscene

In conclusion I will attempt to elucidate a group of phenomena which play a part, important though often ignored, in the emotional life of the present day. They are related to the subject under discussion, inasmuch as they, too, are the result of a lack of harmony between sensuousness and love. As long as sensuousness is felt and understood as a natural element, and one which does not under normal circumstances enter consciousness as a distinct principle, the emotional sphere which may be designated as demoniacal-sexual and obscene, does not exist. Not until sensuousness is confronted by a higher principle, a now solely acknowledged spiritual-divine principle, will natural life, and particularly normal sexuality, be stigmatised as low and ungodly, even as demoniacal. In proportion as the conception of God became more spiritual and divine, the conception of the devil became more horrible; the higher the soul soared, the deeper sank the body. This philosophy of pure spirituality was expressed by St. Bernard of Clairvaux in the following words: "Oh, soul, stamped with the image of God, adorned with His semblance, espoused to faith, endowed with His spirit, redeemed by His blood, the compeer of angels, invested with reason—what hast thou in common with the flesh, for which thou must suffer so much? . . . And yet it is thy dearest companion! Behold, there will come a day when it shall be a miserable, pallid corpse, food for worms! For however beautifully it may be adorned, yet it is nothing but flesh!" The man of the later Middle Ages, and especially the cleric, who was completely dominated by the contrast of the ascetic and the sexual, feared the devil more than he loved God, and regarded the sensual temptations which beset his excited, superstitious and eternally unsatisfied imagination as sent by the devil. The naïveté of sensuality had passed away for ever; as goodness was looked upon as divine and supernatural, nature and natural instincts were condemned. Man was torn asunder.

But the devil was not only feared, he was also worshipped. A devil-worship, the details of which have been little studied, existed from the tenth to the fourteenth century (when it reached its climax), side by side with the worship of God. The greater the dread of heresy and witchcraft, the greater became the number of men who, despairing of salvation, prostrated themselves before the devil, whom they seemed unable to escape (a single evil thought was sufficient to doom their souls to eternal damnation), in the hope that he would at least save their bodies from the stake and vouchsafe them the pleasures of this world. Satan promised his worshippers unlimited pleasure; he became the redeemer of those whom the clergy persecuted. It is asserted that his worship consisted in an obscene parody of the Mass; according to Michelet, the body of a female worshipper served as the altar on which a toad was consecrated and partaken of instead of the Host. The adept solemnly renounced Jesus and did homage to Satan by kissing his image.

Asceticism and libertinism always go hand in hand. They are convertible principles rending their victim. *Temptation* is the fundamental motif of this condition. The devil was believed to send out his servants to win new souls; monks were visited by demons in the shape of a voluptuous woman, the *succubus*; Satan himself, or one of his emissaries, disguised as a fashionable gentleman, the *incubus*, appeared to the nuns. Undoubtedly the dreams of over-excited men and women played a very important part in this connection; many hysterical women felt the devil's kiss and embrace. All these women were themselves convinced of the truth of their hallucinations and imaginings, and once the belief in witchcraft was firmly established (in the thirteenth century) the obvious atonement for their hysteria was the stake.

The fear of witches, which existed parallel with the love of the Madonna, was typical of the declining Middle Ages. The first Christian centuries knew neither the Lady of Heaven in the later meaning of the word, nor did they know anything of witches. In the reign of Charlemagne the penalty for the belief in witchcraft was death. At all times man has exhibited a tendency to see in woman either a celestial or an infernal being, and nowhere was this tendency more strongly developed than in the soul of the mediaeval dualist: he created the beloved and adored Queen of Heaven, the mediator between God and humanity and, as her counterpart the witch, the despised and dreaded seducer, a being between man and devil. Powerless to effect a reconciliation between spiritual love and sensuous pleasure, he required two distinct female types as personifications of the two directions of his desire; love and the pleasure of the senses could have nothing in common, and once the highest value was realised in the spiritual love of woman, pleasure could not appear otherwise than degraded, sinful and diabolical. In this respect, also, woman submitted without a murmur to the dictates of male will.

Mary and the devil became more and more the real hostile powers of the thirteenth century; the classical time of woman-worship was also the climax of the fear of the devil and witchcraft. The Dominican monks who, above all other orders, contributed to the spread of the cult of Mary, proceeded, soon after the establishment of the Inquisition, against the witches, the enemies of Mary. In the second half of the thirteenth century the persecution of heresy gradually gave way to the persecution of witchcraft.

I will not go into these well-known details, for the psychical position is clear enough: to the man whose heart is filled with the love of good and the spiritual love of woman, sensuousness will appear as dangerous and perilous, and will have at the same time the glamour of the demoniacally-sexual. It is the diabolical element of dualistic consciousness in the sphere of eroticism. Many people of the present day will not be able to understand this feeling, for it pre-supposes a completely inharmonious emotional life.

The consciousness of the obscene is allied to the conception of the demoniacal; it accompanies modern synthetic love as its temptation and its shadow. In personal love sensuality and soul are no longer independent, contrasted principles; personality, taking the spiritual as its foundation, includes the sensuous. In this highest stage all eroticism not hallowed by mutual affection is felt as unpardonable. The purely sexual principle continues to exist, but whenever it appears in its impersonal and brutal crudity as an element hostile to personality, it creates the consciousness of the obscene. The obscene is, therefore, the purely sexual, not in its naïve normality, but as a force inimical to a value, as a rule to the value of personality. The obscene expresses scorn and hatred for personal love. It is the seduction of the primitive which is no longer something *earlier*, but something baser (for every age must gauge all things by its own standard). The aesthetic principle—in this connection the sense of the beauty of the human form—so powerful an element in naïve sensuality as well as in every other form of eroticism, is excluded, because in this particular condition the beauty of the human body is not objectively realised, but is looked upon with the eyes of the senses. The moment personality is acknowledged as the only decisive factor in erotic life, chaotic impersonal sensuality stands condemned. The obscene is the darker aspect of modern love, and without modern love it could not exist. Its essence is negative, is the tendency to caricature and mock the highest form of love. The photograph of a nude woman is not obscene; but if the face is hidden, and thus the personal moment intentionally eliminated in favour of the generic element, it approaches the obscene. This accounts for the widely felt pleasure in obscene pictures; the beholder is not personally engaged, he can enjoy these pictures without taking upon his shoulders any kind of responsibility. Even that minimum of respect which the very dregs of humanity may claim is not required of him. The picture is capable of affording pleasure without claiming a grain of human kindness. Thus it would seem that sensual pleasure is possible without any sacrifice of the inwardly professed higher eroticism, a sacrifice which might be a bar to a primitive relationship with a woman of flesh and blood. Actually, however, it is not possible, for with the surrender to the base source of enjoyment, the spiritual position is abandoned, and personally conceived humanity inwardly annihilated.

It follows from the foregoing that the fascination of the obscene can only be fully felt by one who has completely acknowledged the principle of personality in eroticism, and who has also latent within him the possibility of erotic dualism. The more highly evolved the emotional life of a man (all these considerations apply only to a man in whom the possibility of dualism is latent), the more will he realise the purely sexual, the emphasis of the element of pleasure, as something unseemly and disagreeable; something which he ought to deny himself, but which attracts him with the irresistible fascination of the obscene. The man who surrenders himself naïvely to sensuality does not realise it as obscene, but the man who, conscious of his higher concept, strives against it, experiences the reaction of sensuality with the full force of its perverse seduction. Even if only for a brief space, he annihilates the higher element and gives himself up to the pleasure of the base and degraded.

In this connection we are face to face with the strange but still logical fact, that a man who has completely attained to the third stage of love, feels even the purely spiritual love as odious in its incompleteness. It strikes him as unnatural and forced, a feeling which must, however, not be confused with the ordinary contempt of spiritual love.

Primitively constituted man knows only undifferentiated sexuality. He enjoys the nude, and sees no difference between a Venus by Titian and an ordinary photograph of a nude figure; the aesthete, and more especially the artist, can never understand that a work of art may be sensually stimulating. That it may be so will always be bluntly denied by an individual capable of enjoying a beautiful form, but to the uncultivated mind the picture of the female body will only evoke memories of pleasure. This feeling, however, is quite distinct from the obscene; it is neither hostile to the higher spiritual life, nor is it criminal; it is natural and harmonious. But the same feeling may become obscene if a man, aware of higher aesthetic values, ignores art and enjoys the picture merely as a representation of a nude figure. Here, too, the seduction lies in a demoniacal element, namely in the destruction of the aesthetic value. The destructive characteristic of the obscene wars against all higher conceptions; it is the revenge of chaotic sex deposed by a higher principle, and has the special charm of secret wrong-doing.

I might go even further, and maintain that because modern love does not admit pleasure as its foundation and content, and because the craving for pleasure is deeply rooted in human nature, love favours to a high degree the desire to reserve a sphere for pleasure distinct from personal love. This region is the obscene, and one might prophesy that it will grow in proportion as the principle of personal love acquires dominion; for pleasure will always need an undisturbed retreat untroubled by higher demands. This can only be found in the sphere of the obscene in which the element of personality is entirely eliminated.

Modern man is beset by another peculiar temptation. The beauty of woman, which in the days of the past was regarded as sacred, can be made a means of pleasure, and thus drawn from the realm of values into the realm of sensuality. This is a breach with the principle of personal love, for to the latter the beauty of a woman is so much part and parcel of the whole personality that it cannot be enjoyed separately, that indeed it can hardly be noticed as a distinct element. This cleavage has become so nearly universal that we are hardly conscious of its profound perversity. It is the arch-sin of all higher eroticism to realise beauty not as the undetachable and self-evident outward form of a beloved soul, but as a means of heightening pleasure. Although in its essence it is the same thing as the examination of a work of art merely for the sake of the pleasure it affords to the senses, the offence is here aggravated because personality is involved. This degradation of the higher values, whether of nature, art, beauty, knowledge, kindness, religion or the human soul, to serve the ends of sensual pleasure is the expression of a perversity which is possibly the most radical and characteristic of our age. To-day the soul of a woman has frequently the same effect on man as her physical beauty; he enjoys it as a subtile charm instead of respecting it as a mystery.

I can hardly expect to make my meaning quite clear to the multitude, but the tendency to enjoy beauty of form or soul as a distinct element represents a rupture with the principle of synthetic love, the love which does not separate but realises the personality of the beloved as an indivisible entity. The enjoyment of beauty as a separate element pre-supposes a conscious, spiritual division, not only of the beloved, but also of the lover, and is therefore the destruction of the principle of unity. Aesthete and libertine alike sink to the lower level of pleasure, and their emotions become obscene. There is no question of a division when Tristan in his vision of Isolde exclaims, "How beautiful thou art!" For great love can create the beauty of the beloved out of its own soul.

Prudery is based on a similar duality. It expresses a consciousness that the nude can only be alluring, obscene, "indecent," and should therefore be feared and avoided. It is the defensive weapon of sexually excited, for the most part, slightly hysterical women, against the purely sexual, whose sphere they often extend amazingly. Prudery conceives sexuality as a distinct, restricted complex in consciousness. Such division is alien to woman and, where it exists, a hysterical condition, a condition of inner discord, is clearly indicated. We may take it that the obscene which affects normal men, affects only hysterical, inwardly discordant women who try to take shelter behind prudery. To the normal woman the obscene does not exist as a spiritual principle; she turns with a feeling of displeasure from all the lower sexual manifestations, and even finds them absurd. The elimination of personality of eroticism, the charm of which is felt by even the most highly differentiated man, has always been foreign to woman—she lacks the duality of erotic emotion which man is slowly and laboriously striving to overcome—a still further proof of the unbroken, synthetic emotion of woman.

CONCLUSION

THE PSYCHOGENETIC LAW

The Individual as an Epitome of the Human Race

The biogenetic law of Ernst Haeckel teaches us that the human embryo passes through all the stages of development traversed by its ancestors in their evolution from the lower forms of the animal world. Although each successive stage completely replaces the preceding one, the latter is there as its organic supposition. Man is not born as a human being until he has travelled over the principal portions of the road to evolution. This law, which establishes the natural connection of the individual with the whole chain of organisms, is continued in a psychogenetic law, not founded on the heredity of the blood but on the heredity of culture (and therefore quite independent of the doctrine of the origin of species). In the course of his development the individual repeats the psycho-spiritual stages through which the species has passed. But while the human body cannot sustain life until it is perfectly developed, the degrees of psychic perfection vary very considerably; not every individual reaches perfection; most men attain to some degree, but there are others who do not even acquire the rudiments.

It would be an attractive and grateful task to point out the halting-places of the human race in the life of the individual; to fix the moment when for the first time in his life the child says "I"—a moment which usually occurs in his second year, and represents the humanisation of the race, the great intuition, when primitive man, divining his spiritual nature, severed himself from the external world; to perceive the child—like its primitive ancestors in their day—treating all weaker creatures which fall into its hands with almost bestial cruelty; to watch the boyish games reflecting the period when the nations lived on war and the chase, their eagerness to draw up rules and regulations and create gradations of rank and marks of distinction. I am not able to carry out such a task in detail and, moreover, as I am dealing with the erotic life only, such a proceeding would be out of place here.

The psychogenetic law, then, comes to this: Every well-developed male individual of the present day successively passes through the three stages of love through which the European races have passed. The three stages are not traceable in all men with infallible certainty, there are numerous individuals whose development in this respect has been arrested, but in the emotional life of every highly differentiated member of the human race they are clearly distinguishable, and the greater the wealth and strength of a soul, the more perfectly will it reflect the history of the race. The evolution of every well-endowed individual presents a rough sketch of the history of civilisation; it has its prehistoric, its classical, its mediaeval, and its modern period. Many men remain imprisoned in the past; others are fragmentary, or appear to be suspended in mid-air, rootless. The spirit of humanity has lived through the past and overcome it, so as to be able to create its future.

The gynecocratic stage actually survives to this day in the nursery. Here the mother rules supreme; the father is an intruder, the brothers are dominated by their sisters, often their juniors. Women mature at an earlier age than men; this assertion applies with equal force to individual and sex in connection with the history of civilisation. After he has left the nursery, there follows in the life of the boy a period during which he associates only with his school-friends, shuns the society of his mother and sisters, and is ashamed of his female relatives. This represents the revival of the men's unions of remote antiquity in the life of the individual of the present day.

At the period of puberty the sexual instinct makes itself felt for the first time; as a rule, if its nature is not recognised, it is accompanied by restlessness and depression. I do not believe that the instinct is, as soon as it appears, directed to the other sex, or anything else outside the individual. This fact cannot be explained by want of opportunity, shyness or bad example; there is a positive reason for it; the longing for a member of the other sex is still unfelt.

Between his twentieth and thirtieth year a man is often dominated by an enthusiastic spiritual love quite unconnected with the sensuality which has hitherto ruled his emotions. I will not elaborate the growth of this love and the new feelings which arise in connection with it; just as in the remote past the sense of personality was born as the centre of a new consciousness, so the individual now undergoes a period of purification and regeneration; through the love for his mistress he discovers his inmost self, of which, until now, he had been practically ignorant. The generative, undifferentiated impulse is supplanted by the love for an individual and stigmatised as base and contemptible. Guincelli's words characterising the second erotic stage of the race: *Amor e cor gentil sono una cosa*, to-day apply to the second stage in the life of the individual. It also occurs that in the heart of a man whom reality has failed to satisfy an ideal woman gradually wins life and shape. Sometimes it is the idealised counterpart of an actual woman, but not infrequently it is a vague, unsubstantial shadow. Here we have the deification of the woman reproduced in the heart of the individual. To illustrate my point, I will quote the very pertinent conversation between Foldal, the embittered old clerk, and John Gabriel Borkman (Ibsen).

BORKMAN: Indeed! Can you show me one who is any good?
FOLDAL: That's just the point. The few women I've known are no good at all.
BORKMAN: (with a sneer) What's the good of them if you don't know them?
FOLDAL (excitedly): Don't say that, John Gabriel! Isn't it a magnificent, an ennobling thought, to know that somewhere, far away, never mind where, the true woman lives?
BORKMAN (impatiently): Stop your high falutin' nonsense!
FOLDAL (hurt): High falutin' nonsense? You call my most sacred belief high falutin' nonsense?

In conclusion I should like to mention here that I look upon Otto Weininger as a tragic victim of the second stage of love which—in our days—is sick with an almost insurmountable inner insufficiency.

There is no need to elaborate my subject further and point out that—the first stage passed—the prime of life brings with it the fusion of sexuality and love. This union is the inner meaning of marriage in the modern sense—whether it is rarely or frequently realised is beside the point.

In previous chapters I have illustrated various phenomena of the emotional life by showing their reflections on the lives of two or three distinguished men. In conclusion I will endeavour to point out the reproduction of all the erotic stages through which the race has passed, in the psychical evolution of Richard Wagner, and their immortalisation in his works. We shall recognise in him the erotic representative of modern man, a personality in whom all that which as a rule is vague and only half expressed, has become great and typical. Love has been the *leitmotif* of his life. The concluding phrase of the crude fairy tale *Die Feen* ("The Fairies"), composed by the youth of nineteen, is: *the infinite power of love*, and the last words written down two days before his death, were: *love—tragedy*.

The opera *Das Liebesverbot* ("The Prohibition to Love"), written in 1834, is eminently symptomatic of the first stage. It is a coarser rendering of that bluntest of all Shakespearean plays, *Measure for Measure*; its sole subject is the pursuit of sensual pleasure, in which all indulge, and the ridiculing of those who appear to yearn for something higher. To detail the contents of the text—it cannot be called a poem—would serve no purpose; biographically, but not artistically interesting, it exhibits with amazing candour the first, purely sexual, stage of the young man of twenty-one. It was the period when "young Germany's" device was the emancipation of sensuality. Wagner himself says that his "conception was mainly directed against Puritan cant, and led to the bold glorification of unrestrained sensuality. I was determined to understand the grave Shakespearean subject only in this sense." And in his "Autobiographical Sketch" he says: "I learned to love matter." In addition to this Wagner gives us the following synopsis of a (lost) libretto, "*Die Hochzeit*" ("The Wedding"), written at an earlier period: "A youth, madly in love with his friend's fiancée, climbs through the window into her bedroom, where the latter is awaiting the arrival of her lover; the fiancée struggles with the frenzied youth and throws him down into the yard, where he expires."

The second, discordant, stage of love is embodied in *Tannhäuser*, composed when Wagner was twenty-nine years of age. There is probably no modern work of art in which the mediaeval feeling of dualism in the scheme of the universe has been expressed with greater pathos. We see man tossed between heaven and hell, between the worshipped saint and seductive sensuality, impersonated by a she-devil. A man of the Middle Ages would have recognised in this work the tragedy of his soul. Wagner had planned the opera before he had really reached the second period, under the title of *Der Venusberg* ("The Mountain of Venus"), and in this earlier version the purely sexual occupied a far more prominent place, probably in closer conformity with the old legend. For here Tannhäuser returns to Venus unsaved and defying the eternal values, determined to renounce a higher life and give himself up to the pleasure of the senses for all eternity. This idea was retained in a later version up to the decisive final turn; the purely spiritual love for Elizabeth eventually overcomes the unrestrained instinct.

As the despairing monk of mediaeval times, apparently abandoned by the love of God, turned to Satan and worshipped him, so Tannhäuser, cast out of the Kingdom of Heaven by the words of the Pope, and renounced by Elizabeth, again gives himself up to sensuality, which is here contrasted with spiritual love, and represented as demoniacal. Tannhäuser is not vacillating between the love of two women—a spiritualised and a sensual love; he is wavering between the purely spiritual love of Elizabeth and promiscuous sexuality represented by Venus, not centring on her as an individual, but diffused, as it were, through her whole kingdom. The dualism which rends the whole universe is strongly and uncompromisingly emphasised in text and music, and Wagner himself explained to the opera singer, Schnorr von Carolsfeld, that the main characteristic of the principal part was "the intensest expression of delight and remorse without any intermediate stage of feeling, changing abruptly and decisively." The closing words of the first scene: "My salvation lies in Mary!" are the real turning point of the drama. As abrupt as his desertion of Venus for Mary, is his return to her in the third act. By the side of Mary is placed the more human, the more earthly but yet idealised form of Elizabeth, a figure closely resembling Beatrice and Margaret.

The music of *Tannhäuser* (more especially the overture) expresses the contrast between the two erotic world-elements with striking abruptness. The harmonious and musically perfect motive of religious yearning (the chorus of the pilgrims) which forms the beginning and the end of the overture, is assailed by the briefer motives of sensuous seduction and ecstasy of the middle; the quivering, tickling passages of the violins play round the sacred music of the chorale like so many seductive elves. The Venusberg music is probably the most perfect expression of pure sensuality which has ever been reached in the world of music; it is the complete translation of sensual craving and sensual rapture into the language of music. In the Venusberg music composed for the performance in Paris, this motive is still more richly elaborated, and the recently published "sketches" for the scene in the Venusberg contain a number of details which were eliminated from the later version. Here bestial and demoniacal sensuality, not content with human couples, nymphs, maenads, sirens and fauns, calls for beings half-brute, half-human, represented by centaurs and sphinxes, for black goats, cats, tigers, panthers, and so on, finally for obscene representations of antique legends, such as Leda and the Swan,

Europa and the Bull, symbols and illustrations of the climax of perversion. It is a magnificent, poetico-musical picture of untrammelled sexuality, whose queen is Woman, the priestess of voluptuousness, represented by Venus. Tannhäuser's yearning for humanity and divinely pure love gives to this world a tinge of the demoniacal, for the latter is nothing but natural sensuality regarded from a higher standpoint, in this case from the point of view of spiritual love. Whenever it is opposed to the transcendental, the natural is conceived as dangerous and diabolical. At the moment of the abrupt inner change in Tannhäuser, Venus and her world must vanish like a phantom of the night. "A consuming, voluptuous excitement kept my blood and nerves tingling while I sketched and composed the music of *Tannhäuser*. . ." says Wagner in one place, and in another he confesses that sensual pleasure, while attracting and seducing him, filled him with repugnance. He speaks of his longing to "satisfy my craving in a higher, nobler element which, unpolluted by the sensuality so characteristic of modern life and art, appears to me as something pure, something chaste and virginal, unapproachable and intangible. What else can this longing for love, the noblest feeling I am capable of, be, than the yearning to leave this world of facts behind me and become absorbed in an element of infinite, transcendental love, to which death would be the gate. . ."

The dualism in the music of *Tannhäuser* is consistently maintained. The two elements war against each other without ever merging into one. Those parts of the music which characterise Elizabeth are full of noble pathos and a little sentimental. At the beginning of the second act she is not yet herself; she can still laugh like a light-hearted girl, but when she again succumbs to Tannhäuser's unearthly (and to her fatal) charm, and realises how irrevocably he has surrendered himself to Venus, she rises to true greatness and resolutely faces the swords unsheathed to punish the offender. Before our eyes she is transformed into the saint who realises her mission and is ready to take her burden upon her; more heroic than Beatrice or Margaret, she points to him "who laughingly stabbed her heart," the road to salvation. Like her two predecessors Elizabeth prays to Mary for the salvation of her lover—the prayer for the beloved has ever been woman's truest and most fervent prayer.

The thought of achieving a man's salvation through a great and steadfast love, is the subject of the *Flying Dutchman*, and plays, as is well known, an important part with Wagner. Strange to say he has for this very reason frequently been scoffed at by those who call themselves admirers of Goethe. Dante-Goethe's great problem of salvation is represented in

Tannhäuser with the utmost lucidity. The essence of it is that love can positively intervene in the life of a man whose soul is turned towards it, but who is confused and beset by temptations. His vacillating heart feels the love which is brooding over him and ultimately abandons itself to it, to be saved by its unswerving loyalty. Maybe this is as much a miracle as "grace," but it is also a psychical fact, because the love which yearns for the sinner awakens and increases not only his faith in its power to help, but also in his own strength; darkness and evil dismay him and he turns towards the light. In *Tannhäuser* this spiritual condition, which is of such primary importance in the last scene of *Faust*, is clearly expressed; his love for Elizabeth has been strong enough to kill desire kindled in his heart again and again by Venus; yet again he is on the point of succumbing to his senses. The vision of Venus appears before his eyes, but at Wolfram's exclamation, "Elizabeth!" he realises in a flash that Elizabeth has been praying for him day and night, and has given her life to save him. Before this sudden illumination the power of Venus sinks into nothing; divine love falls into his darkness like a ray of light—"Oh, sacred love's eternal power!"—it quickens his own love which is striving upwards, and with the words: "Saint Elizabeth, pray for me!" he sinks to the ground. His way, like Faust's, although one-sidedly emotional, leads from chaos and sin to pure love and salvation, not through his own strength but by the help vouchsafed to him in the love of his glorified mistress.

By the side of the struggling, suffering Tannhäuser, tossed hither and thither between God and the devil, between Elizabeth and Venus, stands Wolfram, the untempted woman-worshipper. The two extremes clash upon each other in the contest of the minnesingers. Tannhäuser, at war with himself, exasperated by the calm, matter-of-fact way in which Wolfram sings the praise of spiritual love, rushes to the other extreme and bursts into rapturous praise of the goddess of love and the pleasure of the senses. I need not lay stress on the fact that at that time of his life Wagner's own heart was the arena in which the conflict was fought out; a work like *Tannhäuser* is not *made*, it is conceived in the innermost soul of its creator. Every one of Wagner's great works bears the unmistakable stamp of sincerity and intensity, while with Goethe, on the other hand, it is not difficult to distinguish the genuine ones, that is to say, those which were written under the pressure of a compelling impulse, from those which owed their existence to the intellect rather than to the soul.

Tannhäuser immortalises the adolescence of the European races of mankind; the third stage is not even anticipated.

Lohengrin, the principal interest of which is other than erotic, represents a transitional phase between the second and the third stage; body and soul are no longer regarded as warring against each other; a greater harmony beyond either is dimly divined. Lohengrin has set out from a distant, transcendental kingdom to find earthly happiness in Elsa's love—but he is doomed to disappointment. I will not analyse the theme, but rather quote a few passages from Wagner: "Lohengrin is seeking the woman who is ready to believe in him; who will not ask him who he is and whence he comes, but love him as he is and because he is so. . . Lohengrin's only desire is for love, to be loved, to be understood through love. In spite of the superior development of his senses, in spite of his intense consciousness, he desires nothing more than to live the life of an ordinary citizen of this earth, to love and be loved—to be a perfect specimen of humanity." Wagner further speaks of his longing to find "the woman"; the female principle, quite simply, for ever appearing to him under new forms; the woman for whom the Flying Dutchman longed in his unfathomable distress; the woman who, like a radiant star, guided Tannhäuser from the voluptuous caverns of the Venusberg to the pure regions of the spirit, and drew Lohengrin from his dazzling heights to the warm bosom of the earth. We find here the new form of love, not yet fully comprehended but desired and anticipated in art.

In *Tristan and Isolde* it is attained completely and in its highest perfection. We possess in Wagner's letters to Matilda Wesendonk, and in the diary written for her, the documents of the personal experience out of which Tristan grew, and which unfold one of the most touching love-stories. As I have already discussed *Tristan and Isolde* in a previous chapter, I will here only quote a passage from a letter written by Wagner and addressed to Liszt at the time of his first meeting with Matilda; it fully expresses the harmony of the third stage. "Give me a heart, a mind, a woman's love in which I can plunge my whole being—who will fully understand me—how little else I should need in this world!"

It is very significant that side by side with *Tristan* we have *Die Meistersinger*, composed a little later on. Here the third stage of love is realised in its idyllic possibility; the synthesis has been given the shape of middle-class matter-of-factness, that is to say, the fulfilment of love in marriage: "I love a maid and claim her hand!" For this reason the work, although the fundamental idea is not erotic, is entitled to be placed by the side of *Tristan* with its demand for the absolute metaphysical consummation of love.

It is an amazing fact that the same genius should have experienced and portrayed both stages so perfectly. Doubtless Tannhäuser and Tristan are the most personal self-revelations of the great lover, pulsating with passion, and far remote from the colossal objective world of the Niebelungs, the lofty serenity of Lohengrin and the wisdom of Parsifal.

Wagner had finished the *Ring* before he conceived the idea of *Tristan and Isolde*. (It was printed in 1852.) In the former he intentionally raised the value of love and its position in the universe to a problem, embodying his knowledge of the world, and more especially of the modern world, in supernatural, mythical figures. The greatest ambition of man is power and wealth, the symbol of which is a golden ring. Gold in itself is innocent—elementary—a bauble at the bottom of the river, a toy for laughing children; but the insatiable thirst for power and wealth has robbed it of its harmlessness and made it the tool and symbol of tyranny. Only a being completely in the grip of the greed for riches and dominion, a being who looks upon the world and all men as objects to be bent to his will, and who has consequently renounced love, could have thus enslaved the world. Love does not impair the worth of a fellow-creature, but sets him above all things; a lover cannot be entirely selfish; his feeling at least for his mistress, and through her for the rest of the world, must be pure and unselfish. The struggle between these two most powerful instincts, both in the race and in the heart of the individual (Wotan), is the incomparable subject of this tragedy. The whole world-process is represented as a struggle between the apparently great, who are yet the slaves of gold and authority, and the truly free man who serves love, and on whom ambition has no hold.

The representatives of the petty, greedy, toiling human vermin, who readily renounced love for the sake of wealth, because the latter will always buy lust and pleasure, are the Niebelungs, the dwellers in the Netherworld who never see the sun. They have but one standard: money; one supreme value: power, the gift of wealth. Mime bewails his people (the small tradesmen as it were), as follows; "Light-hearted smiths we used to fashion gems and trinkets for our wives, gorgeous jewels, the Niebelungs' pretty trifles—we laughed at the labour." But Alberich, the capitalist, through the magic of the ring, has usurped the power and enslaved his fellows. "Now the felon compels us to creep in the heart of the mountains to labour for him. There we must delve and explore and despoil, plunder and smelt and hammer the metal, restlessly toiling to increase his treasure." The really daemonic property of the gold is that everybody succumbs to its seduction and strives to possess it. The former naïve joy of living, embodied in the Rhine-daughters, and their not yet humanised song, which seems to come direct from the heart of nature, is destroyed by the theft of the Rhine-gold. What till then had been a serenely shining "star of the deep," has been transformed into a means by which to win authority. The programme of the greedy and tyrannous never varies; Alberich proclaims it; "The whole world will I win," and it is his daemonic will to depreciate love and set up power as the only value, so that nobody shall doubt his greatness and unique genius. "As I renounce love, so all shall renounce it, with gold have I bought you, for gold shall you crave." Love shall die and lust shall take its place; he will force even the wives of the gods to do his will, for his wealth has made him master of the whole world. Compared to his restless activity, the giant "Fafner" is "stupid"; he is incapable of transforming gold into power; he merely enjoys its possession, content with the consciousness of his wealth.

But the curse of Alberich, the first who transmuted the shining metal into money, rests on gold and power. "It shall not bring gladness—who has it be seared by sorrow, who lacks it devoured by envy. . ." The curse of the eternal concatenation: tyranny—slavery, the care which accompanies wealth and the envy of the have-nots, can only be lifted from the world by a man who is inwardly free, who is neither master nor slave. Siegfried understands the song of the birds and the elementary beings, the Rhine-daughters; he is a stranger to human desires and passions. "I inherited nothing but my body—and living it is consumed." He is proof against the magic of the ring; the only value he knows is love. Alberich, his opponent, says, in speaking of him: "My curse has no sting for the mettlesome hero, for he knows not the worth of the ring; he squanders his prodigal strength, laughing and glowing with love his body is burning away." Half way between Alberich, the inwardly worthless wielder of power, and Siegfried, the truly free man, the embodiment of all virtue, who is murdered by the powers of darkness, stands Wotan, in whose heart both motives, authority and love, are struggling for supremacy, who will renounce neither love nor power. Artistically and symbolically the salvation of the world from the curse of greed and tyranny is brought about by the restitution of the ring, and its dissolution in the pure waters of the river from whence it had been taken; the gold is given back to the Rhine-daughters, to fulfil again its original purpose, namely, to delight the heart of man with its dazzling sheen.

Thus Wagner, the greatest and most inspired exponent of love among modern artists, declared that of all values love was the greatest. His intuitive genius left all the doctrines formulated by Schopenhauer and Buddha far behind and definitely rejected pessimism as a creed. There is an interesting letter from him to Matilda Wesendonk, written while he was composing the music of *Tristan*, and containing modifications of Schopenhauer's philosophy which he considered requisite. "It is a question of pointing out the road to salvation which no philosopher, not even Schopenhauer, discovered, the road which leads to the perfect pacification of the will through love; I do not mean abstract love for all humanity, but true love, based on sexual love, that is to say love between man and woman."

In *Parsifal*, the last and most mature of all his works, Wagner is breaking new ground. Here love between man and woman is deposed from the exalted position it hitherto held, subordinated to the metaphysical purpose of the world, that is to say, "the purpose of attaining to perfection," and absorbed in a higher association of ideas. Sexual love has undergone a change, it is no longer love in the true sense, but the unconditional love of the mystic. The enigmatical figure of Kundry is not the impersonation of one woman, she is woman herself. The incarnation of everything female, she embodies the sensuous, seductive and destructive element together with the contempt of the man who falls under her spell, as well as the motherly, and finally the humbly-administrative principle, which so far had not yet become a part of the erotic ideal. She is both positive and negative, a blind tool of the element of evil which prompts man to forget his higher mission (reminiscent of the second mediaeval period), and passionately yearning for salvation. She dies before the Holy Grail, the religious ideal made visible. Beside Kundry there are the flower-maidens, naïvely sensuous beings, who blossom like the flowers and fade again, unconscious and irresponsible. I refrain from a discussion of this work, which would lead too far, and only maintain that the music, corresponding to the text, is entirely unerotic and unsentimental, absolutely pure and religious. The love of a man for a woman has been superseded by love for the absolute and supernatural. Thus, after Wagner had experienced all the stages of love through which humanity has passed, and embodied them in his works, he reached a new point of view, a stage to which we have not yet attained and which, very likely, we are not even able fully to understand. This fourth stage—not unlike Weininger's ideal—is the overthrow of the female and earthly element in man by a voluntary surrender to the metaphysical.

Wagner's last position, taken up quite deliberately, permits of two explanations which I will point out without pressing either of them. Only a man possessing both the wisdom of the aged Wagner and a knowledge of the evolution of the race, and the road which still stretches out in front of it, would be entitled to speak a decisive word. The first obviously is that Wagner divined a last stage in the emotional life of man, a period which has outgrown sexual love and replaced it by mysticism. In conjecturing a potential fourth stage, the three previous ones must be regarded as one. The second explanation is that Wagner's feeling in his last work is no longer representative of the feeling of the race, but is, as it were, a personal matter, at least in so far as love is concerned. For although the principal subject in *Parsifal* is not love, yet it plays a very prominent part in it. I am only touching upon these two alternatives. But if the latter debatable point be omitted, my analysis of Wagner's emotional life must have shown in which sense the inspired man may be rightly regarded as typical of the race. He leads the broadest and at the same time the most personal life, and yet he manifests in it something which is far greater, far more universal and representative.

My argument proves that the evolution as well as the aberrations of love have affected man alone and, roughly speaking, to this day affect only him. He is the Odysseus, wandering through heaven and hell, ultimately to return home, perhaps, to where woman, the unchangeable, is awaiting him. That which has been woman's natural endowment from all beginning, the blending of spiritual and sensual love, man looks upon and desires to-day as his highest erotic ideal. His chaotic sexual impulse, the inheritance of the past, appears to him low and base in the presence of her in whom sexuality has always been blended with love; his worship, intensified until it reached the metaphysical, seems to him unfounded and eccentric before her who has ever been and ever will be entirely human, and who is perfect in his eyes because she possesses what he is striving after. This and nothing else is the meaning of the vague statement that in all matters pertaining to love woman occupies a higher position than man. She is always the same; he is always new and problematical; never perfect, he falls into error and sin where she cannot err, for her instinct is nature herself, and she knows not the meaning of sin. Whatever burden man has laid upon her, she has borne it patiently and silently; she has allowed him to worship her as a goddess and stigmatise her as a fiend, while all the time she remained problemless and natural, inwardly remote from the aberrations in which her intellect believed so readily. The conclusion which we have to draw, and which touches the foundation of the psychology of both sexes, is that only man's emotions have a history, while those of the woman have undergone no change.

If there is a law by which the human race is reproduced in the individual, then the so-called atavism in the shape of abnormality cannot be the sudden, or apparently sudden reappearance of conditions which once were normal and then disappeared; rather must it be the final arrest of an individual on a previous and lower stage, preventing him from reaching our standard in one or the other emotional sphere. The more humanity a man has in him, the more perfectly will he repeat in his life the stages through which the race has passed, or, in other words: the oftener that which once quickened the heart of man is repeated and surpassed, the greater is the possibility that new things may grow out of it. Atavism therefore is not so much the persistence of the earlier as the absence of the later stages. (This agrees with Freud's conception of the neurotic subject.)

It is obvious that the three stages of love are merely the expression of a period in one definite direction. The emotions of antiquity were entirely earthly, obvious and impersonal; the Middle Ages, on the other hand, attached value only to the world beyond the grave and matters pertaining to the soul. The beauty of spring was to them but a reflexion of another beauty.

> *"How glorious is life below!*
> *What greater glories may the heavens hold!"*

sings Brother John characteristically. But our period is conscious of the need of realising all our desires, and attaining to the highest possible spiritual perfection in this earthly life, and this not by destroying the transcendent ideals, but by stripping them of their metaphysical character, and bringing them to bear on this life, so that it may become a higher and holier one. The will of our intellectual heroes is not the rejection of the doctrine of the survival of the soul, but the comprehension of past transcendental values, so that they may become a safe guide to us in this earthly life; a more perfect blending of realism and idealism; the glorification of life under the aspect of eternity. This applies to love as well: the thought of the infinite, eternal love must transfigure and ennoble all that which is natural and human.

If my theories are correct, they prove the ontological character of historical evolution and the value of the study of history for the comprehension of the human soul. I have shown in a specific and highly important domain that that which we are fond of regarding as the characteristic quality of man was not present from the beginning, but has gradually been evolved in historical time. In other words: history can and must teach us the origin and evolution of the spirit and soul of man, as anthropology teaches us the construction of the body. In philosophically approaching history, it must not be our object to discover "what has been," but "what has become, how we became and what we are." The science of history which loses sight of its bearing on our time, content with its knowledge of the past, is antiquarian and dead; at the most it has aesthetic value, but it is worthless as far as the history of civilisation is concerned. Only that which has been productive in the past, which has had a quickening influence, producing new values, is historical in the highest sense. It creates a new and close relationship between psychology and history. The principal purpose, or one of the principal purposes of psychology, that is the knowledge of the construction of the normal human being, has received a new possibility of solution: every essential quality which the human race has evolved in the course of history must be present in every normally developed individual of our time. The normal man of to-day is not the normal man of the past; every successive century finds him richer and more complex, but he can always be discovered intuitively in history. In this sense history is an auxiliary science of psychology, or rather, the psychology of the human race, for the evolution of the psychology of the individual—which has been studied very little—is merely an abbreviated history of the evolution of the psychology of the species. A past period of civilisation can be traced in the life of every fully developed man, and *vice versa* the stages in the life of the individual point the way in history.

If it can be established that the fundamental emotions of the human heart originated in historical time, the widely spread, but unproved, theory that everything great and decisive existed from the beginning will be contradicted. The other complementary assertion that nothing which once existed ever quite disappears, must be admitted; nothing perishes in the soul of man; its position with regard to the whole is merely shifted by newly intervening motives and values; and even when it does not change its fundamental character, it becomes a different thing in the whole complex of the soul. Sexuality, which in the remote past was a matter of course, unassailable by doubt, became problematical and demoniacal as soon as it entered into relationship with the new factors of erotic life. An existence in harmony with nature was possible as long as the human race was still in evolution, and not yet conscious of itself. But as soon as intellect and self-consciousness had been evolved, civilisation became possible. Nature has no history in the sense of the origin of values; in the case of still uncivilised tribes every new generation is a faithful reproduction of the preceding one. Certainly there is modification caused by adaptation to the environment, but there are no moral values, and consequently there is no history.

I have attempted to explain why tragedy is inseparable from love in its highest intensity, to show the limits which check all deep emotion and the yearning which would overstep them. The emotional life of man, which is capable of infinite evolution, can only find satisfaction on its lower, animal stages. Hunger, thirst, and sexual craving can be satisfied without much difficulty, and therefore no tragic shadow falls on the first stage. But the emotion which overwhelms the soul cannot be appeased. Not only the great thinker's thirst for knowledge, the mystic's religious yearning, the aesthetic will of the rare artist, but also the love and longing of the passionate lover must reach beyond the attainable to the infinite. This earth is the kingdom of "mean" actions, "mean" emotions and "mean" men. And the lover, unable to bear its limits, creates for himself a new world—the world of metaphysical love.

A Note About the Author

Emil Lucka (1877–1941) was an Austrian writer, dramatist, and philosopher. He began writing while working as a bank clerk in Vienna, publishing essays of cultural criticism in philosophical periodicals. With the success of his popular biographies of composers, writers, and artists, he was able to fully devote his time to his writing. His philosophical theories were heavily influenced by Immanuel Kant, and later his plays dealt with Kantian maxims of ethics. He was best known for his revolutionary theories of love and sex, which were elucidated in his books *The Evolution of Love* (1922) and *Eros* (1915).

A Note from the Publisher

Spanning many genres, from non-fiction essays to literature classics to children's books and lyric poetry, Mint Edition books showcase the master works of our time in a modern new package. The text is freshly typeset, is clean and easy to read, and features a new note about the author in each volume. Many books also include exclusive new introductory material. Every book boasts a striking new cover, which makes it as appropriate for collecting as it is for gift giving. Mint Edition books are only printed when a reader orders them, so natural resources are not wasted. We're proud that our books are never manufactured in excess and exist only in the exact quantity they need to be read and enjoyed.

bookfinity

Discover more of your favorite classics with Bookfinity™.

- Track your reading with custom book lists.
- Get great book recommendations for your personalized Reader Type.
- Add reviews for your favorite books.
- AND MUCH MORE!

Visit **bookfinity.com** and take the fun Reader Type quiz to get started.

Enjoy our classic and modern companion pairings!

Classic & Modern

Bookfinity is a registered trademark of Ingram Book Group LLC. © 2023 Bookfinity. All rights reserved.

www.ingramcontent.com/pod-product-compliance
Lightning Source LLC
Chambersburg PA
CBHW022332280326
41934CB00006B/609

* 9 7 8 1 5 1 3 2 6 6 5 2 7 *